Virtue and Venom

Virtue and Venom

Catalogs of Women from Antiquity
to the Renaissance

Glenda McLeod

Ann Arbor

THE UNIVERSITY OF MICHIGAN PRESS

Published in the United States of America by
The University of Michigan Press
Manufactured in the United States of America

1994   1993   1992   1991   4   3   2   1

Library of Congress Cataloging-in-Publication Data

McLeod, Glenda, 1953–
     Virtue and venom : catalogs of women from antiquity to the
Renaissance / Glenda McLeod.
          p.   cm. — (Women and culture series)
     Includes bibliographical references and index.
     ISBN 0-472-10206-0 (alk. paper)
     1. Literature, Medieval—History and criticism. 2. Women in
literature. 3. Classical literature—History and criticism.
4. Literature, Medieval—Classical influences. 5. Catalogs in
literature.   I. Title.   II. Series.
PN682.W6M37   1991
809'.93352042'0903—dc20   91-27466
                                                                CIP

British Library Cataloguing in Publication Data
McLeod, Glenda
Virtue and venom : catalogs of women from antiquity to the
Renaissance.
1. Women
I. Title
305.4

ISBN 0-472-10206-0

Distributed in the United Kingdom and Europe by
Manchester University Press, Oxford Road,
Manchester M13 9PL, UK

Foreword

Charity Cannon Willard

In a day when it is fashionable to interpret the works of medieval writers according to the psychological theories of Freud or even more modern doctrines, it is reassuring to read a study of sources that throws new light on three late medieval texts: Boccaccio's *De claris mulieribus* (Concerning Famous Women), Chaucer's *Legend of Good Women,* and Christine de Pizan's *Livre de la cité des dames* (Book of the City of Ladies). The first two are, of course, well known, but the third has attracted considerable attention only in recent years as it has been translated into modern languages: English by Earl Jeffrey Richards, modern French by Thérèse Moreau and Eric Hicks, German by Margerete Zimmerman, and Dutch by Tine Ponfoort. Through these translations, Christine de Pizan's audience has been considerably increased and her text has given rise to a lively new discussion of whether or not she should be considered a founder of modern feminism, a question that Glenda McLeod considers with admirable reason.

Moreover, this interesting new study of the catalog tradition in literature over a period of several centuries effectively calls attention to one of the most important sources of inspiration for all three writers examined here, but it underscores especially the complexity of Christine's motives in writing the *Cité des dames.* Traditionally, the work has been all too readily dismissed as a partial translation and adaptation of Boccaccio's *De claris mulieribus,* an idea first developed by Alfred Jeanroy in an article published in *Romania* in 1922 and then picked up in the first modern biography of Christine published by Marie-Josèphe Pinet in 1927. Although progress has been made since then in attributing to Christine a more complex intent in writing her book, this study adds a new dimension to our understanding of her aims, as well as her source and the complexity of her methods.

Although it has been impossible to establish a direct link between Christine and Chaucer, even though their lives overlapped to some extent, both were obviously indebted to Boccaccio. Even if the *Cité des dames* was considerably more than a mere adaptation, it nevertheless owed an essential part of its inspiration to the popularity of the Italian writer in Paris around the year 1400. The story of Griseldis from Petrarch's version of Boccaccio's tale was known to French readers as early as 1390 through Philippe de Mézière's use of it in his *Livre de la vertu du saint sacrement de mariage et du reconfort des dames mariées* (Book of the Virtue of the Holy Sacrament of Marriage and of the Comfort for Married Ladies). Its popularity is attested by the anonymous dramatic version that bears the date 1395. Christine was undoubtedly making use of this popularity, with a touch of irony, when she included it in her own book. Furthermore, Boccaccio's *De genealogia deorum gentilium* (Of the Genealogy of the Gentile Gods) was being copied in Paris before the end of the fourteenth century, even if it was not translated into French until somewhat later. It was there that Christine found the definition of poetry that she used in her own writings. Even more important, however, were the first of two translations of *De casibus virorum illustrium* (Fates of Illustrious Men) made by Laurent de Premierfait in 1400 and *De claris mulieribus* in 1401. Christine de Pizan clearly knew all of these works and their popularity in French court circles was undoubtedly a factor in her idea of composing her own catalog of famous women.

Glenda McLeod is thus entirely correct in asserting that Christine probably knew and made use of both these translations, although little has been made up to now of this double influence. This is altogether reasonable in view of the fact that several early copies of *De casibus* were prepared and illustrated in the same workshop that produced the first copies of *Cité des dames*. There is strong evidence of a close relationship between Christine and the artist named by Millard Meiss the City of Ladies Master, who at least supervised the illustration of the early Boccaccio manuscripts, all of which underscores the probability that Christine was familiar with both Boccaccio translations from the start. Moreover, the conversations surrounding her biographies of the ladies recall the *De casibus* more than the *De claris mulieribus*, which merely provides a chronological series of biographies of the chosen ladies. In addition, of course, Christine made use of several tales from the *Decameron*, which had not yet been translated into French.

The question of why the *Cité des dames* did not continue to be copied beyond the end of the fifteenth century and was printed only in an early sixteenth-century English translation is intriguing, and Glenda McLeod gives as good an explanation as any that can be devised. It seems probable that the *Livre des trois vertus* (The Book of the Three Virtues), sometimes called in the printed version the *Trésor de la cité des dames* (Treasury of the City of Ladies), in addressing itself more directly to the problems of contemporary women, had a wider appeal. It was printed three times and read well into the sixteenth century, perhaps until the French translation of Castiglione's *Book of the Courtier* proposed a new model of womanhood. At the same time, the catalog tradition was carried on by others into the sixteenth century and beyond.

Nevertheless, there is evidence from existing records and manuscripts that the *Cité des dames* was in the libraries of a group of women who wielded considerable political power in the late fifteenth and sixteenth centuries: Margaret of Austria and Mary of Hungary, both governors of the Netherlands for the Emperor Charles V, had two copies of Christine's two texts bound into one volume; Louise of Savoy, regent for her son Francis I, had a copy; as did probably Anne of Brittany, whose confessor, Antoine Dufour, composed his own catalog of ladies, *Les Vies des Femmes Célèbres,* in the tradition of *Cité des dames*. One may wonder, however, if by the end of the fifteenth century the idea of constructing a medieval walled city had not become rather outmoded, especially in view of the enthusiasm for an entirely new type of architecture inspired by Italy.

One of the merits of a book such as this one by Glenda McLeod is that it encourages the reader to take a new look at things that are somewhat familiar. Along with reflecting on the evolution of architecture one realizes, for instance, that François Villon must have been recalling these catalogs in writing his "Ballade of Dead Ladies," ending with "Joan, the Good Maid of Lorraine / Whom the English burned at Rouen." It was, after all, Christine de Pizan who first celebrated in poetry the exploits of this heroine. What she wrote about women was by no means forgotten, even if less widely acclaimed than the works of Boccaccio or Chaucer.

Contents

Introduction

Even though the essentialist task of defining woman's nature has recently been a favorite topic of discussion in numerous scholarly works, it did not originate in the twentieth century. Indeed, defining femineity[1] has been a recurrent *topos* since the ancient Greeks.[2] Whether the ancient definitions were provided in a satirical poem (such as Semonides's *On Women*), a philosophical tract (such as Aristotle's *De generatione animalium*),[3] or a rhetorical game (such as the "Quid est mulier?" passages in medieval manuscripts), their framers were most often men who assumed the universality of their viewpoints. In fact, the first woman to handle the *topos* may have been Christine de Pizan, a fifteenth-century writer whose works encouraged (if not inspired) the Renaissance debate on woman's place called the *querelle des femmes*. The recent revival of interest in femineity makes the present propitious for reinvestigating these earlier polemics. This study will trace a general history of one form that polemics took—the catalog of women—focusing especially on one important period of intense interest in the topic, at the close of the Middle Ages.

Catalogs of women are lists—sometimes found in other works, sometimes found alone—enumerating pagan and (sometimes) Christian heroines who jointly define a notion of femineity. Because of their focus on the past, catalogs attempt to cull this notion from the testimony of history.[4] They

---

1. Eric Partridge in *Usage and Abusage* (1942; reprint, New York: Harper and Row, 1981) points out that *femineity* has now replaced *femininity* as the noun signifying the quality or nature of the female sex. I have adopted Partridge's usage throughout this book because the connotations of *femininity* often make this word inappropriate.

2. Pomeroy (1975) discusses this concern.

3. This treatise is the classical source for defining women's biological inferiority to men.

4. In fact, early catalog verse—such as the genealogical tables in the Bible—functions as a kind of crude history.

therefore offer a unique perspective on the problem of defining femineity by promising to review women as entities participating in and formed by historical currents. Such an approach is of immense significance at any time of great change but was especially so in the fourteenth and fifteenth centuries, when historical perspectives were undergoing transformations and when a differentiation between poesy and history was beginning to emerge. Additionally, late medieval catalogers who used their lists inside fictional works were intrigued by the catalog's relationship to *auctoritas,* the works of important authors cited as authorities. When a cataloger mustered authorities to argue for a virtuous femineity, the catalog form neatly mirrored a tension between personal opinion and authoritative dictum, between content (the thesis of woman's virtue) and form (a catalog built from older texts that more often had argued differently). That problem could and often did speak to whether a living *auctor* should authenticate his role by his personal experience.[5] There is little wonder, then, that all sorts of writers were attracted to the catalog genre and that these included not hacks (until late in the tradition) but the finest writers of their age.

Modern readers have not been so inclined to the catalog even though they have admired specific compilations (such as the general prologue to the *Canterbury Tales*). They have dismissed these works with charges of monotony, formlessness, and a general lack of artistry or point. But while we may find catalogs boring, medieval readers and writers were clearly fascinated by them, to an extent not often recognized.[6] They appear alone and within almost all genres, and they are not as mediocre as often proposed. Not only does Chaucer use them in several of his works,[7] but much of Dante's *Divine Comedy* can be considered a catalog as well. And the form survived well into the Renaissance. Castiglione's *The Book of the Courtier* and Ariosto's *Orlando Furioso* contain catalogs of good women. Catalogs were used by both sides in the *querelle des femmes,* often with the very same exempla

---

5. This problem is, of course, supremely important to Chaucer's later work, but Minnis (1988) has shown how a concern for the writer as a human being is evident in scholastic commentaries of a hundred years before.

6. J. Allen (1982) has pointed out the importance of the catalog to fourteenth- and fifteenth-century letters. But even as late as 1987, in his posthumously published biography of Chaucer, Donald Howard, a distinguished Chaucerian, speculated that Chaucer may have been bored by *Legend of Good Women* because the work "must have lost some of its luster after the first few years" (1987, 396).

7. Among Chaucerian works with catalogs are the *Legend of Good Women, The Book of the Duchess,* and, of course, the general prologue to the *Canterbury Tales.* The Monk's Tale is also a catalog.

arguing for opposing opinions.[8] Such popularity, diffusion, and versatility invite us to take a second look at the form and at its applicability to defining femineity.

Perhaps an important key to the catalog's popularity lies in what an educated medieval audience expected from a text. As modern readers, we tend to look for entertainment, amusement, and originality when we read. Medieval readers, however, wanted edification, a moral example to imitate, and (in an age when books were expensive items) ample erudition and facts.[9] The catalog could supply all of these needs. In form and in function, it was related to the popular genre of the florilegium,[10] whose sole raison d'être was to transmit the wisdom of written authority. Like medieval florilegia, which compiled excerpts from classical, patristic, and ecclesiastical sources, the catalogs of women gathered classical heroines together into an easily accessible volume or an easily remembered format. Like our own reference books—useful *because* they were seen as unoriginal—these collections seem to have conveyed a general consensus about a given subject, such as women, a consensus based on a culture's written legacy.[11]

This claim to representation may explain the catalog's wide appeal and its special application to the task of defining femineity. Catalogs lent a work credibility. Moreover, for authors seeking a shield behind which they might assert a personal voice or a reinterpretation of their sources, the catalog's staid format could make new or even startling ideas seem acceptable. Catalogs can, then, not only illuminate the stubborn persistence of western misogyny but also reveal struggles and doubts about this line of thought.

More specifically, catalogs can disclose two processes at work in the fashioning of new notions (and hence new *figurae*) of femineity. On the one hand, a new interest in historical perspective and in reinterpreting older texts could force a reexamination of past heroines. On the other, authors with a changing sense of the literary often identified their dissident poetics (fre-

---

8. For a discussion of the *querelle des femmes*, see Kelly 1982; Bornstein, *Distaves and Dames: Renaissance Treatises for and about Women* (Delmar, N.Y.: Scholars' Facsimilies and Reprints, 1978); Kelso 1956; Suzanne Hull, *Chaste, Silent, and Obedient: English Books for Women 1475–1640* (San Marino: Huntington Library, 1982); MacLean 1983; and Woodbridge 1984. The best source for the continental debate continues to be Kelso 1956.

9. Many late medieval books appealed to readers in this fashion, as, for example, Pierre Bersuire's *Reductorium morale*, Christine de Pizan's *L'Epistre d'Othéa*, and almost all of Boccaccio's Latin works.

10. Florilegium is a translation of the Greek word "anthology" and was not named as a genre until the early Renaissance. The later Middle Ages produced numerous florilegia which had formative ties to the summa and encyclopedia traditions.

11. See Rouse and Rouse 1979 on this point.

quently linked to emotion, the private life, pleasure, and the senses) with women, who, ontologically, were frequently linked to the same things. Neither process has been addressed before in a study of the catalog tradition, but both are needed to help us understand later debates and strategies in the Renaissance *querelle des femmes*.[12]

As this double emphasis on history and literature implies, one point of departure for this study could be Virginia Woolf's striking insight that women dominate poetry but are all but absent in history.[13] Woolf's dichotomy, however, cannot be unreservedly applied to ancient texts, which often mix historical and literary components. From the beginning of the genre, catalogs had a historical dimension even when found in "literary" works such as the epic or satiric verse. Conversely, historical examples, such as Messalina, often show up in literary texts, such as Juvenal's *Satire Six*. In fact, one of the most troublesome problems in studying these catalogs is the real absence in many eras of literature or history, in the modern sense of the terms. Medieval readers, for example, often treated "literary" texts as ethical lessons. And while we have medieval histories—chronicles, sagas, universal histories—they are quite different from our own and quite devoid of that sense of historical distance that the Renaissance is popularly credited with discovering. Many early audiences read the same catalogs as either literature or history or (most confusingly) as both.[14] The later medieval catalogs, which began to distinguish between the two disciplines, often did so imprecisely or haltingly, as was the case with Boccaccio's *De claris mulieribus*. Since women function in poetry as the objects of desire while in history they are (or should be) the objects of study, the conflation or differentiation of these two approaches is important in determining how each individual catalog defines women. All catalogs in this study will be examined in the context of whether and how they distinguish between history and literature, of whether and how they challenge authorities in both areas.

Like all other medieval genres, the catalog of women has its roots in classical antiquity. Chapter 1 thus examines classical Greek and Roman catalogs. These date back to the ancient Greek epics of Hesiod and Homer,

---

12. The only study of the catalog tradition that I know of is McMillan 1979. Katherine Henderson and Barbara McManus in *Half Humankind* (Urbana: University of Illinois Press, 1985) do set the documents of the Pamphlet Wars in England within a social context.

13. Virginia Woolf, *A Room of One's Own* (New York: Harcourt, Brace and World, 1929) 62.

14. For example, Boccaccio's *De claris mulieribus* mixes the two categories, and Chaucer assures us his tale of Cleopatra in *Legend of Good Women* is "storyal soth, it is no fable" (1961, 702).

both of whom wrote in a period of cultural ferment every bit as intense as that of the later medieval catalogers. Like them, Hesiod and Homer use their listings to define a sense of cultural continuity. A satiric catalog by Semonides (*On Women*) introduces structure and techniques often repeated in later satiric treatments, and Plutarch's *Mulierum virtutes* (The Virtues of Women) offers us an example of a rare catalog explicitly equating men's and women's virtue.

Because medieval writers didn't have these Greek works, they are important to this study only for their influence on the Roman catalogs, which date principally from the first two centuries of the empire. Vergil's list in the Underworld of *Aeneid* 6, Ovid's *Heroides,* and Juvenal's *Satire Six* are all of immense significance for medieval catalogs because they were avidly read and frequently cited. Because of its differentiation between the male and female catalogs of the Underworld, Vergil's epic (the earliest list) sets an important example for the exclusion of women from history. Ovid's *Heroides* confirms this exclusion by associating its feminine *figurae* with a dissident poetics that stresses the private over the public life. Both poets, with very different poetical programs, consequently separate the catalog heroine from the politics and history of the empire. While Juvenal's satiric catalog associates women with history and the community, it is the history of decadence and the community in decline. These catalogs, then, helped to establish an authoritative pattern for the isolation of the heroine from important social and historical contexts.

Chapter 2 examines contributions from the patristic period and the curious scarcity of catalogs in the early and High Middle Ages. The major catalog from Christian Rome is found in St. Jerome's defense of chastity, *Adversus Jovinianum* (Against Jovinian). It sets forth the Christian hierarchy of feminine worth—sublime virgins; chaste wives and widows; sexually active females—and orchestrates a pantheon of feminine characterizations still dominant by the time Christine de Pizan wrote her catalog in 1405. *Adversus Jovinianum* also isolates the heroine in another important way, for by viewing the virgin as a woman who has transcended her femineity, Jerome neatly severs the good woman from her gender. *Adversus Jovinianum* is our best source for studying how the classical legacy was absorbed into the Christian catalog and (since it is the first true florilegean catalog) how the catalog's call to authority could mask an essential rewriting of sources. The awareness and use of this pattern in the High Middle Ages are exemplified in Walter Map's *De nugis curialium* (Courtier's Trifles) and Jean de Meun's *Roman de la Rose* (Romance of the Rose).

While all major periods of catalog compilation—Archaic Greece, imperial Rome, the later Middle Ages—saw intense social ferment, the simple fact of change is not enough in and of itself to stimulate catalog compilation. The High Middle Ages was an era of many transformations but very few catalogs, even though the Gothic period fostered an active tradition of defense and attack against women.[15] In the midst of major paradigm shifts, authors would logically seek to redefine the cultural legacy, including the notion of femineity, but to do so in a catalog seems to require a special interest in the past, a need to reinterpret—but not necessarily replace—older authorities. In the later Middle Ages, this interest appears in the new humanist scholarship, an increased willingness to trust empirical knowledge, and a certain fondness for using the image of women to mediate between old and new authorities. Catalogs by nature drew upon *auctoritas;* they gathered information from written sources. But the compiler could also reinterpret that knowledge in light of his or her experience or opinions. In the last three catalogs of this study, we shall see how individual interpretation—construed as a reliance upon empirical knowledge, an interest in humanist scholarship, or a new grounding for the author's voice—became more and more openly a part of the catalog of women.

Chapter 3 examines the first of these works—Giovanni Boccaccio's *De claris mulieribus*—as an example of humanist scholarship. Boccaccio himself claims *De claris mulieribus* represents a new type of collection of famous women, one modeled on similar collections of famous men.[16] Yet despite his boast, *De claris mulieribus* is very much a mixed bag. Like Jerome's collection, it emphasizes the importance of a woman's chastity, associates femineity with vice, and portrays the woman whose virtues lead to accomplishments as both rare and "virile." In other words, it continues to exclude women from virtue, public life, and history. At the same time, however, it does treat the *mulier clara* according to the traditions of epideictic rhetoric (the rhetoric of funeral orations and occasional speaking, which had long been associated with civic virtue).[17] It thus anticipates future links between the good woman and the good state. Rhetoricians had advocated that epideictic encomiums generate praise from the topics of *notatio* (the deeds of character) rather than *effictio* (the goods of fortune, beauty and birth, usual loci for

---

15. See Hentsch 1903 and Meyers 1817 for a discussion of this tradition.
16. Boccaccio makes this statement at the very beginning of his Proemio for *De claris mulieribus.*
17. This connection between the literature of praise and civic virtue goes back to Plato. For a discussion, see Hardison 1962.

praise of women). This switch from ontological statement to the review of women's actions would bear further important fruit in Christine de Pizan's collection.

Despite these changes, however, *De claris mulieribus* is still largely conservative in its approach. Not only do its standards for judging women's virtue often coincide with Jerome's, but the word claris in its title indicates an interest not in illustrious (in the sense of admirable) but in famous (with the sense of notorious) women.[18] Most important, while Boccaccio makes a rudimentary attempt to apply new humanist ideas to his catalog of women, his organization here differs significantly from that in *De casibus virorum illustrium* (On the Fates of Illustrious Men), his catalog of famous men, which was linked to history in many important ways. *De claris mulieribus* suggests interesting changes and was an important inspiration for other catalogs, but more often than not it transmitted the tradition of isolation that had marked the catalogs since imperial Rome.

Chapter 4 examines how Chaucer used that tradition for an exploration of poetics in the *Legend of Good Women*. A revival of Ovid's *Heroides*, the *Legend of Good Women* experiments with new understandings of poetics by exploring tensions between experience and authority. While not a true florilegium, it is often a florilegean sampling of late medieval generic conventions. Most important for this study, it surveys the relationship between a catalog and its compiler (one of the four possible roles available to a medieval writer).[19] Furthermore, the relationship between prologue and legends uses women and their relations with lovers to comment on the writer's relationship to his art. Finally, in a collection whose title provocatively couples secular heroines and blessed saints, Chaucer speculates on the value of empirical knowledge by playing on woman's traditional ties with the senses.

For all these themes, the Chaucerian narrator is central. By framing his treatment of the pagan heroines as a self-defense—the poet-narrator Chaucer must write this catalog in penance for having offended women—Chaucer illustrates how the compiler's bias, experiences, and cultural milieu can shape his collection. By emphasizing the narrator's empirical exploration of his relation with Queen Alceste, Chaucer explores the relative values of experience and authority in art. Finally, by making the narrator central to his

---

18. Boccaccio himself gives this flexibility as his reason for describing his heroines as *mulier clara*. Catalogers who used the same heroines often spelled their names differently. The original spellings as used in individual catalogs have been perserved in this study. Some inconsistences between catalogs should be expected.

19. See Minnis 1987, esp. chap. 3, for a discussion of these roles.

plot, Chaucer the author calls on older Ovidian associations between poetry and woman, casting the main feminine character in the poem (Queen Alceste) as the narrator's muse as well as his lover. In attempting to define a virtue that does not exclude the temporal world or contradict the eternal, Chaucer reveals how women's characterizations have always been more descriptive of their creators than of women themselves. Chapter 4 examines how Chaucer manipulates the older, misogynistic patterns to advance these speculations and reveals the extent to which *Legend of Good Women* really concerns not women but poets and a newly valued type of knowing.

Such knowing plays a central role in the final catalog examined, Christine de Pizan's *Livre de la cité des dames* (Book of the City of Ladies). The first catalog to be written by a woman and the first to defend women against institutionalized misogyny, this book in many ways represents a culmination of medieval catalog development. In fact, it is a remarkable, groundbreaking text that synthesizes many older implementations to produce a wholly new type of catalog and a wholly new definition of femineity.

In its attempts to reinterpret traditional exempla, *Cité des dames* sets up important precedents for the *querelle des femmes* and also offers one resolution of the experience-authority dialectic that had plagued Chaucer. This dialectic is central to the book's subject. A medieval woman struggling toward a new identity had to reconcile her experiences with the written books that would deny or limit her power. In the process, she also had to grapple with the catalog's triple exclusion of women from virtue, public life, and history. To do less would be to undermine her own authority to speak.

Cité des dames engages all these endeavors by constructing individual and gender identities based on a new sense of cultural history. All three are implied by the construction of a city. The city ultimately provides not only a history of woman and a symbol of feminine solidarity but also the image of an individual's self-defense. A woman narrator, calling on her experience and her sense of reason, rectitude, and justice, reinterprets authority. Through her work, women achieve the connections with universal veracity, history, and the plan of providence, which had not been supplied in earlier collections. Indeed, Christine's book, as Joan Kelly noted, initiated a "four hundred year tradition of women thinking about women and sexual politics in European society" (1982, 8), and she modeled the confrontation with misogyny as a complex mixture of reclamation, appropriation, and subversion. In terms of her catalog's structure, Christine also challenges the florilegean form by making the compiler's experience an open and important source of the truths she wishes to convey. Chapter 5 investigates how

Christine implements these changes through her allegorical frame, her reinterpretation of individual exempla, and her investigation of her predecessors' misogynic assumptions.

In general, this study treats all catalogs as attempts to express or critique cultural attitudes toward women. Catalog definitions—whether in detraction or defense—will be evaluated in terms of how women's relation to the historical and cultural legacy defined the compiler's sense of his or her society. If woman is included within these concepts, her contributions are evaluated as positive or negative influences on the community. If she is excluded, her association with other abstractions is determined. The focus on the catalog genre perforce implies an approach that borrows from the disciplines of history and literature. This study does not simply examine the image of women in literature, nor does it try to reconstruct the actual condition of women in the past; yet it verges on both endeavors. Consequently, important points to be addressed about each catalog will include what types of women the compilers are interested in; what roles dominate; whether the exempla support a model of feminine virtue or vice; how those abstractions are defined; what cultural or historical forces surface in the texts; and finally, if the characteristics, structures, and presentations of the catalog are comparable to criteria for similar collections of men (if extant). By the study's end, lines of descent or simple similarities between individual catalogs should be clear.

Since the thinkers of earlier periods (all the way back to Homer and Hesiod) shaped their works in terms of existing literary tradition, the truth these catalogs express had a remarkable durability. That truth—and the way it was transmitted—deserve our study.

I have been fortunate to receive generous help in preparing this manuscript and would like to acknowledge it here. Francis Teague, Frank Warnke, Steven Grossvogel, and Bill Provost read the manuscript in total or in part and offered intelligent and useful observations. The readers' comments from the University of Michigan Press were also enlightening and encouraging. I would like to thank Guy Mermier for providing a forum at the University of Michigan for some of the ideas in chapter 5. And I would like especially to thank Charity Willard for reading this manuscript several times and always offering excellent advice. Finally, I owe a great deal of what is valuable in this study to Katharina Wilson. Her good influences will be apparent to anyone who knows her work.

Chapter 1

A Fickle Thing Is Woman

Catalogs of women were found in nearly every genre of classical literature. In satires, epics, polemical treatises, and lyrics they provided a principle of organization, an appeal to authority, or a recognized mode of persuasion. They were linked in origin to a very ancient verse form called catalog verse, which is found in the early literature of virtually all Western societies.[1] Catalog verse, metered lists organized around some central common denominator, was usually educative in function, presenting moral instruction (as in rhymed rules of conduct) or rudimentary history lessons (as in genealogical listings).[2] An excellent example of an early catalog detailing rules of conduct is Proverbs 31, which describes the good wife. Genesis 10, on the other hand, which gives the descendants of Noah, Japeth, Ham, and Sham, is a representative catalog genealogy. Both edification and historical transcription remained important purposes of the classical catalogs of women even as they developed into more sophisticated forms.

During the course of antiquity, catalogs also developed toward the florilegium, a genre unnamed until the Renaissance and largely unstudied even today.[3] The florilegium was like the catalog in that its loosely enumera-

---

1. Catalog verse is simply a metered or rhymed list. The catalog developed, however, toward a gathering of exempla and with this association came links with rhetoric (exempla were often considered rhetorical arguments) and with history (exempla were a preferred method of historical instruction among the Greeks and Romans). For more information on the exemplum, see Aristotle's *Rhetoric* (1356a35–1958a35) and *Prior Analytics* (2.23.68.b.30-6919). See also Bremmond and LeGoff 1982.

2. For a fuller discussion of catalogue verse, see *Princeton Encyclopedia of Poetics*, 1965 ed., s.v.

3. For a discussion of florilegia and their usefulness to the student of the past see the entry under florilegia in *The Dictionary of the Middle Ages*, 1982 ed.; Rouse and Rouse 1979; and

tive structure purported to transmit conventional wisdom and cultural consensus. It also presented itself as authoritative, a claim widely accepted despite the fact that a compiler's biases clearly shaped his or her collection. Unlike catalog verse, however, which can be found in cultures at all levels of complexity, florilegia are only written in older, more urbane cultures possessing a considerable written heritage. Such societies need, in Chaucer's memorable phrase, a "key of remembrance" to the past and its values. As its generic name indicates, the florilegium harvests the choicer parts of this past: it gathers (*legere*) flowers (*flores*).[4] From such an etymology, we can expect heterogeneity, beauty, and variety; and indeed as catalogs move toward this genre, they become further and further displaced from the early unity of catalog verse. In fact, the later florilegean catalogs present intricate, even contradictory pictures of womankind, often attempting to reconcile older standards with new realities and ideals.

All catalogs of women define and reflect upon the status of women, but as Marilyn Arthur points out in her essay on the origins of Western attitudes toward women, this status is always an aspect of a whole social movement.[5] In the Western world, the definition of femineity expressed in the early catalogs first emerged in consort with the Greek creation of the *polis*. During the eighth century B.C., archaic Greek society replaced the older clan structures of Bronze Age Greece with a social structure that based itself explicitly upon the nuclear family.[6] Considerable evidence of this change exists. In Athens, for example, the new bases were even written into Solon's law code. This shift brought women a new chance for prominence. While their functions did not really change, the attitude toward them did (Arthur 1984, 14). As the sole source of legitimate heirs, the Greek wife acquired an importance not commanded by her predecessor in the harem. In the early epics, particularly the Homeric ones, women consequently seem to

---

Henri Rochais, "Floriléges spirituels, floriléges latins," in *Dictionnaire de spiritualité ascétique et mystique,* 1964 ed.

4. *The Dictionary of the Middle Ages,* 1982 ed., s.v. "florilegia."

5. See Arthur 1984.

6. Arthur (1984) builds up a convincing picture for this development, drawing for example on Solon's law code, which made the family a basic social unit. See also Victor Ehrenberg, "When did the *Polis* Rise?" *Journal of Hellenic Studies* 57 (1937): 147–59; Donald Richter, "The Position of Women in Classical Athens," *Classical Journal of Midwestern States* 1971: 1–8; A. R. W. Harrison, *Law of Athens: Family and Property* (Oxford: Clarendon, 1968); H. J. Wolff, "Man, Law, and Family Organization in Ancient Athens," *Traditio* 2 (1944): 49–95; Pomeroy 1975; and Fustel de Coulanges, *La Cité antique: Etude sur le culte, le droit, les institutions de la Grèce et de Rome* (Paris: Hachette, 1916).

enjoy greater prestige as wives and mothers.[7] Two early epic catalogs of heroines, by Hesiod and Homer, also testify to this change. Both lists are genealogical; both focus on the mothers of Greek heroes. Hesiod's epic, the *Eoiae,* is shaped as a catalog; in Homer's *Odyssey,* the catalog is found within a larger tale. Textual evidence is far from conclusive, but many classicists feel that Homer's collection is patterned on Hesiod's.[8] The *Eoiae,* then, may be the earliest Greek catalog of heroines that has survived even if only in fragmented form.

Too little of Hesiod's work remains to reconstruct with certainty its structure and purpose, but in antiquity it was clearly a poem of major importance (Lattimore 1959, 8). Many classicists, among them Hugh Evelyn-White, believe the *Eoiae* forms a sequel to the *Theogeny,* Hesiod's epic of divine genealogy.[9] As that work ends with an invocation to the muses to sing of the tribe of women, the *Eoiae's* tales of love between the gods and mortal women may well answer the request. If Evelyn-White is correct in suggesting that the legends were originally interspersed with tall tales—he hypothesizes that several now separate poems, such as the *Shield of Hercules* and Theseus's descent to Hades, once formed part of the catalog—then this genealogy furnishes context and frame for the oral history of the Greek tribes. Such an organization makes sense for Hesiod. In his native Boethia, descent was customarily traced through the mother rather than the father. More important, by cataloging Greek heroes through their divine engendering, Hesiod establishes each hero's requisite link with divinity and justifies his elevated status among men.

The fame of the *Eoiae's* heroines rests solely on their biological function; no individual characterization is attempted as far as can be detected, nor does Hesiod view women apart from their relationships with men. Indeed, the women seem to be interesting primarily as referents to their heroic sons. In the fragments that survive, they play no active role in their own stories. Centuries later, the Virgin Mary would fulfill a similar function for Christians, who often saw her as the passive channel of the divine seed.

---

7. Among other things, Arthur (1984) points to a difference between Achilles, the older warrior hero whose heroism is based solely upon interactions with men, and Hector, the newer warrior hero, who is seen in domestic as well as militant postures. See Arthur for a discussion of how the *Iliad* and the *Odyssey* demonstrate this challenging of older standards.

8. For a discussion of why Homeric scholars feel that the episode in Hades is a later interpolation, see Page 1955, 21–36.

9. See Hugh G. Evelyn-White, Introduction to *Hesiod: The Homeric Hymns and Homerica* (Cambridge, Mass.: Harvard University Press, 1959), xx–xxi.

A similar situation exists in the *Odyssey*. Homer's catalog, included in his description of Odysseus's trip to Hades, enumerates the dead heroines whose shades Odysseus encounters there. As the catalog appears immediately before the hero meets his dead comrades from Troy, the heroines help to set the Trojan War in context by reminding readers of other stories concerning the Greek clans.[10] Like Hesiod, Homer uses his heroines as convenient referents to history. All are memorable simply as the incubators of heroes who collectively represent the various Greek tribes. Tyro and Khloris are related to early rulers of Pylos, the home island of Odysseus's friend Nestor. In like manner, Antiope, Alkmene, Megare, and Epikaste refer to Thebes; Leda and Iphimedeia to Sparta; Phaidra, Prokris, and Ariadne to Crete; and Myra, Clymene, and Eriphyle to Mycenea. The last member of the collection is Eriphyle, who betrayed her husband for gold. She connects the catalog with Odysseus's subsequent encounter with Agamemnon, who is still obsessed with Clytemnestra's murderous infidelity, but she is not representative of the list as a whole; the Greek hero—not woman as traitor—is Homer's common denominator. Unlike the heroes whom Odysseus meets in Hades— Achilles and Agamemnon—the heroines give speeches that are for the most part unrecorded, and Odysseus's reactions to them are not personalized. Homer's hero only gives details about Poseidon's rape of Tyro and even here, makes no attempt to describe or characterize the famous queen. His descriptions of other catalog heroines tell more about their husbands and sons than the women themselves. Such abbreviated treatment makes for a lack of individuation curious for a poet as gifted as Homer was in the quick character sketch. As women, the heroines simply have no distinctive features. They are cyphers.

Because of their historical bases, these two epic catalogs foreshadow later collections, which illustrate a notion of cultural history. In Homer and Hesiod, woman's biological role defines not merely the individual but also her social and historical importance.

The Greek woman's new prominence in the nuclear family gave rise to a hostile and satiric tradition in Greek literature as well, but it may prove more fruitful at this time to trace subsequent developments of Homer and Hesiod's treatments. One, Vergil's *Aeneid,* continues the epic tradition; the other, Plutarch's *Mulierum virtutes,* anticipates the expository form that late medieval and Renaissance catalogs often assumed.

Vergil and Plutarch's catalogs were composed within a hundred years

---

10. Finley characterizes Homer's catalog as "historical and synoptic" (1978, 119).

of each other and, like the early Greek catalogs, were conditioned by a general context of social change. In Vergil's case, the change involved Rome's transformation from embattled republic to ruling empire, a change orchestrated in very precise ways by Vergil's patron, the Emperor Augustus Caesar, who had become emperor by defeating Anthony and Cleopatra's forces at Actium. Augustus never claimed any title but *Princeps* (first citizen) and throughout his lifetime maintained that he had not established the empire but restored the republic. One of the things he felt most imperiled the republic was a pervasive Greek influence that threatened to degenerate the stern Roman spirit. As part of his campaign to save this spirit (and redirect it to imperial ends), Augustus commissioned Vergil to write the *Aeneid*, a national epic demonstrating the superiority of the Roman character.

The *Aeneid's* famous love story of Aeneas and Dido, which forms book 4 of the epic, must be seen in light of this history and purpose. Like Anthony, Aeneas falls in love with an African queen. Unlike Anthony, however, he forgets neither his duty nor Rome, and when ordered to resume the quest for Italy, chooses his destiny over his pleasure. This is not to say that Aeneas simply inverts the story of Anthony or that Dido simplistically reincarnates the notorious Cleopatra. She is victimized and often appealing. He frequently seems ungrateful and exploitive. But in the poem, Dido clearly helps exemplify a Greek *ethos* that finally proves inferior to the Roman spirit embodied by her lover. Finally, in Dido's case, this *ethos* largely amounts to a wrong-headed elevation of private over public duty.

Since Vergil's catalog of heroines is associated with Dido, the catalog members are similarly portrayed. The *Aeneid's* situation thus differs from that in the *Odyssey*, although Vergil's catalog is part of his larger imitation of Homer's underworld sequence. Homer's catalogs of heroes and heroines are connected within a history; Vergil, however, specifically differentiates his catalogs of heroes and heroines through the historical marker of their relationship to Rome's destiny.

In adopting Homer's list of heroines, Vergil retains the biological basis of the Greek catalogs—sexuality is the common denominator in both—but he treats woman's biological relationship to man as destructive passion.[11] In the *Aeneid's* catalog of heroines, women's association with the individual and private life severs their connection to Roman historical contexts, which Vergil clearly defines as male in character. Additionally, Dido and the hero-

---

11. There is much precedent for this shift. The characterization of love as suffering and of passion as dangerous is also seen in the poetry of aristocratic Greek poets such as Alcaeus, Sappho, Ibyais, and Anacreon.

ines are portrayed, if not without compassion, as especially vulnerable to love, and thus to character failings. Vergil's heroines are famous *and* unhappy, a new depiction in the epic catalogs[12] and one implying vexatious moral questions about the heroines' lives.

Like Odysseus, Aeneas meets the heroines in the realm of Persephone. They are confined, however, to a dismal spot called the Fields of Mourning (*Lugentes Campi*). In part, these women's unhappy and unenviable fate derives from the *Aeneid*'s particular view of history. Vergil's poem organizes human history into a universal plot in which the founding of Rome is presented as a turning point. The epic proceeds teleologically to this climax, which influences every part of the narrative, even if the event itself does not take place in the poem. The heroines happen to be associated with the wrong side of that historical turning point. When Aeneas goes to Orcus for directions (which prove, unlike Odysseus's simple sailing instructions, to be a moral blueprint and justification for the Roman Empire), he meets two important figures from his past: Dido, his former lover, and Anchises, his father. The former (and her catalog of heroines) are associated with all that Aeneas has left behind, while the latter (who appears with the catalog of Rome's heroes) points to the future.

This opposition between a dead past and a glorious future marks every aspect of the catalogs, from the appearances of Dido and Anchises to the contexts of the listings. The heroes are found in the Elysian fields, where they appear as a unit with purpose and direction, marching toward the light in a crisp, direct line. The heroines are scattered and isolated, aimlessly wandering the hidden paths of the gloomy *Lugentes Campi*. Additionally, while Dido is silent, bitter, and crazed, Anchises is a fountain of words, eloquently justifying Rome's future position as ruler of the civilized world. In short, Vergil associates the heroines with confusion, stagnation, and isolation. They have no purpose, no future, no sense of dedication, qualities all represented in the catalog of heroes. By submitting to passion, Dido and her companions have obviously refused to accept a "wider historical perspective" (Bono 1976, 215). Since Anchises is the ancestor of Vergil's patron, Augustus Caesar, and since Dido is associated with Rome's two greatest enemies— Carthage (her city) and Cleopatra (the African queen)—the contrast is hardly surprising, but it does negatively affect this catalog's image of femineity.

Whether or not one takes Dido's side in her quarrel with Aeneas, her behavior and placement also suggest that her fate is a warning against the

---

12. See Finley 1978 for an argument that Homer's heroines are also unhappy.

very un-Roman idea of abandoning one's duty.[13] Her appearance in Orcus is not without ominous signs. When Aeneas first spots her, she is compared to the moon half-glimpsed through a cloud—"qualem primo qui surgere mense /aut videt aut vidisse putat per nubila lunam."[14] The simile carries overtones of lunacy and disorder both in its evocation of visual unreality (Aeneas is not even sure he sees Dido) and in the association of Dido with the moon. Since one of the *Aeneid*'s most persistent image patterns portrays the march toward Rome as a march toward light,[15] Dido's description as a visually vague figure—a cloud-veiled moon—excludes her from a purposeful pattern of ascent.

Aeneas's exchanges with Dido also indicate her antithesis to the poem's heroic themes. Unlike those of Homer's heroines, Dido's words do not merely go unrecorded; she refuses to speak. This intransigence is modeled in part on Aias' refusal to speak in the *Odyssey,* another silence born of insanity and great loss. But Vergil emphasizes the passion behind Dido's agony with two significant metaphorical descriptions. Her still burning ("ardentem" [442]) eyes pick up on the fire imagery of *Aeneid* 4 which describes Aeneas and Dido's destructive love. Her face of stone ("si dura silex aut stet Marpesia cautes" [471]) vividly conveys her imprisonment in that state of insane passion. Dido is trapped in her last minutes of misery, an exemplum of how passion can destabilize one's life.

The secret, winding pathways of the dimly lit *Lugentes Campi* suggest this isolation and romance—isolation from social and historical context, the romance of private passion. When Vergil says that Dido wanders through these fields, his word for the movement is "errabat" (451), a significant choice.[16] *Errare* translates not only as directionless wandering but also as wandering that misses the right way. It can also mean to lose one's self, a description that certainly applies to Dido if we compare her appearance in Orcus to her first appearance as the competent ruler of Carthage. Dido has

---

13. Perret (1964) argues that just such an inference can be made. For a dissenting view on Dido's culpability, see Perkell 1981. She argues that in respect to Aeneas's reactions to Creusa and Dido the book exhibits a pattern of "departure, female casualty, denied responsibility, and *pietas* . . . intended to reflect an incomplete humanity in Aeneas and in the *pietas* which he exemplifies" (1981, 370).

14. All quotations of the *Aeneid* are taken from Virgil 1956. These lines are from 6.453–454. Further references to this work appear in the text.

15. For a discussion of this pattern see Poschl 1962 and Brooks Otis, *Vergil: A Study in Civilized Poetry* (Oxford: Clarendon, 1964).

16. Perret also points out this word choice, which he sees as an "evocateur de l'instabilité essentielle à l'amour humain" (1964, 258).

thus wandered into error. The heroines who accompany her reinforce this impression, for these other women share her fate. Among the seven, three come from Homer—Phaedra, Procris, and Eriphyle—while four are Vergil's additions—Evadne, Pasiphaë, Laodamia, and Caeneus. All seven die violent deaths, but the real common denominator among them is that they lived, as classicist Jacques Perret points out (1964, 250), for passion. The *Aeneid* classifies them as victims of love—"quos durus amor crudeli tabe peredit" (442). Yet though Vergil never directly accuses the heroines of error or misjudgment in this respect, the catalog's structure suggests that the heroines, like Dido, are not simple victims. Vergil's choice of exempla purposefully combines three women whose love is innocent (Procris, Evadne, and Laodamia) with three women whose love is at fault or abnormal (Phaedra, Eriphyle, and Pasiphaë), thus inscribing Dido's own mingling of guilt and innocence within the grouping of heroines. The final example of Caeneus also emphasizes that love is a typically "feminine" tragedy. Like Dido, Caeneus vacillates between a male and female "nature." Raped by Neptune, she requests that he change her into a man so that she may avoid a second victimization. Here in Orcus, however, she reappears as a woman. Just as the catalog's grouping of innocent and guilty echoes Dido's innocence and guilt, so Caeneus's integration of sexual vulnerability and femineity illustrates the role of passion in Dido's life, as Perret has argued (1964, 252). As Caeneus passed from woman to man to woman, so Dido passes from the feminine wife to the manly ruler to the feminine lover. Love "emasculates" the vigorous sovereign of Carthage and returns her to the subordinate sex. This vulnerability also disfigures her public role, rendering Dido unequal to the authority she once wielded. In truth, Dido's passion removes her from history; in the *Lugentes Campi* she is confined to a poetic emblem of the private life, which becomes in a special way her prison, locking her away from the history of Rome. With the *Aeneid*, the catalog of heroines acquires new notes of pathos and despair, partly derived from the heroines' new isolation.

Plutarch's catalog, however, returns to many old themes found in Homer and Hesiod and specifically reverses the distinction between male and female found in Vergil's catalog. Like Hesiod, Plutarch was a native of Boethia, and like the *Eoiae*, *Mulierum virtutes* includes several stories that link the founding of cities to the tales of the heroines. But Plutarch was also, like Vergil, a Roman citizen who lived through a succession of bad rulers and civil war before ending his days under relatively enlightened imperial rule. This experience may account for the emphasis on civic virtue in *Mulierum virtutes*.

In the time of Augustus, Roman historians customarily described the Greek influences as pernicious and emasculating, but in Plutarch's lifetime, the Roman East was on the threshold of its second- and early third-century renaissance. As Christopher Jones notes in his study of Plutarch's attitude toward Rome, Plutarch himself exemplifies "the absorption of Greek men of culture into the social and administrative conditions of the Empire" (1971, 138), for he speaks, even when critical of Rome, as a citizen. It's tantalizing to think that Plutarch writes about the unrecognized talents of his heroines at the very time when Rome began to recognize the talents of the "effeminate" Greeks. (A major theme in *Mulierum virtutes* is the Greek heroine's service to her city.)

But whether or not this change in the status of Greeks affected Plutarch's treatment of his heroines, he clearly had philosophical traditions to draw on for his praise of women. While Greek philosophers such as Aristotle often denigrated women, the Stoics (whom Plutarch admired) often argued the opposite side. Cleantis, for example, wrote a treatise entitled "Concerning the Proposition that the Virtue of Men and Women Is the Same," and Musonius wrote that women also should be allowed to practice philosophy. In addition, between Homer and Hesiod's catalogs and *Mulierum virtutes* lies a sporadic but vital catalog tradition in Greek literature.[17] Sopater, a first century Alexandrian satirist, reportedly excerpted material from three such collections—Artemon of Magnesia's *Accounts of Deeds Done Courageously by Women,* Apollonius of Tyre's *Women Who Were Philosophers or Otherwise Accomplished Something Noteworthy or through Whom Houses Were Joined in Good Will,* and an anonymous collection, *Women Lifted to Great Fame and Brilliant Reputation.* None are extant, but all three are suggested sources for an existing, anonymous collection entitled *Women Intelligent and Courageous in Warfare.*[18] As the titles of these works indicate, such catalogs take a more multifarious approach to femineity than did earlier Greek collections. Suidas also mentions a Charnos of Carthage, who supposedly wrote biographies of women in four books.

The most important of these later Greek catalogs, however, is clearly Plutarch's own, written in the first century A.D. Even though unknown to

---

17. A brief history of this tradition can be found in Stadter 1965, 7–8.

18. This catalog, included in Anton Westermann, *Paradoxographoi, Scriptores rerum mirabilium Graeci* (Braunschweig: Anton Westermann, 1839), 213–18 contains fourteen sketches. Ten heroines are barbarians (Semiramis, Zarinaia, Nitocris of Egypt, Nitocris of Babylon, Dido, Atossa, Rhodogyne, Lyde, Tomyris, and Onomaris). Four are Greek (Argeia, Pheretime, Thargelia, and Artemisia). Following this catalog is a collection giving another picture of femineity: "Houses which were ruined through women."

medieval catalogers, it deserves our attention as the first catalog to argue for women's civic contributions and for the equality of male and female virtue.

Besides continuing features from the Greek epic catalogs, Plutarch's *Mulierum virtutes* changes how and why its heroines are praised. To begin with, the circumstances of its composition link it with epideictic rhetoric, the branch of oratory concerned with occasional speeches, funeral orations, and the literature of praise.[19] Written for Clea, the priestess of Delphi,[20] the essay is intended as a memorial for a woman named Leontis, recently deceased. In his introduction, Plutarch reminds Clea of their conversation at the time of Leontis's death and surprisingly argues that men and women have one and the same virtue. He goes on in this essay to dispute the Athenian leader Thucydides, who once claimed that a woman is distinguished by not having a public reputation, whereas the opposite is true for men. Plutarch also embraces the Roman practice of publicly honoring women after their death, and hopes his catalog will honor Leontis. The opening thus promises not only to praise women but also to do so within an essentially public frame, just as for men. In combination, these two approaches delineate a starkly new stance in the catalog tradition.

Plutarch's second innovation is to present the catalog as a form of historical exposition and argument. These stories are not meant to "beguile," but to convince and persuade (even though Plutarch maintains that entertainment in the service of learning is not to be eschewed). The catalog's exempla thus function explicitly as arguments, a classification of obvious importance for the texts of the *querelle des femmes*. Moreover, Plutarch stresses his heroines' historicity by calling attention to his scholarship. He asserts that he will offer Clea rare examples, not the usual individuals recited on such occasions. This explanation effectively publicizes Plutarch's shaping presence within the collection, making his defense of methodology a case for his own integrity. This conventional rhetorical strategy would become important in later medieval collections.

The problem of where Plutarch obtained his examples brings us to his final innovation, the structuring of *Mulierum virtutes* as a florilegium. Philip Stadter has proven that Plutarch gleaned his material from the original Greek histories themselves, thus demonstrating that the catalog is a florilegium in the truest sense of the term, even if Plutarch, like most compilers, occasion-

---

19. The genre of the encomium, for example, falls within epideictic rhetoric.
20. Plutarch was a high priest of Delphi; Clea is a historical character.

ally made creative use of his sources.[21] Like all florilegia, then, *Mulierum virtutes* exhibits a heterogeneity not found in the epic catalogs of Homer, Hesiod, or Vergil. While most of Plutarch's examples illustrate women's courage—in defiance of courage's traditional position as the preeminently male virtue—he also praises the heroines for their piety, intelligence, beauty, chastity, patriotism, and generosity.[22] As such attributes imply, the catalog's heroines occupy a variety of roles far beyond their biological function in the epic catalog. Telesilla of Argos is a poet, the Celtic women are judges, and the wife of Pythes (Plutarch's crowning, final example) is a wise and effective ruler. Finally, Plutarch's pattern of exemplification treats women both as a group and then as individuals, thus establishing that women have claims to virtue as individuals and as a gender. As we shall see, this argument sharply diverges from one of the persistent patterns of isolation in later catalogs, which frequently include a virtuous heroine only to deny her femineity.

Any of these innovations would make Plutarch's essay significant; together they account for a new catalog form and argument that define virtuous femineity in the same terms as those invoked in collections of famous men. *Mulierum virtutes* treats as virtuous the women who make active contributions to the good of the community and who are thus integrated into rather than isolated from it. In fact one of the reiterated patterns in the collection is that of the Greek heroine's struggle against a foreign despot. Plutarch also proposes that such actions are equal in kind to men's. While he never advocates social reform, and does uphold the model of feminine subservience in other works, this advocacy marks a significant milestone in the catalog tradition. In terms of methodology, *Mulierum virtutes* also sets a new standard of public praise by applying the principles of epideictic rhetoric from within a florilegium. Finally, Plutarch's concern with the integrity of his methods underscores his utilization of the catalog as a polemic. Such authorial integrity would later become a vital argument in scholarly catalogs asserting women's worth—that is, in catalogs that went against received assumptions about the authoritative notion of femineity. While *Mulierum virtutes* did not directly influence medieval catalogs, its innovations make it the first of a

---

21. Stadter (1965) notes that Plutarch often worked from memory and sometimes forgot what were, to him, irrelevant details, i.e., incidents that did not directly relate to the virtues under examination. He also sometimes combined sources for a more complete account.

22. Among the twenty-seven stories, the women of Miletus and Ceos exemplify chastity; Aretaphila, wisdom and beauty; Camma, fidelity; and Statonice, generosity. Several are lauded for their struggles against tyrants—Timocleia, Eryxo, Aretaphila, and Xenocrite, for example.

type, and since Plutarch was widely read in the Renaissance, a study of this essay's influence is needed. As it stands, however, the book offers an intriguing instance of how the early epic catalogs of feminine fame led to a very early argument for women's virtue.

The use of the catalog to exemplify the opposing, misogynic stance is best articulated, if not argued, in various satiric catalogs that trace their origins back to ancient Greece. Like the epic catalog, the satiric collections emerged in late archaic Greece and were also conditioned by the rising importance of the family. But where the epic catalog reflects women's concomitant rise in prestige, the satiric catalog builds upon the husband's heightened preoccupation with his wife's potential infidelity.

Why misogyny played such an important role in Greek culture is not entirely clear, but one theory presented by Arthur (1984) suggestively links literary misogyny with woman's new economic importance within the family.[23] The success of the nuclear family logically depended on the wife's willingness to support her husband. Likewise, in the Greek *polis,* the continuance of the family's claims over land rights was contingent upon a woman's ability to produce an heir. These issues were of paramount economic importance in early Greece, where the availability of land was greatly restricted.[24] Women were transferred on marriage from one family to another. Denied any major social or political freedom, they had little concrete stake in any particular family or group. With women's loyalties thus suspect, it is not surprising that men came to believe women required male supervision and control.[25] In time, this belief influenced even the Greek cosmologies. Hesiod's *Theogeny,* for example, portrays women as hostile to civilization and lacking in moral dimension. In other philosophical works, the lower station occupied by femineity is expressed through a tendency to think in warring opposites.[26] The Pythagoreans' Table of Opposites, whose earliest stage is thought to be preserved in Aristotle's *Metaphysics* 986.A, aligns

---

23. See Arthur 1984, 23–52.

24. See, for example, Aristotle, *Athenian Politics* 2; Plutarch, *Solon* 13; William J. Woodhouse, *Solon the Liberator* (1938; reprint, New York: Octagon, 1965); Douglas M. MacDowell, *The Law in Classical Athens* (Ithaca, N. Y.: Cornell University Press, 1978); and Hans J. Wolff, "The Origin of Judicial Legislation among the Greeks," *Traditio* 4 (1946): 31–87.

25. As Arthur notes, the "perception of woman as a threat and the hostility towards them as sexual beings, implicitly expects them to assert their claims . . . and implicitly understands the need to justify the prevailing order against such claims" (1984, 50).

26. For a discussion of the ways in which oppositions were used and related to each other, see Lloyd 1971.

femineity with such negative qualities as darkness and evil. Satiric catalogs, while less inclined to philosophy, build on the same assumptions.

The earliest example of a satiric catalog is Semonides of Amorgos's *On Women*, which classifies vicious feminine behavior by type. The fact that Semonides names these types after animals and elements is part of his joke— women are, *sui generis*, inhuman. The poem reveals its middle-class origins by basing its definitions on daily behavior, but the outlines of its stereotypes accord perfectly well with the *Theogeny* and Aristotle's discussion of Pythagorean opposites. Three pragmatic feminine vices are emphasized in *On Women*—sexual impropriety, idleness, and disobedience, the latter usually exhibited through speech. The donkey woman and the cat woman, for example, indiscriminately bed with all comers, embodying the threat of illegitimate heirs. An aristocratic type termed the mare woman[27] combines all three vices in her flirtatious life style. Lazy and provocative, she mates (i.e., works to produce an heir) only if forced. Other idle types are less finicky but no less disruptive. The pig woman, the donkey woman, and the earth woman all thrive on their husbands' labor, consequently shrinking the family's financial base. Finally the sea woman, dog woman, vixen woman, and ape woman represent the rebellious side of the gender. The ape woman is a particular misfortune since she is clever *and* oblivious to ridicule. *On Women* is perhaps the first catalog to decry women's intelligence.

Semonides's collection also contains an example of virtuous womanhood, but it is ironic. The bee woman is industrious, loving, fertile, and submissive. More important, she increases her husband's wealth. Unfortunately she is atypical and rare. Further, her name recalls one of Hesiod's most violently misogynic passages in the *Works and Days*,[28] where he compares the abused husband and the lazy wife to worker and drone bees. The woman, like the drone, stays home and grows fat while the husband, like the worker, lives a life of unceasing toil. So while the bee woman reveals the economic base of Semonides's definitions—their roots in a subsistence economy—she does nothing to diminish the collection's satiric bite.

As Semonides's poem demonstrates, even at this early stage the satiric catalog is associated with "certain distinct conventions" (Arthur 1984, 47) which through the Roman, patristic, and medieval periods were frequently

---

27. In one poem, for example, the aristocratic poet Anacreon compares a young girl to a Thracian filly he wants to mount, a comparison that soon became a literary cliché.

28. See Hesiod, *Theogeny, Works and Days,* ed. M. L. West (Oxford: Clarendon, 1988), 302–6. For a discussion of this passage, see Sussman 1984.

used, clearly demarcated, and seldom changed. The persona's definition of vice simply inverts the virtue defined by the bee woman, whose conduct is represented as restricted and rare. The persona makes sweeping, unsupported generalizations and is guilty of giving only one side of the argument. He is thus an unreliable guide to conduct, and the discerning reader then and now is not encouraged to take his accusations at face value. Such a characterization naturally leads the reader to question whether the author is satirizing women, the persona, or something else entirely. The catalog's tone is also ironic and often humorous. Its heroines exemplify the same use of feminine stereotype found in modern comedies, as, for example, the character of Sibyl Fawlty in *Fawlty Towers*.[29] While the economic basis of the poem sounds realistic enough, *On Women* is, like many other satires, best understood as an extended joke fueled by acerbic, at times bad-tempered observations of human nature.

The most important Roman satiric catalog also implements many of these conventions, but it employs them with a much sharper tone. Written around the same time as *Mulierum virtutes,* Juvenal's *Satire Six* responds to a perceived decline in Roman values and moral strengths. Like all Juvenal's satires, it is marked by an extraordinarily skillful use of *vituperatio*.[30] It preserves *On Women*'s economic concerns but adds a sociohistoric frame that greatly enlarges the consequences of feminine vice and that mimics the historical referents of epic catalogs. Partly because of his rhetorical training, which emphasized the use of exempla, Juvenal also moves his catalog toward the florilegium by invoking actual women in addition to simple satiric types.[31] The charges he makes remains essentially the same as these in *On Women*—women are sexually insatiable, morally depraved, and dangerously idle. But the exempla that support these accusations characterize a whole society rather than a single gender. They move women's wickedness from the sphere of domestic strife to the sphere of cultural history, with the clear implication that the depraved woman appropriately symbolizes (if not causes) the present Roman decline—the satire's true target.

While the internal unity of *Satire Six* has long been recognized as problematic, the satire itself, as W. S. Anderson (1956) has argued, clearly

---

29. Hugh Lloyd-Jones's introduction to Semonides (1975) also argues that the purpose of the poem was entertainment.

30. Anderson (1961) argues that Juvenal's satires are most closely associated with the *genus demonstrativum* and with the style *vituperatio*.

31. Juvenal often uses exempla to structure his satires. Anderson (1956) argues that his skill lay in arranging the exempla to build up a complex, interacting portrait.

falls into two loosely related sections. In general, the persona's pretext for speaking is that he must dissuade his friend Posthumus from marriage. From lines 1–286, he speaks of women's failings as wives. An opening reference to the Golden Age introduces a quasi-mythical frame for the discussion by charging that unchastity (*impudicitia*) signaled the end of man's early utopia and the beginning of his present moral decline. The second section (ll. 287–661) speaks in general terms of women's vices. It opens with a historical reference to the wars with Hannibal and discusses the dominance of *luxuria* in Roman society, which is then held responsible for the decay of Roman virtue and integrity.

In addition to this division, Juvenal's persona bases his attack on two historical commonplaces. The first dates at least to Aristotle and charges that a society affording too much freedom to women is emasculated and vulnerable. The second, a favorite of older Roman historians—Juvenal is being rather old-fashioned—blames Rome's present decline on money and the eastern luxuries it can buy, temptations that Juvenal associates with his female exempla.[32]

In making his attacks, the persona begins with an offensive against wives' sexual insatiability, a charge also dominant in *On Women*. Tuccia cannot command—"imperat"—herself;[33] the rustic Thymele is easily seduced by the pantomimist's sensual movements; Eppia and Messalina, the most striking historical exempla of the poem, are controlled by their passion. The last two heroines also illustrate the persona's special invective against the monied upper classes, for Eppia, a senator's wife, deserts her family to run away with her gladiator lover Sergius (82–114), and Messalina, the wife of the former Emperor Claudius, is led by her perverse tastes to masquerade nightly as a prostitute in a local brothel (114–33). Each woman's escapade is rendered vividly, sensually, even coyly. The persona dwells, for example, on Sergius's disgusting deformities, which, like his "sword," are the source of Eppia's attraction. We are also treated to an especially close look at Messalina in the brothel, lying amid soiled coverlets with her gilded breasts and belly exposed. Later, as she slinks back to the palace, we are reminded that she carries the smell of the brothel to her emperor's pillow, thus betray-

---

32. The first commonplace dates at least to Aristotle, who attributed the decline of Sparta to the special freedoms enjoyed by its female population. References to the Eastern corruption of Rome are numerous in Roman literature; see, for example, Sallust, *De Catilinae coniuratione* 2.5 and Seneca *Epistulae*. 90.8.

33. Juvenal 1956, line 64. All line references to this work appear in the text.

ing her country along with her husband (another mingling of domestic and historical themes).

An essential part of Juvenal's savagery is his vicious treatment of the satiric catalog's lone virtuous exemplum. His persona goes beyond Semonides's, claiming that this relative of the bee woman, evoked as a "rara avis . . . nigroque simillima cycno" (165), does not exist.[34] Nor, he holds, is that necessarily bad. As Anderson points out in his many discussions of the poem, the examples of the good wife in section 1 are intentionally ambiguous (1956, 75). While Juvenal's cave woman is certainly virtuous in all the traditional ways—subordinate, industrious, fertile, obedient—she is also singularly unattractive and primitive. In like manner, Niobe and Cornelia meet the old standards of fertility but only delight in their children for the glory thus conferred on themselves. Such presentations highlight the persona's extreme point; one shouldn't marry because there are no desirable women. Their apparent virtues only hide their real flaws.

As Juvenal's persona explores the implications of this truism, he expands his theme to link Rome's savage women with Rome's present immorality. In our city, he notes, women rule and men obey. Wives use their sexual charms to acquire power over their husbands; they stage wholesale assaults on traditionally male spheres of power—the law (242–43), gladiatorial exercises (253), and (worse still) rhetoric (280–84). They order the rewriting of their husbands' wills and conspire with their eunuchs against him. They behave as they please. Such social displacements are fed by the women's unchastity, which is funded in turn by Roman wealth.[35] Because of their newly acquired affluence, Roman women can trade heavily in the Eastern luxuries. They turn against traditional religions by either sullying the old rites or abandoning the old faiths entirely for Eastern cults and superstitions.[36] They lead a hedonistic and idle life which Anderson sees as symbolized by *Venus ebria* (1956, 300), the drunken Venus who embodies the women's self-indulgence. In Juvenal's portrait, other sins of the flesh also proliferate— greed, gluttony, cruelty, all the excesses of a dull and witless character. The speaker graphically describes how a drunken hostess arrives late for a dinner, drinks to a point beyond inebriation, and then vomits up the wine before her

34. While *rara avis* became a standard appellation for the virtuous woman of the satiric catalog, the name is not necessarily original with Juvenal. It also occurs in Persius and, as G. Hagendahl (1967) points out, might well have been proverbial.

35. For a longer discussion of this problem see Anderson 1956.

36. Juvenal makes specific reference to an actual scandal of his time. The rites of the *Bona Dea*, a native Roman goddess, were supposed to be open to women alone, yet disguised men were found attending the rites for sexual purposes.

guests. In the persona's words, she "souses the floor with the washings of her insides"—"dum redit et loto terram ferit intestino" (429). The coarse language often used in satires emphasizes the odious physicality of her actions. Such women are "gravis" (418), heavy and hardened beneath their cosmetics and their numbing life styles.[37] In their confusion, tyranny, and irrationality, they measure Rome's fall through wealth, for as the persona notes, when wives were kept chaste by poverty, Rome defeated Hannibal. Now Rome is a victim of the peace—"nunc patimur longae pacis mala" (292)—and is conquered by luxury—"saevior armis /luxuria incubuit victumque ulciscitur orbem" (292–93)—both qualities the persona classifies as "feminine."

The ultimate viciousness of the persona only emerges in his last one hundred lines, where Juvenal's monsters become not merely immoral but criminal. Here the speaker totally reverses women's role in the early epic catalogs. Where Homer and Hesiod's women were celebrated as mothers, Juvenal's *matronae* abort their fetuses and poison their husbands. Claudius was poisoned by Agrippina; Metallus was killed by Clodia. These incidents echo Juvenal's other themes by concentrating on the upper class and evoking a general picture of Rome as a nightmare world. Since these exempla are actual, they are strategically placed at the end to bolster the speaker's most outrageous contentions. They also provide continuity with the past, for the speaker identifies the current models of feminine conduct as Medea, Clytemnestra, Procris, and Eriphyle, the last two being also found in Vergil's and Homer's catalogs. Their appearance at the end of *Satire Six* negates women's most widely recognized contribution to society—their fecundity— while crowning the picture of Rome as a doomed and sterile community. Here woman becomes, as Semonides once characterized her, the greatest evil visited on man. If later catalogs would characterize women as excluded from a culture's public life, *Satire Six* became a source for arguing the disaster that would occur if that exclusion were removed.

Although the poem is hostile to women, it would be simplistic to argue that Juvenal himself shares this view. If *Satire Six* is unkind to Roman women, it is no less harsh on Roman men. Among the men mentioned by the persona, Sertorius is only in love with his wife's beauty (a parallel to feminine sensuality), Censennia's husband marries her only for her money (an instance of male greed), and Ursidius wishes to marry only to be eligible for

---

37. Anderson (1956, 88–89) regards such a description as an intentional play upon the Roman virtue of *gravitas* or earnestness.

benefits under the Augustan marriage laws (a case of clear self-seeking).[38] The persona himself is the most compromised male of all.[39] His inconsistent, wandering narrative betrays a most un-Roman frivolity. Moreover, his violent anger is entirely misplaced by the standards of Roman virtue, as Anderson shows in his article, "Anger in Juvenal and Seneca" (1970). Within the context of Stoic ideals of reason, prudence, and moderation—ideals long recognized as central to *Satire Six*—he hardly appears trustworthy when advising Posthumus to seek a homosexual liaison or his wife's abortion.[40] His recurrent, detailed evocations of the sleazier side of Roman life are also prurient. And his parting remark that husbands should protect themselves by swallowing prophylactics aligns him with the women who abort their own children. He, too, is an avatar of sterility. Juvenal seems to see vice and ignorance as attributes of the Roman populace in general, male and female.

But even if women in *Satire Six* only indicate a general social malaise, they are indisputably Juvenal's main symbols of its decadence. Thus, his use of the feminine *figura* justifies a Vergilian separation between women and history on the grounds of women's immorality. The characterization of social decline as "feminine" does not originate with *Satire Six,* but the work does mark its forceful and influential introduction into the catalog tradition. Later medieval readers and writers, often clerical and frequently celibate, took these accusations seriously. Juvenal's satire arguably treats women as complex symbols for an equally complex phenomenon, but given its scathing attack upon sexuality, it can be read as another affirmation of Vergil's divorce between women and authority. Whether Rome is sick because women hold authoritative positions or women hold authoritative positions because Rome is sick, the message is the same: in healthy societies, women remain home.

This divorce between women and the active life offers one reason why the catalog heroine was found unworthy of the epic's heroic standard but appropriate for the satire's emblem of decadence; it also proved instrumental to one last catalog of antiquity, Ovid's *Heroides,* composed a generation after Vergil's masterpiece. Like the satiric and epic catalogs, the *Heroides* also

---

38. See Wilson and Makowski 1991 for a more complete discussion of such patterns in the poem.

39. This characterization of Juvenal's person has been studied at length. See, for example, Anderson 1970 and Martin Winkler, *The Persona in Three Satires of Juvenal* (New York: Hildesheim, 1983).

40. For a discussion of Juvenal's Stoic sympathies see C. Schneider, *Juvenal und Seneca* (Ph.D. diss., University of Wurzburg, 1930); for a dissenting view see Clarence Mendell, *Latin Poetry and the Age of Rhetoric and Satire* (Hamden, Conn.: Archon, 1967).

focuses on female sexuality, albeit in the form of a suffering fidelity exemplified in the stories of abandoned but faithful lovers. Unlike the satiric cataloger, however, Ovid is interested not in social mores or historical processes but in literary composition, how heroines are characterized. He uses the heroines' situations to parody older texts and explore new tensions in poetics. In fact, the *Heroides* is unique in that it lets the heroines tell their own tales. Each chapter in this collection purports to be a letter written at the crisis point in the heroine's myth. Our impressions of these women arise directly from their own words, although the poet's guiding hand is never far from view. This "layering" of voices—the heroines' under the poet's—gives the *Heroides* its intricate appeal and tone. It also makes the reader focus on how the poet is fashioning his characters and pulling his literary strings.

There are twenty-one letters in the *Heroides,* but the first fifteen are most directly related to the tradition of the catalog of good women.[41] Unlike the other six, these are ostensibly written by abandoned women faithful to their lovers. The authors include many of antiquity's most famous figures— Penelope, Phyllis, Phaedra, Oenone, Hypsipyle, Dido, Hermione, Briseis, Deianira, Ariadne, Canace, Medea, Laodamia, Hypermnestra, and Sappho. All fifteen regard themselves as alone and deserted; they call themselves "sola," "deserta," "relicta." Their letters address absent lovers who have either abandoned them or proven indifferent. The writers are thus harried, often obsessed by the thought of rivals. They plea for their lovers' return, evoking as persuasive arguments the memories of past happiness and past services. Over and over they assert their own sense of worth as lovers. Occasionally they charge their beloveds with ingratitude and perfidy; usually they end with a threat of suicide or revenge. Because the reader is already familiar with the stories, he or she knows that the heroines' hopes and pleas are in vain; consequently, the letters—no matter how ridiculous, self-centered, or silly—appeal to what one critic has called a "sophisticated humanity" (Anderson 1973, 55) on the part of the reader. Yet while one can be genuinely moved by the epistles, their ridiculousness is also unavoidable as well, a juxtaposition that makes for a very peculiar tone.

Not all readers have appreciated the mix; John Dryden, who translated the *Heroides,* and Joseph Addison, who reviewed them, disapproved of

---

41. Thematically and linguistically there are differences between the first fifteen and the last six of Ovid's *Heroides.* At present, critical opinion favors Ovid as the author of all twenty-one letters, but it is also thought that the last six were composed several years after the first fifteen. For a discussion of the many problems associated with this text, see Jacobson 1974, Canon 1971, and H. Dorrie, *Der heroische Brief* (Berlin: W. de Gruyter, 1968).

Ovid's "intrusive" wit.[42] Other and more recent critics have voiced similar complaints.[43] Still other critics, however, have opened new approaches to the poem by accepting the mixed tone as a stylistic feature rather than a flaw. Their work gives us insight into Ovid's parody of genre.[44] This approach will be used here in considering the *Heroides'* metaliterary dimension, an aspect that sets important precedents for at least one medieval catalog.

One of the recurrent problems in Ovid's *Heroides* has been the text's innovative nature, for nothing quite like these epistles exists before them. They were undoubtedly influenced by many other genres, the most important being the Latin love elegy. In fact, an early prototype of sorts exists in Propertius's elegies.[45] As customary in an elegy, the *Heroides* speak of love in a tone of complaint.[46] Even more striking, they are composed in elegiac couplets. Ovid changes the elegiac situation in three important ways: by focusing on women, not men; by modifying a heroic situation rather than heroicizing an erotic one; and by distancing the poet from the speaker, which allows Ovid to satirize the third person in the first.[47] As each epistle in the *Heroides* concentrates on one person's private life, Ovid's play is often directed at parodying the elegiac persona. But while parodic features have long been recognized in the poem, another long-standing critical commonplace is that the *Heroides'* realistic characterizations are its major and most original achievements. Pinpointing the nature of the heroines thus captured on paper has long been an important problem.

Since the recurrent combination of Ovidian wit and effective pathos often makes it impossible to tell whether or when the poet is satirizing his characters, a more fruitful approach is to accept the mixture and look at how Ovid has built on the ruins of older portraits. Throughout the fifteen poems, each heroine systematically emerges from the author's frustration of his

---

42. See *Ovid's Epistles with his Amours,* trans. John Dryden (London, 1761) i–xv, and no. 62 of the *Spectator,* 11 May 1710.

43. Wilkinson remarks that Ovid's heroines "are not too miserable to make puns" (1965, 98).

44. See, for example, Verducci 1985, Anderson 1973, and Jacobson 1974.

45. In *Elegy* 4.3, Propertius portrays a Roman wife writing her soldier husband in the East to express her loyalty and unhappiness. For a comparison of Ovid's and Propertius's techniques, see H. Merklin, "Arethusia und Laodamia," *Hermes* 96 (1968): 461–94.

46. Anderson notes that Ovid employs the verb *queror* in this work fourty-one times, or more frequently than in any of his other texts (1975, 69–70). He also notes that Horace, Propertius, and Ovid defined the standard mood of the elegy with the word *querela.*

47. Anderson (1973) speaks of the first two formations; E. Rand, *Ovid and His Influence* (1925; reprint, New York: Cooper Square, 1963), comments on the satiric tone of the letters. The book-length studies by Verducci (1985) and Jacobson (1974) also comment at length upon Ovid's parodies.

readers' expectations. For example, it is impossible to read Dido's epistle without thinking of Vergil's queen, but in the *Heroides* we do not meet the *Aeneid*'s maddened and tragic Dido. Instead, we see a polished rhetorician contriving her plea with a self-evident artistry entirely missing in Dido's famous confrontation with her lover.[48] Likewise, Canace, who has a child by her brother, reveals none of the volatility, passion, or stricken introspection traditional in an Ovidian heroine caught up in incestuous passions. Innocence and passivity are her keynotes, a surprising combination in light of her story.[49]

The humor of the parodies makes it tempting to think of the heroines as diminished by what they say, and Ovid's epistles do sometimes lower the tragic stature of their ostensible authors. For example, Ariadne was famous in Latin literature through Catullus's portrait of her as the "maiden of Dia . . . midway between human and divine love, between doomed futurity and the consolation of ecstatic apotheosis" (Verducci 1985, 245). But in the *Heroides* she becomes a self-conscious poser. Her complaint, overly rich in visual pictures and artificial postures, makes us see "too graphically" her groping in the empty bed for her lover, her race across the island, her prostration with grief (Verducci 1985, 267).

But despite these nuances in his letters, Ovid is not consistently satiric.[50] As some critics have noted, the Dido of *Heroides* 7 is far more sophisticated and intelligent than the Dido of *Aeneid* 4 (Anderson 1973, 53). And Briseis's letter has a genuinely affecting pathos. It is clear from her epistle that Ovid's characterization makes a sharp divergence from the one that appears in Homer's *Iliad,* where Briseis's brief appearance provides a scene of lucid self-realization. Bereft of Achilles or Agamemnon's love, having lost family, freedom, and land, the slave girl's tears for Patrokolos are also tears for her own fate, seen with perfect and unflinching clarity. As Florence Verducci points out, Ovid obscures this clarity and gives us instead a creature on the brink of self-annihilation (1985, 101). Torn between her positions as slave and lover, Ovid's Briseis literally comes to pieces before our very eyes. Instead of situating herself, she abdicates her "self," actually referring to it as *materiam* (1. 152) or "thing." Her abundant use of the passive voice also suggests a disintegration of will, making for a greatly moving portrait. Nor is her case unique in this respect. Most of Ovid's

---

48. See Anderson (1973) for a detailed analysis of this letter.

49. Verducci's analysis of Canace's letter shows that Canace violates almost every feature of the usual Ovidian heroine of incest (1985, 194–200).

50. Anderson (1973) argues that the heroines are "charming" rather than silly and that Ovid created from older portraits a series of "modern" women with a gift for argumentation.

heroines, even when they are conniving like Dido or posturing like Ariadne, are painfully isolated. Many are suicidal. All write under tremendous psychological pressure. Separated from loved ones, parents, and community, they are close to losing their very sense of self. Indeed, their identities seem fixed only by the songs of loss they sing in their solitude.

Such portraits clearly do not connect women with history or with the community, but as the above discussion suggests, they strongly associate the catalog with literary experiment. By combining antithetical elements (such as humor and complaint), by mixing different generic conventions (such as using heroines from the epic in elegiac situations), Ovid explores a new poetics in the *Heroides,* one that certainly stands outside the literary propriety suggested by Vergil's *Aeneid.* For such a poetics, the isolated, abandoned heroine, who also stands beyond traditional social ties, is a perfect correlative. Nowhere does Ovid make this link more dramatically than in Epistle 15, ostensibly written by Sappho. It's worth examining this letter in some detail not only because it is the last of the first fifteen poems, but also because its author is herself a lyric poet.

Sappho is unique among Ovid's other heroines in this collection in that she is a historical, not a legendary, character, and a poet as well as a lover. As Howard Jacobson notes, these roles parallel Ovid's own, just as Sappho's Leucadian leap to suicide (mentioned at letter's end) is a "metaphor for Ovid's leave-taking of the corpus" (1974, 299). In addition, Sappho's epistle is the only one to speak directly of literary composition. Significantly, she connects her isolation with her waning poetic powers and anticipates many aspects of the Ovidian persona in the *Tristia* and other poems of exile.

Because of Sappho's roles as poet and lover, one important focus of the letter is obviously the relationship between art and life. In the beginning, Sappho mingles these themes by announcing herself with her genre. She will write in the elegiac rather than the lyric mode because her subject—Phaon's desertion—is close to tears. She does indeed call upon numerous elegiac *topoi* in the poem, as Verducci has shown, among them the betrayed lover's complaint, the visit to former romantic haunts, the erotic dream, the warning to successors, the satirical remarks of saner relations, and the equation of love and poetry in the farewell (1985, 137). But her letter has often been recognized as a parody of the elegy, not an elegy itself. In fact, the poem is sometimes classified as a failure because Sappho, by midpoint, confesses to a failing of her poetic powers. While *Heroides* 15 is indisputably weak at points—it is by far the longest and least organized of the first fifteen letters— calling it a failure dismisses the effective contrasts between its successful and unsuccessful passages. It seems far more likely that these protestations, like similar ones in Ovid's *Tristia,* are not accidental. In fact, they evoke the terror of an artist's fall from creativity.

The reasons for this fall are never directly enumerated in the poem, but Ovid draws implicit ties between the decline and Sappho's circumstances. At one point Sappho claims that what you love makes you what you are— "sive abeunt studia in mores" (l. 83)—that in loving the beardless youth Phaon, she has made herself as subtle as her poems. This interaction of life and art proves fatal for her, as writer and woman. She notes that poetry demands a mind at rest, but she burns with a destructive fire. Verducci maintains that this excess of feeling ruins Sappho's art (1985, 137); Howard Jacobson maintains that Ovid's purpose is to parody the elegiac persona (1974, 299). In any case, when it fails, Sappho's epistle undeniably makes a case for the artfulness of art, its disingenuousness, coolness, and removal from life. Involvement with one's subject destroys both art and creativity, whether the subject is love or the founding of Rome. On the other hand, with the right poetic distance a fit subject can be found even in the private life of passion, which Vergil abandons in his poem as antithetical to the Roman spirit. This connection between artist and subject will become important to later catalogs modeled on the *Heroides,* a catalog that examines this problem with regard to a writer's relationship with his sources.

Sappho's portrait also asserts the writer's prerogative to independence. In transforming the real Sappho into a character of the *Heroides,* Ovid exercises his right to make the Greek lyric poet into something simultaneously "literary, legendary, and Ovidian" (Jacobson 1974, 299), a shaping power often applied to other catalog heroines. In fact, considering the echoes of the *Heroides* in the *Amores,* the *Tristia,* and the *Epistulae ex Ponto,* it is fair to see this epistle as part of Ovid's ongoing perfection of a representative persona.[51] The heroine's various parts—poet, lover, and exile—speak to the characteristic Ovidian voice. They are also integral to Ovid's authorial program, his preference for an art of play that, in opposition to the Vergilian poetics of the *Aeneid,* focuses on the individual. In the *Heroides,* then, Ovid embraces the very qualities that Vergil's *Aeneid* had dismissed—passion, absorption in the individual life, alienation from history. Buried in that embrace is a recognition that the heroine, because she is isolated from usual contexts, presents a convenient blank sheet for "indecorous" literary acts.

---

51. For parallels between the *Heroides* and Ovid's later poems, see, Jacobson's (1974) discussion of Sappho's epistle; Helmut Rahn, "Ovids elegische Epistel," *Antike und Abendland* 7 (1963): 105–20; and Betty Nagle, *The Poetics of Exile* (Brussels: Latomus, 1980).

Just as the satiric catalogers project fears, desires, and expectations upon the misogynic stereotype, so Ovid wittily projects literary fears, desires, and expectations on his heroines. As in *Satire Six* and *On Women*, the *Heroides* often realize such projections with humor, but they always do so with a profound literary self-consciousness missing in other classical catalogs. Both the humor and the self-consciousness would attract later medieval poets.

One final point should be made about Ovid's catalog and its relationship to the catalog's development toward the florilegium. While the *Heroides*, unlike *Mulierum virtutes*, can in no sense be considered a florilegium, Ovid's collection does exhibit the kind of variety associated with this genre. What he excerpts, however, are techniques, not content. As Verducci's study of the poem (1985) shows, the *Heroides* gather and then parody other characterizations of the heroines from the genres of myth (Deianira), epic (Dido, Briseis), and elegy (Ariadne). While other florilegean catalogs exploit the authority of the past, this catalog flirts with the authority of literary precedent, insisting on the poet's right to remake conventional techniques. Chaucer's use of the *Heroides* in the *Legend of Good Women*, will build on these ideas in important ways.

While this brief survey of classical catalogs has traced the emergence of catalogs in a number of different scholarly and literary genres, it is important to note that although this diffusion existed, it did not always produce radically different characterizations. Aspects of women's definition remained remarkably consistent from the Greeks to the Romans. Women are viewed in terms of biological function or sexual desire. But the extraordinarily durable conventions also proved extraordinarily diverse in how they might be applied. For example, while Homer and Hesiod use these aspects to associate women with cultural contexts, Vergil and Ovid both assume women's isolation from history and public commerce. Finally, Juvenal uses the idea that women's association with a communal public life and with history is destructive. From its earliest appearance as a simple genealogical list to its later use as a laboratory for literary experiment, the catalog of women remained remarkably flexible. It could invoke, mock, transmit, and transform the authoritative view of womankind, or it could associate that view with other, peripheral concerns, as in Ovid's text. As Christianity transformed the Western world, as medieval Europe crystallized around the fragments of Rome, the catalog's adaptability would prove a useful way to recreate and reuse the notion of femineity. In this re-creation, the reconciliation of authority and ideology would become paramount.

Chapter 2

Woman's Peculiar Virtue

Early Christian literature gives us nothing like the abundance of catalogs found in Greece and Rome, a change that can be explained in several ways. The church fathers, fixated on heaven rather than earth, did not fancy a form whose roots lay in social structure, historical perspective, and earthly love. Moreover, the catalog was firmly associated with a classical heritage they were trying to displace. This association remained strong throughout the medieval period and explains why few catalogs were composed until the revival of classical studies in the twelfth century.[1] Finally, the catalog's association with sexuality—in the form either of passion or reproduction—did not accord with the church fathers' admiration for abstinence as a moral standard.

Yet the early Christian era's one important work containing catalogs of women, St. Jerome's *Adversus Jovinianum,* has an importance that far outweighs its number, for it greatly influenced catalogers to come. While its examples were not often taken up, its methodology was. Jerome's role in devaluing women's status in Christianity is well known, but understanding *Adversus Jovinianum*'s listings within the general catalog tradition can yield new insights. For one thing, Jerome's lists complete the evolution toward the florilegium. They also illustrate how a compiler can manipulate his sources without that manipulation being apparent to general readers.[2] Furthermore,

---

1. Another reason for this neglect might be that the catalog of heroines was replaced in the Middle Ages by *vitae* of female saints. Geoffrey Chaucer recognized this inherent relationship when he called his tales of good women "legends," a word that had only heretofore been used for saints' tales in Middle English. In his preface, Boccaccio also says *De claris mulieribus* does for pagan women what other collections had done for Christian women.

2. This innovation exerted its most powerful influence in the latter half of the Middle Ages when florilegia were composed in great numbers.

they represent the first scholarly catalogs to use the authoritative weight of history to argue a misogynistic view of women's nature.

This view was funneled through the early Christian obsession with chastity, which was not only the leading but the sole index of feminine conduct for Jerome.[3] Such a monopoly of interest did not return the catalog to the single-mindedness of catalog verse—far from it. The chaste ideal both here and in numerous other texts of the faith was divided into three categories of interrelated worths: virginity, continent widowhood, and faithful marriage. The relationships between these states were often convoluted, and reconciling Christian and pagan standards proved complex. But woman's conduct—her virtue or lack thereof—was more than likely measured by the single ruler of her sex life. The new values Christianity placed on sexual mores were therefore paramount to the early Christian era of catalog history, and they must be understood in the context of how these values historically came to hold for women.

While scholars have only recently studied how Christianity's revolution in sexual values changed women's lives, it is fairly clear that the changes provoked traced the same general pattern as in early Greek societies. Initially beneficial, the social shift later worked to women's detriment.[4] At first many women saw the new faith as offering unique opportunities. A number of Christianity's earliest and most enthusiastic converts were women. Educated pagans routinely and derisively referred to the sect as a "cult of women and slaves" because the hatred of social barriers inherent in Christ's teaching attracted large numbers from both groups. Christianity also tendered women the opportunity of life lived without men, or, conversely, a life of equality with men, both offers stemming from the early eschatological orientation of the church. Their faith strongly ascetic from Greek, Jewish, and Oriental roots, early Christians believed they were living in the last days of history. They saw no purpose in procreation and encouraged both men and women to devote themselves exclusively to religious duties.[5] Surprisingly egalitarian

---

3. A great deal of work has been done recently on the topic of virginity as a virtue. See, for example, John Bugge, *Virginitas: An Essay in the History of a Medieval Ideal* (The Hague: Martinus Nighoff, 1975); Demetrius Dumm, *The Theological Basis of Virginity According to St. Jerome* (Thesis, Pontificium Athenaeum Anselmianum, 1961); and McNamara 1976.

4. See Ruether 1974 for a detailed acount of the background to this ideological shift.

5. See McNamara 1983; Stevan L. Davies, *The Revolt of the Widows: The Social World of the Apocryphal Acts* (Carbondale, Ill.: Southern Illinois University Press, 1980); and Leonard and Arlene Swidler, *Women Priests* (New York: Paulist Press, 1977). I am particularly indebted to McNamara's work for my discussion here.

attitudes emerged as a consequence.[6] St. Paul, for example, proposed a society without marriage, with neither male nor female. Even more radically, passages in scripture such as Galatians 2:20 assured women of their spiritual equality in Christ. Evidence in the New Testament and other early Christian documents shows these ideas were implemented as well as discussed. In fact, an early formula for the ordination of women priests survives even today in the Apostolic Conventions, and women were not expressly barred from the priesthood until 352 A.D.

As Christians began to realize that Christ's coming was not imminent, attention turned from heavenly issues to organizing and administering the church as an earthly institution. Egalitarianism was one of the first casualties. As early as the second century A.D., the church began to bar women from authority and even spoke of restricting them to the home. Existing celibate communities of women fought to maintain their rights, aided by the fact that during the years of Roman persecution, church leaders were reluctant to lose a valuable group of converts. In addition, many of the early Fathers sincerely supported the bilateral chaste ideal, no matter how deeply they distrusted feminine sexuality. Beginning with Tertullian in the second century A.D., a number of them—Cyprian of Carthage, John Chrysostom, Methodius, Ambrose, and Origen—threw their support behind women celibates.[7]

Accepting these communities created ideological and practical problems, however, for Christian leaders had to define a social place for such women. No real classical precedent existed for a group of women pledged to life-long celibacy. Moreover, neither the church hierarchy nor the early Fathers were willing to surrender patriarchal control of their faith. To maintain this status quo, they had to reconcile existing secular models, which called for women's subservience, with a new ecclesiastical model, which glorified the virgin. The Pauline marriage model placing wives in submission to their husbands had been justified by the notion of woman as a "weaker vessel."[8] The spiritual perfection of female celibates called this idea of woman's inferiority into question. Most specific, the church was nervous lest the woman celibate be elevated over priests, who were frequently married. A solution was found by redefining gender. In the first century A.D.,

---

6. Biblical passages also refer to this earlier Christian spirit of egalitarianism. See, for example, I Timothy 6:3; Revelations 2:20; and I Timothy 3:16.

7. See, for example, Cyprian, *De habitu virginem;* St. John Chrysostum, *Hom. XIX ad I Cor. VII 1, 2* and *De virginitate;* Tertullian, *Ad uxorem, De exhortatione castitatis,* and *De pudicitia;* and St. Methodius, *The Symposium of Ten Virgins.*

8. The term "weaker vessel" comes from St. Paul's comments in Ephesians 5:22–33.

Clement of Alexandria asserted that women were female only in their roles as wives and childbearers. The church now reasoned that if the female religious removed herself from these roles, she removed herself from her gender as well. A celibate woman thus became, in moral terms, a man. Social control over women celibates was preserved by returning to the marriage model. On earth, such a woman was a "bride of Christ" and like an earthly wife derived her excellence from her husband.[9] This compromise preserved the gender's inferior position but granted the woman celibate both her virtue and her right to social place. Both virtue and place, however, came at the cost of a feminine capacity for virtue.

The pagan catalog of heroines could illustrate and defend this view because, like the Christians, pagans frequently thought of femineity as categorically inferior. As early as the Pythagoreans, classical philosophers had associated femineity with vice and chaos, maleness with virtue and order. In fact the fit between Christian and pagan misogyny was very close on this point. If the lifestyle of a woman celibate was new, the ideal of marital chastity was not. Nor had chastity been without its special privileges in antiquity. The Romans had honored women with only one husband as *univirae*. The priestesses of Vesta, Diana, and Apollo had always held virginal offices for the terms of their tenure.[10] A literary tradition of the virago or manly woman accorded quite well with the idea of the woman celibate as virile. Christianity's early ascetic bias simply adapted these views to new contexts. The basis of comparison was already present.

Even so, a Christian catalog of women was not written until rather late in the history of Christian Rome and by St. Jerome, a Father very different in education and outlook from early church leaders. By the fourth century A.D., stewards of the church were educated men, well able to meet the catalog's special demands for learning. More important, they knew how to justify using pagan material in a Christian text, an approach still very controversial among the new Christian elite.[11] It is not surprising that St. Jerome introduced the catalog into the Christian tradition, for Jerome forged the

---

9. Tertullian was the Christian thinker who actually coined the term "bride of Christ." He introduced it, almost casually, in *Adversus Haereses*. Although a fervent supporter of celibate women, Tertullian was enraged when some women virgins in his African church saw themselves as equal to men and therefore qualified to participate in sacerdotal services. In *De velandi virginum,* he rejected this stance out of hand and recommended that women celibates be cloistered and veiled as a sign of their submission.

10. These priestesses, however, generally married on completion of their services.

11. St. Ambrose had studied the Greek philosophers but opposed using them. St. Jerome, a humanist and philologist, provided a whole arsenal of reasons for citing pagan *auctores* in his

most enduring arguments for consulting pagan learning in the service of the faith. A brilliant scholar as well as a doctor of the church, he took pride in his learning and rhetorical skill. And his catalogs in *Adversus Jovinianum* show an exquisite knowledge of antiquity.

Yet even so, this knowledge does not appear gratuitously as rhetorical flourishes. Jerome musters his exempla to refute ideas voiced by the heretical monk Jovinian, who had criticized the chaste ideal as "unnatural" and specific to the Christian time and place.[12] In *Adversus Jovinianum*, St. Jerome uses his heroines within a rhetorical *persuasio* to prove that pagans had also valued chastity, albeit with an inferior understanding. While his catalogs are only indirectly concerned then with defining woman's nature, they imply definite attitudes toward femineity.

As we can anticipate from Jerome's faith and purpose, these listings are restrained in their praise of chaste pagans and clearly portray pagan virtues as unfocused and inadequate. Jerome specifies that classical exempla are not cited to praise the heroines but to shame inadequate Christians. But in spite of all this, the catalog illustrates a distinct notion of femineity and a long-lived hierarchy of possible roles for women.

Jerome assembled two distinct catalogs for his treatise—one illustrating feminine virtue, the other feminine vice. By including both, Jerome defines the entire spectrum of behavior open to women and suggests that the difference between virtue and vice lies more in degree than in kind. Later medieval catalogs adopted the same attitude; they also borrowed Jerome's structure, treating first the manly virgin, then the continent widow, and finally the faithful wife.[13] At the very bottom of the order, Jerome and his successors place the antipole of virtue—unchastity, a label that (in *Adversus Jovinianum*) applies to widows who remarry as well as unfaithful or abusive wives. In all groups, women are considered evocations of the physical, and women's virtue depends on the successful restraint of their nature. In the positive

---

70th Epistle. Medieval writers justifying their own citations mined this source over and over again. St. Augustine never clearly formulated a relationship between the new and the old learning, although his *De doctrina christiana,* which defends the rhetorical eloquence of the Bible, was widely accepted as legitimating the study of pagan sciences. For a discussion of this problem, see Curtius 1973, 39–42.

12. Jovinian's tract has been lost, but he appears to have revived the ancient Stoic ideal that all vices and virtues are of equal weight. There should be no difference, he argued, between the virgin and the married Christian, once baptized. For a detailed account of this argument and Jerome's subsequent influence see Delhaye (1951).

13. This hierarchical definition of the chaste ideal was not, of course, original with Jerome. It can also be found in Augustine, Tertullian, and other fathers of the church.

catalog, virginity is logically highlighted and supreme, but the widow also attracts a great deal of Jerome's attention because the status and virtue proposed for her are new. Widowhood in the ancient world had meant a loss in money, power, prestige, and good fortune. In making her second only to the virgin, Jerome helped to create a new class without real historical precedents in the West.[14] But although his reworking of classical material was greatest in respect to this category, he modified exempla for all three states to fit the new Christian context.

Jerome's catalog begins with the viragoes (the virile virgins) who, like the woman celibate, transcend their gender through their chastity. Women athletes and warriors such as Atlanta and Camilla illustrate the virgin's manliness while women religious figures such as the Sibyls, Cassandra, Chryseis, Vesta, and the priestesses of Apollo, Juno, Diana, and Vesta speak to the virgin's "knowledge of the counsel of God."[15] A host of pagan "martyrs"— women who killed themselves or were slain in defense of their chastity— roughly parallel the Christian martyrs of the recent persecutions. And a rare catalog of virgin births—including Minerva, Buddha, Plato, and Romulus and Remus—testifies to pagan parallels to Mary. This latter and climactic listing combines the points made by the other two. The viragoes' virility is represented by the males of the catalog while the piety of the women priests is echoed in the divine or prophetic status of each member. The virgin births also associate virginity with holiness (Buddha), wisdom (Plato and Minerva), and power (Romulus and Remus). Within *Adversus Jovinianum,* the list proves that even pagans acknowledged the intrinsic connection between virginity on one hand, and physical prowess, social fame, spiritual holiness, philosophic wisdom, and physical courage on the other. It is significant, however, that Jerome celebrates virginity itself, not the heroines. Not only does he focus on the children rather than on the virgin mother (even including sons, like Plato, as well as daughters, like Minverva), but the "martyrs" are not given individual names. Neither the gender nor the individual heroines are celebrated.

After the virgin, the section devoted to praising married chastity focuses on both widows and wives; it draws heavily on Roman admiration for

---

14. The new respect given widows can be seen in St. Ambrose's *De Viduis,* which provides a comprehensive definition of widowhood as Christianity accepted it. Lightman and Zeisal (1977) discuss the evolution of the term.

15. St. Jerome, "Against Jovinianus," trans. W. H. Fremantle, in vol. 6 of *A Select Library of Nicene and Post Nicene Fathers of the Christian Church,* 2d series (1892; reprint, Grand Rapids, Mich.: N. Eerdmans, 1978), 379. All English quotations are from this text. Latin quotations are from Jerome 1844–64. Further references to these editions appear in the text.

the *univirae*. As Jerome describes it, this epithet was awarded both to women who refused to marry after their husbands' death and to women who showed extraordinary affection for their only husband. The prevalence of widows in this section betokens Jerome's concern for legitimizing a uniquely Christian standard, but, as we shall see, he distorts history to establish its pedigree. We hear that Dido stabbed herself on her husband's funeral pyre (the same myth Boccaccio later used in his catalog), that Indian wives immolate themselves at their husbands' funerals, and that Rhodogune slew a nurse who advised her to take a second husband. Clearly, we are to approve. Despite the interest in chastity, some of the approbation for both widows and wives rests on traditional social values—modesty, obedience, and loyalty, all familiar emblems of feminine submission since the ancient Greeks. Intelligence and achievement are ignored. Nor are deeds enumerated. Among the faithful wives, for example, the ridiculous Bilia proves her chastity by believing that all men have bad breath because her husband does. Whether she was really this naive or merely endured her husband's fault is immaterial, Jerome says. Either behavior deserves praise in a wife.

At a cursory glance, or to a reader unfamiliar with classical culture, these *exempla* seem to prove that the ancient Romans valued chastity in widows as a moral value. In truth, they did not; Jerome is actually changing, blurring, or omitting facts in many of his *exempla*. An obvious case in point is when he "proves" pagan recognition of virginity's spiritual worth by listing virgin "martyrs" whose suicides accord with a *social* standard.[16] Even more striking is the treatment of widowhood. By even suggesting that continent widowhood was admired, Jerome is falsifying his sources. *Univira* was a term of approbation in ancient Rome, but it never applied to women who survived their husbands. As Marjorie Lightman and William Zeisal have demonstrated, the term's exact connotation changed over the course of history.[17] First applied only to patrician wives with living husbands, by the late republic and empire it referred to women of all classes who had predeceased their spouses. The Christian use of the term for widows was entirely new.

---

16. For example, the daughters of Phidon in *Adversus Jovinianum* committed suicide rather than be raped by their father's murderers. Their response says a great deal about Greek social standards and their own personal preferences, but nothing about Christian martyrs for chastity, who preferred death for spiritual reasons.

17. Lightman and Zeisal (1977) argue that Jerome and other Christians writers expanded the meaning of the term. For another opinion see Jean Gagé, *Matronalia* (Brussels: Latomus, 1963); J. B. Frey, "Signification des termes 'monandros' et 'univiri,'" *Récherches de Science Religeuse* 20 (1930): 48–60, and Michel Hubert, *Le Remariage à Rome: etude à histoire juridique et sociale* (Milan: A. Giuffrè, 1972).

Jerome also ignores the different virtues attributed to the *univira,* whose definition changed not only between pagan and Christian Rome but also within the centuries of pagan rule as well. Originally, such women were examples of propriety and good fortune.[18] Their propriety lay in their obedience to the *pater familias,* be he father or husband. Their good fortune lay in his survival. Jerome retains the first association with obedience but discards, as did later Romans, the reference to good fortune. Chaste widowhood is not a misfortune for him, and when his exempla refer to these older associations, he obscures the difference.

We can best see these and other alterations by looking at two examples Jerome borrowed from Seneca's lost essay *De Matrimonio.*[19] Neither of the two support the Christian ideal, even though Jerome proposes that they do. The first, a widow named Porcia Minor, told a woman: "The fortunate and proper matrona marries only once" (382) ("Felix et pudica matrona numquam praeterquam semel nubit" [275]). This advice embodies the old Roman definition of the term by referring to propriety and good fortune. And when the second widow, Valeria, says that she won't remarry because for her "her husband . . . always lived" (382) ("sibi semper maritum Servium vivere" [276]), she may mean, as Jerome implies, that he lives in her love. But she may also mean that he lives in her hatred. In either case, neither of these examples really supports Jerome's contention that pagan Rome valued the chaste widow because she avoided sexual pleasure since sexuality is not mentioned.

Throughout the opening catalog of chastity, similar misfits also occur in instances unconnected with the *univira.* The wife of Hasdrubal jumps into the flames of Carthage to "escape capture" (30) ("cum se cerneret a Romanis capiendam esse" [274]), but that does not necessarily mean she is concerned only with preserving her chastity, as Jerome infers. Moreover, since her actions deliberately reproach her husband, who is considering surrender, she hardly exemplifies a woman who entertains "a marvelous affection for the only husband" (381) she ever had ("quae mire unicos amaverunt maritos" [273]). An even more startling inclusion is Candaules's wife, who is praised for murdering her husband because he allows a friend to spy upon her in the

---

18. In fact the term may have been originally associated with the early Roman cults. Even in the Principate, the wives of Jupiter *flamines* had to be *univirae. Univirae* also figure in Roman wedding ceremonies described in Tertullian's *De exhortatione castitatis* 13 and *De monogamia* 17.4.

19. Ernst Bickel (1915, vol. 1) traces this source and collects the edited existing fragments of Seneca's essay.

bath. The sequel to the story is still more discordant since the wife remarries after Candaules's death. Neither action exemplifies married chastity or wifely affection.

It is impossible to believe that Jerome was unaware of these inconsistencies in the catalog of good women. He was a highly educated and intelligent man thoroughly trained in classical sciences. Moreover, in a passage from *Adversus Jovinianum* he playfully alludes to possible manipulations or subversions in his lists:

> I feel that in giving this list of women, I have said far more than is customary in illustrating a point, and that I might be justly censured by my *learned* reader. But what am I to do when women of our time press me with apostolic authority, and before the first husband is buried, repeat from morning to night the precepts which allow a second marriage? Seeing they despise the fidelity which Christian purity dictates, let them at least learn chastity from the heathen. (383, italics mine)

> (Sentio in catalogo feminarum multo me plura dixisse, quam exemplorum patitur consuetudo, et a lectore erudito juste posse reprehendi. Sed quid faciam, cum mihi mulieres nostri temporis, Apostoli iugerant auctoritatem; et necdum elato funere prioris viri, memoriter digamiae praecepta decantent? Ut quae Christianae pudicitiae despiciunt fidem, discant saltem ab Ethnicis castitatem. [276])

The passage reads very like the apologia of a formal verse satire, where the persona justifies his attack by characterizing himself as a plain, honest man moved to speak by the injustices surrounding him. Jerome does modify the formulaic pose in one important way; he uses the disclaimer to justify his method, not his attack (which he sees as justifiable). A reasonable man driven to desperation by the women around him, the speaker must resort to distortion in order to communicate his point. If the learned should detect his changes, the speaker dryly implies, these women certainly won't. Better to speak to them in the barbarous style they seem to understand than to haggle with them uselessly. Such a stance would be consistent with Jerome's many castigations of Jovinian's style and the widows' arguments.

As David Wiesen recently argued, Jerome was a master of satiric technique,[20] and I would like to argue that the catalog of *Adversus Jovinianum* shows traces of it even in this positive collection. *Adversus Jovinianum* is not a satire, but it is sometimes shaped by conventions of the genre.

---

20. See Wiesen 1964. Rand (1957) also describes a satiric strain in Jerome's writings but not in connection with *Adversus Jovinianum*.

Jerome's comments on his method could indicate an extension of his attack against Jovinian, whose barbarous style and method of argumentation are explicitly castigated in the opening of Jerome's treatise. (Indeed, Jerome opens *Adversus Jovinianum* more like an incensed classical rhetor than an indignant Christian.) Pagan inadequacies, the rhetorical shortcomings of Jovinian, and the failings of modern Christians are all targets of the satiric tone, but in the process several misogynistic assertions about women's intelligence and fidelity are pressed.

These assertions are also vigorously reinforced later in the treatise by Jerome's negative catalog of wicked wives, a compilation excerpted, Jerome claims, from a lost philosophical tract by the Greek philosopher Theophrastus.[21] At this catalog's inception, an abrupt and puzzling switch occurs in tactics and audience. While women figure as possible ethical temptations in both catalogs, the first catalog of chaste women appears to be directed, at least in part, to widows who wish to remarry. They should read and "imitate the fidelity of concubines" (380) ("Imitentur matronae, et matronae saltem Christianae, concubinarum fidem" [274]) that they might "at least learn chastity from the heathens" (383) ("discant saltem ab Ethnicis castitatem" [276]). The second catalog appears to address men, specifically scholars, whom Jerome tries to dissuade from marriage with his examples of deadly, dangerous, and predatory wives.[22] Both catalogs emphasize women's association with the corporeal, but the negative list aligns women with physical decadence. If these vigorous tales of vice and lust seem out of place in a Christian treatise of virginity, that's because they are. But this kind of combination of lively tale and high moral tone is an effective rhetorical strategy, and one that has attracted readers's interest for centuries.

Most vices attributed to women in *Adversus Jovinianum* would be familiar to readers of *On Women* or *Satire Six*. Since this catalog addresses learned men, however, women's principal threat is different. Women here imperil a scholar's studies, not a husband's control. Because of their sloth, avarice, and lust, wives rob a scholarly man of the peace he needs for his work. Disobedient, contentious, and nagging, they are a constant drain. Xantippe abused Socrates; Actoria Paula insulted Cato; and Cicero's wife, Terentia, married his enemy. Some, like Clytemnestra, murder their husbands; others, like Helen, incite wars. Most important, all incarnate lust.

---

21. In the most complete study of Jerome's sources, Bickel noted that Jerome probably used Seneca and Porphyry for the excerpt.

22. This address to a male audience perhaps explains why this catalog was more frequently imitated by male clerks than was the first.

Jerome argues that woman is sexually insatiable and emphasizes his earlier proposition that wives are among the greatest of evils. Not only can their husbands not satisfy them, but they go to other men to quench their passions and thus bring misfortune. L. Sulla and Cn. Pompey's wives made both men look like fools in the public eye. Pasiphaë, who mated with a bull, produced a monstrous offspring. And Clytemnestra went so far as to murder. Since woman is most representative of her gender in *Adversus Jovinianum* when she is most sexual, this accusation makes the feminine woman a monster of iniquity on the very point Jerome's treatment equates with virtue—chastity. Thus virtue for a woman becomes a matter of denying what she is, a process of rejecting rather than realizing her inner self. In fact, Jerome asserts that chastity is woman's crowning virtue, equal to eloquence, military glory, and political achievement in man.

The idea of a difference between male and female virtue was not new, nor was the idea that the male involved exertion and the female restraint. Aristotle says in the *Politics,* for example, that where a man's virtue lies in command, a woman's lies in obedience; where a man should be eloquent, a woman should be silent (I.13). But since Jerome's preeminently feminine virtue is chastity and since that involves woman's restraint of her sexual and physical nature, the obvious corollary is that femineity is naturally vicious as well as inferior. Jerome's compilation thus illustrates one last isolation added to the catalog tradition—the isolation of the active and virtuous woman from her gender. Here Jerome also found his greatest correlation to pagan material, for the catalog of wicked wives, unlike the other list, needed very little manipulation.

In accusing women of infidelity and sexual insatiability, in associating femineity with the body, Jerome builds on satiric stereotypes common to Greece and Rome. He also portrays feminine virtue in the same way as satiric catalogers, simply by inverting the more common female vice. Unlike Semonides or Juvenal, however, Jerome is making a serious argument, and his catalog carried unusually authoritative and scholarly weight. He creates a continuous spectrum between virginity (and the manly woman) and unchastity (and the feminine one). In the middle, he places the exceptional "womanly" woman of virtue (the good wife) who achieves her status by self-effacement. Her appearance in the positive catalog is quite brief, however, and in the negative one, she appears as a satiric rara avis, not only unusual but useless. If her husband loves her, Jerome says, if she avoids all other failings, she still distracts him from his business by worrying him about her health and safety.

This final mating between the rara avis and the ideal of chastity makes *Adversus Jovinianum*'s definition of virtue bear an unfailingly male face. Pure virgins, continent widows, and faithful wives either act in, defend, or passively acquiesce to an image of male superiority.[23] At the highest levels, women have active roles, but their actions are commensurable with the deeds of male heroes who guard the status quo. They are, in spirit, men. Women who "fall" into marriage but refuse to do so more than once are still admired for controlling their sexual threat. Their lot is passive, however, and their virtue lies in self-restraint. They are obedient to their husbands; their only active gestures are an affirmation of loyalty or an embrace of death. Wives who go their own way and indulge in or use their sexuality are the very emblems of corruption, as Cleopatra had been to Augustan historians. Vicious, petty, contentious, and dangerous, they deny that conventional morality has any claim upon them and act through purely selfish motives. They manipulate men through their sexual wiles and often lure them to their deaths.

Yet, independent, deeply disruptive and potentially fatal as they are, wicked wives are also a source of literary allurement, although it's doubtful that Jerome intended to emphasize this aspect. As noted above, the catalog of wicked wives attracted far more attention than the catalog of virtuous heroines in the years of Jerome's greatest influence. One of the reasons may be the relish of its stories. Even today, these women's outrageous behavior makes for more scandalous and interesting reading than does the passivity of the virtuous heroines, making it tempting to say that in terms of literature, a woman character had to be bad to be good.

Despite the use of the rara avis, then, *Adversus Jovinianum*'s catalogs are not satiric in the same way as Juvenal's or Semonides's. They seriously espouse the chaste ideal for women *and* for men. They also give women some defined opportunity for prestige, limited though it may be. Most important, Jerome does not adapt the pose of a characteristic satiric persona despite his manipulative use of exempla. In *Satire Six* and *On Women*, the speakers are untrustworthy men, implicated in the very vices they condemn. By the nature of their comments, they indict themselves as well as the women they accuse. In contrast, Jerome's comments are all directed against Jovinian, his audience, and his wicked exempla. Instead of highlighting his presence in the catalog proper and making that presence, like Plutarch's, an ethical

---

23. In tracing this schema, I am indebted to ideas in Maureen Fries' unpublished paper, "Women Heroes, Heroines, and Counter Heroes: Images of Women in Arthurian Literature."

argument, Jerome vanishes beneath a cloak of references, which he is (supposedly) only repeating, not shaping. Only the learned reader would ever detect changes. Not all later readers were so learned or so quick. Certainly many of the medieval clerks who read Jerome could not have known that *Adversus Jovinianum* misrepresented both pagan and church history. In its day, Jerome's treatise was a controversial document. Shocked at its abuses since they had hoped it would bring their leader back to Rome, Jerome's own followers went so far as to buy up as many copies of the essay as they could to prevent its dissemination in the capital.[24] Yet the treatise gives no hint of this storm, even though *Adversus Jovinianum* opens with a defense against possible charges of Manicheism.[25] The exempla effectively pose as well-known truisms, information a reasonable person would have expected Jovinian to know when he claimed the Christians invented the chaste standard. When Jerome's popularity was at its peak in the High and late Middle Ages, this use of the compiler's stance would speak to educated clerks and show them a way to manipulate pagan material.

Before leaving *Adversus Jovinianum,* a word should be said about its invocation of the past. Because Jerome calls upon pagan examples, the above discussion may suggest that his catalogs strive to situate woman within a relationship to history. They do not. Historical relevance is unimportant in *Adversus Jovinianum,* whose most important frame is ideological and heavenly. Jerome, like the classical catalogers, chose his examples from the past, but his selection does not consequently argue that no virtuous women exist in the present.[26] If anything, Jerome's treatise exemplifies the striking lack of historical perspective—the blinkered stare toward eternity—that shaped the way medieval people viewed the past.

This flattened view of history also may explain why the early medieval period produced almost no catalogs of women, laudatory or otherwise. The writers of this early period weren't interested in tidbits from pagan history. Additionally, a catalog requires access to libraries or other florilegia, both of which were rare in early Europe. There were no urbane, sophisticated societies to indulge in literary catalogs such as the *Heroides;* no real social controversies brewed over woman's place, such as those which had nurtured the classical and patristic lists. In fact, women enjoyed a peculiar degree of autonomy in the early Middle Ages, and led largely separate lives in the

---

24. The storm surrounding *Adversus Jovinianum* is amply documented in Jerome's own correspondence; see Jerome 1957–80, nos. 48, 49, and 50.

25. This defense occurs in section 3 of *Adversus Jovinianum.*

26. Boccaccio limits his subject similarly in *De claris mulieribus.*

upper and literate classes. As David Herlihy has demonstrated, early medieval lords were often absent from home, waging war or exploring new lands.[27] Left to manage on their own, their wives often enjoyed remarkable scope for their talent in the day-to-day business of running their husbands' estates. Separation between a feminine private and a male public sphere simply did not exist as it had in early Athens or imperial Rome, or as it would again in the early Renaissance.[28] Not surprisingly, then, the early medieval epics feature heroes like Beowulf or Roland, who define their prowess through their relationships with men. They may encounter women in powerful positions, but they are not pictured in the domestic scenes of the Homeric epics nor are they implicated in a sense of cultural history.

On the other hand, writers in the convents and monasteries neglected the catalog for different reasons. Often segregated by vocation, monks and nuns lived lives in which the distinctions between public and private were largely moot. Much of their literature was hagiographic or exegetical. The former did not exploit pagan subject matter; the latter used women as figures for abstraction. Occasional commentaries on Old Testament catalogs, such as the description of the good wife in Proverbs 31:10–31, avoided the wife's gender altogether. The Venerable Bede's commentary, one of the first, equates the good wife with the church. Such a reading is entirely within the normal bounds of medieval exegesis. As Joan Ferrante points out in her study of the medieval image of women, Judith, Esther, Ruth, Mary, Martha, and even reformed prostitutes such as Raab and Mary Magdalene were treated in precisely the same way (1973, 26).

In the twelfth century, circumstances more favorable to catalogs emerged. Society underwent tremendous expansion. Large cosmopolitan centers appeared, culture became secularized, and a learned clerical class was beginning to be trained in cathedral schools (rather than monasteries) where a large number of texts were reintroduced into the West from the Arab world. Reared to fear women, these clerks also compiled catalogs. Since they were taught from childhood that women were impediments to scholarship and avatars of physical temptation, since their attitudes were shaped by a long program of misogamous (anti-matrimonial) and misogynic texts similar in kind to the Theophrastian excerpt from *Adversus Jovinianum*, it is not

---

27. See Herlihy 1976.

28. Stuard (1976) also remarks upon this phenomenon in her introduction. For a reexamination of what the private life meant in different historical eras, see *A History of the Private Life*, ed. Philippe Ariès and George Duby, 4 vols. (Cambridge, Mass.: Harvard University Press, 1988–90).

surprising that they often mined Jerome for exempla and precepts. These early clerical compilations, usually found in texts of misogamous propaganda, argue for the same celibate life-style that Jerome had advocated. But clerical misogamy is much less ascetic in nature than the misogamy of *Adversus Jovinianum.*[29] Clerks wrote for other clerks, who frequently lived active, secular lives beyond monastery walls. As scribes, bureaucrats, or teachers, they were men of the world and consequently were seldom as prudish about sexuality as their cloistered counterparts. In fact, their catalogs frequently cater to a secular audience.

Walter Map's *Dissuasio Valerii ad Rufinum de non ducat uxorem* (Valerie's dissuasion to Rufinus against taking a wife) (ca. 1190; found in Map 1983) is one such catalog. Map himself was no monk, but a witty courtier who served King Henry II of England.[30] That he was not unique can be seen from his publication record. *Dissuasio Valerii ad Rufinum de non ducat uxorem* was one of the best sellers of the High Middle Ages. It was held in such regard that it was even falsely attributed to pagan authors, the greatest possible compliment in medieval letters.

Its popularity tells us a great deal about the catalog's relationship to social condition. Map writes in Latin, a choice of tongues that argues he writes for educated readers, but his wit and style show that the audience is courtly, not monastic. By this time, a courtly audience would have had some pretension to learning, for Map puts his erudition on display. His exempla are often drawn from the classical world. He makes repeated allusions to mythology and frequently quotes pagan philosophers. His ironic and humorous tone suggests that, unlike Jerome, he values amusement. Some of his arguments even go against church teaching, as when the persona tells Rufinus it is better to commit endless adultery than to wed. Marriage, not lust, is the object of his attack, a significant change from *Adversus Jovinianum,*[31] and as Valerius tells Rufinus, the problem with matrimony is that it leads not to sin but to slavery. It binds man by the chains of Vulcan to a creature who

---

29. Wilson and Makowski (1991) propose three branches of misogamous literature—philosophic, ascetic, and general. Although all three argue for the single life, they support it for different reasons. Ascetic misogamy sees celibacy as a spiritual good; philosophic sees it as conducive to good scholarship; general argues that only a fool would marry a woman.

30. Map's friend Giraldius Cambrensis includes some biographical notes about him in *Speculum Ecclesiae.* He describes Map as a favorite courtier of Henry II, who admired Map's learning, his rhetorical flair, and his courtly manner. Although the dissuasion against marriage was originally a separate work, Map included it in *De Nugis Curialium,* which discusses life at Henry's court.

31. Wilson and Makowski (1991) and Delahaye (1951) make the same distinction.

cannot be a moral or agreeable companion. Like Juvenal and Jerome, Valerius uses the misogynistic stereotype to argue against matrimony. Like Juvenal's persona, Valerius also sees little good in women, although his judgment is open to question.

Like any medieval work, Map's catalog is derivative, especially in the accusations it brings against women as physical temptations. Unlike Jerome, however, Map uses women's sexuality mostly to provoke and sustain interest. As was fashionable in his time, he displays his learning by intertwining classical references with more familiar ones from the Bible. Valerius begins with four Old Testament exempla—Eve (disobedience), Bathsheba (bad influence), Delilah (deceit), and Solomon's harem (apostasy)—and then refers to the rara avis (here compared to the phoenix), saying that women such as Lucretia, Penelope, and the Sabines no longer exist. Instead, modern women imitate Scylla (betrayal) and Myrrha (unnatural lust). In this group, Jerome's lack of a historical perspective is carried to its logical limit. Valerius indicates no difference between his pagan and Hebrew examples.

In the next paragraphs, classical exempla balance off the earlier biblical citations. Each illuminates the deleterious effect of love on the male, thus skirting the direct definition of femineity. Europa brings Jupiter to bellow like a bull (male lust as beastliness); Leucothoe causes Apollo to lose his light (male loss of power), and in taking Mars to bed, Venus renders him vulnerable to Vulcan's chains (public ridicule). A reference to Pallas Athene (a rara avis of wisdom) complements the earlier reference to the phoenix.

Having thus dispensed with biblical and mythical examples, Valerius draws upon Jerome's excerpt from Theophrastus. Heroines who appear in both Jerome and Map include Terentia (Cicero's wife), Lais of Corinth (Demosthenes's tempter), and Sulpicius's spouse (whose husband characterizes her as a pinching shoe). Like Jerome, Valerius accuses wives of murdering their husbands, but he qualifies their motives as *either* malice or stupidity. Livia, Lucilia, and Deianira do not mean to kill their husbands, but in all stupidity they do. (The emphasis upon women's stupidity in a witty and erudite work by a man parallels Jerome's emphasis upon women's lechery in a treatise on chastity.) Finally, Valerius touches upon woman's physical insatiability. Danae, whose virginity is melted by the golden shower of Zeus, makes fleeting reference to the economic concerns of the pagan satires. Perictone, Plato's mother, illustrates women's lust. The latter example comes directly from Jerome's *Adversus Jovinianum*, but instead of using Perictone as an instance of a virgin giving birth, Map makes her illustrate the frailty of woman's chastity.[32]

Obviously, then, Valerius, like most satiric personae, uses all his pagan exempla in a deeply ironic way. His arguments, contradictory and confusing, are impossible to trust. His exempla often contradict his contentions. While he claims that women are insatiable, his catalog illustrates male lust. Jupiter rapes Europa; Mars lusts after Venus; Apollo pursues Leucothoe. Moreover, these exempla apply to love affairs, not marriages, which is Valerius's ostensible subject. Valerius's dominant image of Mars in chains is equally discordant, for Mars is the lover, not the husband, of Venus. Furthermore, since he appears at a banquet in the treatise's closing section, it seems he suffers no ill effects from his dalliance.

Such inconsistencies illuminate the poem's point: even when men are aware of the dangers, women can befuddle and confuse them. This observation was apt to be appreciated at the court of a king who had had tremendous troubles with wife and mistresses. But far from castigating sex with a Jeromian indignation, Map uses sexuality to amuse and appeal. His language is laced with sexual innuendoes, usually conveyed metaphorically. Gold "breaking through the barrier of the towers of Perisus" ("Irrupit aurum in propugna cula turris Acrisii") draws upon a conventional circumlocution for coitus.[33] We are told to "pass through rough places" (196) to attain even moderate pleasures, that "stern beginnings are rewarded with a sweet ending," and that "a strait path leadeth to stately mansions" (196) ("Arta enim est uia que ducit ad uitam, nec est semita plana qua itur ad gaudia plena; immo eciam ad mediocria per salebras euadimus" [310]). He also touches on the story of Jason, who must "voyage through a sea that up to this time had not been deflowered by ships or oars" (196) ("quod per mare adhuc tunc nullis deuirginatum ratibus aut remis" [310]). As "deflowered" suggests, the sea is often associated with passion and here is another metaphor for a woman's body. This metaphoric play with words would become central to the action of later catalogs such as Chaucer's *Legend of Good Women,* and it accords nicely with Jean de Meun's style in the *Roman de la Rose.*

In short, Rufinus's problem is not how to remain continent but how to enjoy women safely, how to master his sexuality like a man rather than allow it to rule him like a woman. Medea's two appearances among the exempla of the *dissuasio* illustrate this point and demonstrate the heroine's growing

---

32. Delahaye also notes this revision.

33. Walter Map, *Master Walter Map's Book: De Nugis Curialium,* trans. Frederick Tupper and Marbury Ogle (New York: MacMillan, 1924), 194. The Latin quotation is from Map 1983, 306. All further references to these editions appear in the text.

ability to exemplify opposing ideals. At the conclusion, Medea appears as an *exemplum in malo,* summarizing the evil of all the other exempla cited before her. Like Eve, she is disobedient; like Bathsheba, a bad influence; like Delilah, a liar. While she enables Jason to defeat the bulls (an echo of the Jupiter/Europa story), she also lessens his power (a reference to Apollo) and leads him to public ridicule (as with Mars). Yet earlier on, Rufinus is compared to Medea because, like her, he takes no thought for himself. Use of the same exemplum to signify both tempter and tempted is a rhetorical tour de force that takes full advantage of satire's double edge and woman's double bind. Woman as tempted is the weaker vessel; woman as tempter is the evil seed. Rufinus must learn to avoid becoming one by not yielding to the other. Map is clearly having fun while showing off his learning and wit. He is ironically arguing for the bachelor state, through laughter and without a high moral tone. Map's dissuasion shows how sexuality had come to dominate the catalog, replacing earlier historical and economic frames.

While Map's dissuasion was popular among the educated classes, the new secularism it exemplified was found in more populist forms as well. The most important of these was the large body of sermon literature that later satiric catalogers mined as a fertile source of material.[34] Women were a favorite target of the medieval pulpit, and since sermons were delivered in the vernaculars, these orations reached a much broader audience than did the Latin texts of the clerks. They also built more explicitly on vignettes from daily life, a trend toward realism that later catalogers exploited.

The accusations brought against women in these homilies are identical to those brought by satiric catalogers. Woman is lecherous, gluttonous, vain, proud, and lustful. But the preacher illustrates these tendencies by reference to daily life, not classical exempla. Annual May Day sermons, for example, dwell on woman's beauty and clothing, the drinking and merriment in the meadow, and the contrast with the recent austerity of Lent. The May meadow at the opening of the *Legend of Good Women* owes something to sermon descriptions such as this one:

> Good men and wymmen, now is passed the holy tyme of Ester, and iche man and wyman is shryven and houseled, so that thei have forsaken the devell and all is werkes and been turned to God and to is servyce . . . for the feend hase lost is preye and therfore he is full sorye . . . ffor nowe he seis that the tyme is fayre and warme, and metes and drynkes amenden and been more delicious than thei were, and many beth now fayre clothed, and wymmen nycely arrayed:

---

34. This is Owst's (1961) main thesis.

all this hym thenketh that is conabull to hym, and thus with many othur colours he disseyvith the pepull.[35]

Like this anonymous preacher, Chaucer also warns against Satan, presented as a fowler with traps; speaks of the fair May meadow; describes women's courtly dress; and contrasts the holiday with the austerity of his usual dedication to books. Women's dress was in fact a favorite target of these sermons. As with Alison of Bath, much is made over women's headgear—frets, kerchiefs, jewels, and especially the horned headdress of late medieval costume. John Bromyard, a medieval preacher, sarcastically describes women thus outfitted as "the devil's owls that have high head and little sense." He especially criticizes the "horned variety who resemble devils" (Owst 175–76). The length of dress trains and the cost of costumes never fail to excite comments such as this:

> Such ladies often sin in the matter of length, who drag long tails after them, "clothing" the earth with precious raiment and caring nothing for the nakedness of Christ in his poor folke.[36]

Sermon descriptions of the married life also attack women. One preacher describes them as "the devil's nets with which he fishes in God's fish-pond."[37] Another objects that "those that lay wait as fowlers and hunters are the demons; their snares, decoys, and traps are wicked and foolish women, who in their pomps and wiles catch men and deceive them."[38] Jean de Meun and Chaucer call on these patterns of entrapment in their work.

Classical examples in sermons are rare, but several exempla did become integral to the wicked wife theme. Most prominent are the five proverbial strong men who fell to women's tricks. Among those commonly cited are David (and Bathsheba), Samson (and Delilah), Solomon (and his harem), Hercules (and Deianira), and (sometimes) Vergil. Their examples are enshrined in the middle English proverb: "Who was strenger than Sampson, wyser than Salamon, holyer than David? And zit thei were al overcomen by the queyntise and whiles of women."[39]

Because of their drama and realism, such vignettes and details passed

---

35. Quoted in Owst 1961, 400.
36. Quoted in Owst 1961, 398.
37. Quoted in Owst 1961, 395–96.
38. Quoted in Owst 1961, 386.
39. Quoted in Owst 1961, 386.

easily from vernacular sermons to vernacular literature, as Gerard Owst (1961) argues. Works by Chaucer, Jean de Meun, and Eustache Deschamps all betray evidence of the link. In Jean de Meun's *Roman de la Rose,* arguably the biggest best seller of the Middle Ages, we see the new realism join a confluence of traditional sources—authoritative quotations, classical exempla, and conventional metaphors. This union forges a poetical language that later catalogers would manipulate to their own ends.

There are no sustained catalogs in the *Roman de la Rose,* but there are extended exempla used by two characters on opposing sides of the debate about love. With very different arguments, Le Jaloux and La Vielle nevertheless promote much the same view of womankind, a view consistent in many ways with Jerome's. Like most satiric personae, they are unaware of all the implications of what they say, but what they do say accords well with traditional sources.

Le Jaloux, a portrait of the jealous husband locked in struggle with his wife, relies most heavily on the learned tradition. Neither celibate nor clerical, this character nevertheless calls upon the whole clerical repertoire against women. He alludes to passages from Juvenal, Jerome, Valerius, Ovid, and Peter Abelard's famous love, Heloise. As he laments the lack of virtuous women, he draws his female exempla (and many of his metaphors) from old books, specifically past treatments of the rara avis. From Jerome, he picks up the virtuous examples of Penelope and Lucretia. Like Map, he compares the good woman to a phoenix; like Juvenal, to a black swan. In praising Heloise, he also raises the old saw of the good woman's nonexistence in modern society. In every instance, his speech refers back to clerical clichés.

But while he leans heavily on medieval authorities he does not limit himself to quoting the *auctores* and so infuses the catalog with a new social realism. To prove his points, Le Jaloux uses the examples of Samson and Hercules from the sermons. His specific complaints about his wife also come from sermon stories; her headdresses ("coiffes et ces dorees bendes"); [40] her tight shoes ("tant estroit vous rechauceés" [9289]); and her costly dresses with long trains (". . . tant est longue et tant vous traine / . . . Ceste robe cousteuse et chiere" [8844–45]) are all mentioned with disapproval. He also berates her for dancing, singing, and alleged adultery, phrasing his complaint in words that closely recall the May Day admonishments of the pulpit:

---

40. Guillaume de Lorris and Jean de Meun 1974, 9272. Translations are from *The Romance of the Rose,* trans. Harry Robbins (New York: Dutton, 1962). Further references to these works appear in the text.

"Mes n'en avés, ce croi, talent,
Ains alés chantant et balent,
Par ces jardins, par ces praiaus,
Avec ces ribaus desloiaus,
Qui traïnent ceste espousee
Par l'erbe vert, sor la rosee.

(9111–16)

(I don't believe your practice that would be
When you go tripping through the garden lanes
Or singing through the fields with traitors vile
Who, though the green grass glistens wet with dew
Chase after you, who are my wedded wife.

[21–25])

A decided economic bias characterizes all these complaints, despite the fact the material bears a great deal of resemblance to sermons. One of Le Jaloux's main problems is that his wife is draining his resources. In that respect Jean de Meun is returning to Juvenalian overtones, which would have been familiar from his training.

In contrast to Le Jaloux, La Vielle emphasizes realistic detail. While Le Jaloux speaks of the chains of married life, she speaks of the freedom of a life lived according to nature—nature in the sense of uninhibited sexual activity. Her speech thus builds on the satiric picture of the insatiable woman. As she attacks marriage, she draws on metaphors from sermons but uses them to her own advantage by arguing that if matrimony is a snare—and she agrees that it is—we should free ourselves to live promiscuously. She thus equates the married woman with a bird in a cage pining for the freedom of the fields (13940– 66). The monk is compared to a fish in a net (13985–89), a clear reversal of the usual descriptions of married men as netted fish.

Like Le Jaloux, she also does not limit herself to one source of material. In addition to the realistic details and metaphors of sermons, she touches upon traditional catalog heroines to support her eccentric arguments. Man, she says, is naturally deceitful (an interesting inversion of the usual stereotype of the guileful woman). Women should seek as many lovers as possible (an interesting return to stereotype). In support, she lists heroines from Ovid's catalog: Dido, Phyllis, Oenone, and Medea were all betrayed by men. The women from Ovid's epistles are not evoked as interesting psychological portraits but as examples of feminine fidelity. Chaucer later uses this facetious mating of the Ovidian catalog and the Jeromian chaste standard in his *Legend of Good Women.*

The principle differences between Le Jaloux and La Vielle, however, lie in the frames surrounding their speeches. These too illustrate how completely Jean de Meun understood satiric technique. Together, Le Jaloux and La Vielle reassemble the three major cornerstones of the earlier satiric portraits. Le Jaloux's speech, which frequently cites Juvenal, immediately follows a discussion of the Golden Age, a major motif in *Satire Six.* Like Juvenal's persona, Le Jaloux also stresses economic issues. One of his principal laments is that his wife costs him too much money. On the other hand, La Vielle frames her speech with references to Venus and Mars, the story Map used in *Dissuasio Valerii ad Rufinum de non ducat uxorem.* She thereby introduces the two other major themes of the old satires—woman's sexual insatiability and her disobedience. Both speeches enrich Jerome's single-minded focus on chastity. They also expand the social contexts of Map's collection.

The greatest triumph of the *Roman de la Rose,* however, may well be its revival of the satiric persona. Both Le Jaloux and La Vielle are undercut by their arguments. La Vielle's ideas mark her as the stereotypical wicked wife come to life, for she advocates deceit, is sexually motivated, and acts from greed. Le Jaloux, however, lacks self-control and judgment. Such deficiencies are critical in a husband who should rely on both qualities to guide his wife. Neither character is to be identified with the author, Jean de Meun. In fact, Le Jaloux is invented by another *Roman de la Rose* character and is thus at least three times removed from the author. In addition, Jean de Meun also invokes his role as compiler (as opposed to author) to excuse any offense he may have given in the *Roman de la Rose.* Women should not blame him for what he has said about them, Jean notes. He is simply repeating the words of the *auctores.*

> S'il vous semble que je di fables,
> Por menteor ne m'en tenés,
> Mais as actors vous en prenés
> Qui en lor livres ont escrites
> Les paroles que j'en ai dites,
> E celes que j'en diré
> Que ja de rien n'en mentiré,
> Ne li prodhomme n'en mentirent
> Qui les livres anciens firent.
>
> (15216–24)

This clever dodge of authorial responsibility (so similar to Jerome's misuse of his sources) would later be used—and examined in detail—by many other writers, including John Gower and Chaucer, whose *Legend of Good Women* is ostensibly written to atone for translating the *Rose*.

Jean de Meun's subtlety helped make the *Roman de la Rose* a sophisticated and rewarding reading experience, as its medieval popularity attests.[41] His indirect approach influenced later catalogers such as Chaucer, who also wrestled with problems of voice and the living author's responsibility for his text. In fact, the distance between the speech and the speaker in *Roman de la Rose* often reproduces the effects of Ovid's parody of genre in the *Heroides*. Le Jaloux, a jealous husband, is an unusual character to be quoting clerical misogamous literature. La Vielle is also an unlikely character for reviving Ovid's catalog. For the catalog tradition, the heroine listings in the *Roman de la Rose* indicate not only that the catalog had returned, but that audiences were once more interested in sophisticated literary self-references and social realism. Approximately a hundred years after Jean de Meun, a catalog born of the new Italian humanism would address a new interest in history as well.

---

41. A great deal of this medieval popularity, as well as the work's vogue with more modern critics, lies in Jean de Meun's skillful use of narrative voice. The critical literature on the *Rose* is vast. See, for example, Charles Dahlberg, "Love and *Roman de la Rose*," *Speculum* 44 (1969): 568–84; D. W. Robertson, "The Doctrine of Charity in Medieval Literary Gardens," *Speculum* 26 (1941): 24–49; and Tuve 1966.

Chapter 3

The *Mulier Clara*

It is hardly surprising to find an early Italian humanist attracted to the catalog of women tradition, for the tradition spoke to many of the early humanist interests. Boccaccio's earlier vernacular corpus is also dominated by various treatments of women, who seem to have appealed to him as a subject. To understand *De claris mulieribus,* then, both aspects of Boccaccio's work— humanist scholarship and vernacular literature—must be addressed.

Early Italian hmanism was, above all, a literary and educational movement with direct ties to a strong Italian medieval tradition of rhetoric.[1] In fact, the emminent Renaissance historian Paul Oskar Kristeller places the origins of humanism in a "fusion between the novel interest in classical studies imported from France toward the end of the thirteenth century and the much earlier tradition of medieval Italian rhetoric" (1961, 109). The early Italian humanists devoted themselves to what some ancient Roman authors had called the *studia humanitatis,* generally interpreted as including grammar, poetry, rhetoric, history, and moral philosophy.[2] Most important, in all these areas the major emphasis lay on studying and imitating classical Latin

---

1. There is, of course, an extensive bibliography on the subject of the humanist movement and the early Italian Renaissance. For representative treatments see Kristeller 1961, Hans Baron, *The Crisis of the Early Italian Renaissance* (Princeton: Princeton University Press, 1966); Hanna Gray, "Renaissance Humanism: The Pursuit of Eloquence" *Journal of the History of Ideas* 24 (1963): 497–514; Hay 1962; Seigel 1968; Brucker 1962; Larner 1980; and Pullan 1973. *The Earthly Republic: Italian Humanists on Government and Society,* ed. Benjamin Kohl and Ronald Witt (Philadelphia: University of Pennsylvania Press, 1978), contains a representative sampling of writings by early humanists.

2. Kristeller notes that the term *studia humanitatis* was used in the sense of a liberal education by Cicero and Gellius and was revived by Italian humanists in the late fourteenth century (1961, 9).

(and later Greek) masters, usually in a more comprehensive fashion than their medieval predecessors had.

As a form, then, the catalog offered several enticements to Boccaccio. First, it was a legitimate way to contribute to the field of classical studies. Indeed, Boccaccio says in his preface that *De claris mulieribus* is the first collection to assemble the lives of famous pagan women from the past, and its subsequent popularity testifies that it was in fact valued as a reference book for many centuries.[3] Secondly, the biographical sketches of the collection lent themselves to use as moral exempla, a practice with classical and medieval roots but one especially dear to the humanists, who were especially interested in moral philosophy. The book is also written in Latin, an intriguing choice of tongues for a book addressed to women, who were generally unschooled in Latin, but one perfectly consonant with humanist interests in classical prose style.

Most important, however, both the catalog's historical and its literary referents had ties to the rhetorical study that was humanism's home base.[4] This conflation of the two disciplines is more confusing to us than it would have been to Boccaccio or his contemporary audience. Neither poetry nor history was taught as a separate discipline in the Trecento universities of Italy. History generally fell under the umbrella of rhetoric, and although poetry in the Middle Ages was traditionally associated with grammar, the humanists eventually succeeded in connecting it to rhetoric on the university level.[5] Both pursuits—literature and history—used many of the same source materials and (at least initially) had many of the same aims, such as conveying ethical truths and promoting eloquent speech. It is important to remember, however, that in the Renaissance these two scholarly endeavors diverged and that the seeds of this divergence are present in Boccaccio's time. Early humanists (especially Boccaccio's friend and mentor Petrarch) were acutely aware of their own historical position. They defined the classical period as

---

3. For information on the translations of these volumes into French and English, for example, see Bozzolo 1973, Gathercole 1969, and Wright 1957. The popularity of *De claris mulieribus* was quite long-lasting. Five hundred years later, Laurence Sterne (the author of *Tristram Shandy*) owned copies of Boccaccio's catalogs.

4. The close links between literature and history can be seen in the diploma Petrarch received on being granted the laureate crown, for it authorized his abilities "tam in dicta arte poetica quam in dicta historica arte," and Robert of Sicily questioned him in both areas. Similarly, Coluccio Salutati, the Florentine Chancellor and student of Roman history, wrote an elaborate defense of poetry in the next century and is in fact responsible for first noting the different periods of development in ancient Latin.

5. For a discussion of this change, see Kristeller 1961, 109.

an age of perfection, the Middle Ages as a period of decline, and their own age as a return to classical standards. Such a viewpoint argues these scholars were developing a new sense of historical difference between the present and the past, a sense quite separate from the medieval view of continuity with the Roman past. Eventually this stance would mold a distinctive historiography.

On the side of poetics, many humanists, including Boccaccio and Petrarch, were also aware of aesthetic standards in a way their predecessors were not. That awareness is obvious in the vernacular masterpieces of the age and in their concern for Latin prose style. Boccaccio himself wrote the most important Italian prose piece of his century, and among his Latin classics, one finds the most important defense of poetry to come out of the late medieval period. This preoccupation with poetry along with the new sense of historical perspective shape Boccaccio's catalog, producing interesting ambiguities in his treatment of the heroines.

By the time Boccaccio began work on *De claris mulieribus,* he was an old man. The project, which took shape from 1361 to 1375 in nine separate editorial stages,[6] chronologically belongs to the period when Boccaccio, who may have taken priestly orders, was primarily working on his scholarly works in Latin. He was certainly retired from active life, for in 1371 he left Florence for the Tuscan countryside, where he practically lived an eremitical existence of study and meditation. Yet even in retirement, he never repudiated his earlier works or the interests that informed them.[7] Just as Petrarch worked on his canzonieri at the same time as his Latin epic *Africa,* so Boccaccio revised and recopied the *Decameron* at the same time that he was writing *De claris mulieribus.* The catalog itself exhibits both a *contemptus mundi* and a relish for the details of earthly existence that often seem contradictory. That melange, however, mirrors the ambivalences in much of Boccaccio's work.

Boccaccio used catalogs frequently in both his vernacular and Latin

---

6. Branca (1976) says that work on *De claris mulieribus* probably began in 1361; the first four editorial phases apparently occurred in one year, 1362. For a study of this editorial process, see Vittore Zaccari "Le Fasi redazionalie del 'De claris mulieribus'" *Studi sul Boccaccio* 1 (1963) 255–332.

7. Until recently, it was widely believed that such a repudiation took place, primarily because of an event recorded in Boccaccio and Petrarch's correspondence. A fanatic from Siena announced that the "blessed Petroni," a local religious leader, had had a vision foretelling Petrarch's and Boccaccio's imminent death. He warned them to renounce poetry. Petrarch took the suggestion in his stride, but it distressed Boccaccio. He briefly considered giving up his work and selling his library, but he eventually went back to work on his texts, both Latin and Italian. We know, for example, that he prepared a revised version of the *Decameron* only four years before his death. Found today in the Staatsbibliothek in Berlin, this manuscript is undoubtedly in the hand of Boccaccio's old age.

texts. As his biographer, the eminent Boccaccio critic Vittoria Branca, notes, even in his youth, he was drawn to the medieval summa (1976, 41). Many of his early works, such as *Filocolo,* include catalog displays of erudition. Furthermore, the exemplum tradition, so integral to the catalog, was a great influence on his narrative style.[8] He routinely compiled, expanded, and edited catalogs throughout his career, making the florilegium an ingrained work habit by the time he wrote *De claris mulieribus.*[9] The most direct inspiration for the collection, however, was Petrarch's catalog of famous men, *De viris illustribus* (Of famous men).[10] Such collections go all the way back to classical Rome in origin (St. Jerome also compiled one), but Petrarch's is shaped by his humanist orientation. On his death in 1374, it included some thirty-six biographies, arranged chronologically from the beginning of history to the Roman Empire. In his preface, Boccaccio identified *De viris illustribus* as the model for *De claris mulieribus,* a curious link since one catalog features heroes and the other heroines and since Boccaccio's collection of famous men, *De casibus virorum illustrium,* makes no such claim. As we shall see, however, this odd lineage is but the first of many interesting anomalies in Boccaccio's work.

In *De claris mulieribus,* Boccaccio gives two specific reasons for his decision to write a catalog of women. Both are the reasons of a humanist scholar. His dedication, to Andrea Acciaiuoli, claims that the catalog was written for "the pleasure of my friends."[11] His preface also describes the project as one that needed doing. There may have been additional incentives. Women dominate Boccaccio's vernacular corpus and figure significantly in the *Decameron,* which is dedicated to them.[12] *De claris mulieribus* may continue this fascina-

---

8. Branca notes that the "exemplary inspiration, moreover, is not so much a characteristic peculiar to the design of the *Decameron* as it is a constitutional inclination of Boccaccio's imagination and medieval poetics in general" (1976, 315).

9. Examples of florilegia that Boccaccio worked on over his lifetime include *Zibaldone Magliabechiano* and his copy book, *Zibaldone Laurenziano;* Branca (1976, 95) claims that the first is an influence on both *De claris mulieribus* and *De casibus virorum illustrium.*

10. At least two of Boccaccio's biographers, Branca (1976) and Bergin (1981) also assert this connection.

11. Boccaccio, *Concerning Famous Women,* trans. Guido Guarino (New Brunswick, N.J.: Rutgers University Press, 1963), xxxiii. The Latin, taken from Boccaccio 1967–70b, reads "et ac amicorum solatum . . . potius quam in magnum rei publice commodum" (18). All further references to these works appear in the text.

12. In fact, the *Decameron* is dedicated to a specific class of women—women of leisure, who might suffer too greatly from the pangs of love. Like women, secular literature, was frequently characterized as an "erotic snare." Mazzotta (1972) discusses how Boccaccio played on this idea in his *Decameron.*

tion, especially since it often uses many of the same stories as the *De-cameron*. Moreover, Boccaccio's mention of pleasure and novelty in his explication of the work's genesis also suggests a connection between the two. Love, adventure, ingenuity, and fortune—all important themes in the *Decameron*—were often given feminine faces in medieval literature. Vernacular literature itself was sometimes specifically associated with women since most women did not read Latin and most vernacular tales concerned decidedly unscholarly (and hence inferior) subject matter and generally love. By compiling a scholarly catalog of women, Boccaccio united the subject of his vernacular works with the form and language of his Latin ones, thereby dignifying the one and providing some connection to the other. For the moment I'd like to suggest that the new humanist interests in fame and earthly struggle may have struck Boccaccio as more appropriate to a catalog of women, who were, after all, generally associated with the world of nature and fortune.

In its organization and use of sources, *De claris mulieribus* is clearly a scholarly florilegium.[13] As in most such collections, its prologue elucidates the compiler's purpose (to bring these neglected heroines to the reader's attention), explains his methods (to gather excerpts on famous and infamous heroines from old books), and specifies his intent (to give examples of proper and improper conduct). One hundred and six biographies ranging from approximately fifty to fifteen hundred words make up the catalog proper. As mentioned, these sketches often echo stories from the *Decameron,* but Boccaccio does not unite his entries under any specific theme. He does impart a rudimentary chronological order identical to that in Petrarch's *De viris illustribus;* that is, he begins with Eve and ends with Joanna of Sicily, but there is no central narrative tying the catalog entries together as in Chaucer and Christine de Pizan's collections. The heroines are by and large pagan (98 out of 106) with three Hebrews and five Christians. Boccaccio explains the emphasis on the classical era by noting that famous Christian and Hebrew heroines are well publicized elsewhere and his task here is to recover information that has been ignored. Together the one hundred and six heroines offer an impressive diversity. Some are presented as virgins, wives, and

---

13. In the preface, Boccaccio notes that while numerous collections of famous men have been compiled, "I have been quite astonished that women have had so little attention from writers of this sort that they have gained no recognition in any work devoted especially to them, although it can be clearly seen in the more voluminous histories that some women have acted with as much strength as valor" (xxxvii). These are the words of a medieval anthologist who seeks to propagate knowledge by compiling information into a single, easily accessible volume.

widows, as in St. Jerome's treatise, but others are depicted as whores, philosophers, rulers, scholars, courtesans, and painters. Boccaccio's reactions to them are equally diverse.

This variety of portraits may reflect a continuing influence from Jerome's *Adversus Jovinianum,* which also includes both vicious and virtuous women. But Boccaccio differs from Jerome in the way he judges his heroines. Chastity is important but is not the sole index of women's conduct. Also, even when discussing his heroines' sex lives, Boccaccio does not limit chastity to a sexual definition. It often implies a social role, as when it includes the values of obedience and submission as well as continence. Most radical, Boccaccio sometimes discards chastity entirely and judges his exempla by their personal achievements. He praises the prostitute Leaena (chap. 48), for example, for refusing to betray her coconspirators in a plot against a tyrant. Jerome would have dismissed her out of hand.

Such changes support Boccaccio's claim that *De claris mulieribus* is a new type of collection of women, an orientation possibly augured by the collection's title. There Boccaccio uses the adjective *clarus* in place of the word *illustris,* which is generally found in similar collections of famous men.[14] This change has important implications for genre because of *illustris*'s firm rhetorical connections with history. Classical as well as medieval rhetoric teachers instructed students to remember topics, facts, or great men by placing them in imaginary, well-lit places called *loci illustres.*[15] Using the word *illustris* for catalogs of men connected such lists to this science of memory and (by inference) to history. Boccaccio claims that *De claris mulieribus* also records deeds worthy of memory. Why then did he describe his heroines with the word *claris* and emphasize the change by pointing it out? He gives one reason when he writes that since *clarus* unlike *illustris* can mean notorious, the word seemed more appropriate for a book of infamous as well as famous women. Jerome, however, had similarly mixed categories in *Adversus Jovinianum,* leaving us with the problem of why Boccaccio claimed that his catalog was such a novelty.

Etymological differences perhaps hold the key. *Illustris* derives from the Latin phrase *in lustro* (in the light), hence its denotations of clear, bright, or lustrous.[16] *Clarus,* however, derives from the Latin verb *clamo,* which

---

14. Jerome and Plutarch both entitled their catalogs of men *De viris illustribus;* Boccaccio's is *De casibus virorum illustrium.*

15. Frances Yates (1966) discusses this science of artificial memory. Cicero described these imaginary places as being well-lit, *illustres.*

16. *A Latin Dictionary,* ed. Charlton Lewis and Charles Short, 1962 ed., s.v. "illustris."

means to declaim or to celebrate.[17] Its denotations of clear and distinct originally referred to the audible, not the visual. The difference is suggestive because while light almost universally indicates divine truth, speech is almost always the province of humans, and hence of confusion, opinion, and (naturally) eloquence.[18] Furthermore, *clarus* historically denoted public recognition. In the superlative, it was a favorite epithet of the honor-loving Roman and hence part of the official title of consuls, pontifices, and senators as well as their wives (*clarisssimae feminae*). Etymologically, then, the word *claris* in *De claris mulieribus* not only warns the educated reader of ambiguous meaning and confused purpose but links them with earthly affairs and rhetoric, both important to the humanist program. None of these overtones exist in *Adversus Jovinianum* or in the clerical collections of women heroines. All three are clear portents of changes in *De claris mulieribus'* s style and presentation.

Boccaccio's interest in earthly fame and his allegiance to a Jeromian catalog of virtue and vice create many such anomalies within his "little book in praise of women" (xxxiii) ("in eximiam muliebris sexus laudem . . . libellum" [18]). Several chapters do not praise women at all, despite attempts to do so (see chap. 67 "praising" Sulpicia's chastity). Others are Juvenalian in their invective (see chap. 88 dealing with Cleopatra). Both types diminish the impact of original chapters praising women's achievements within structured encomia (such as chap. 47 which details the biography of Sappho).

Complicating and intensifying this ambivalence is the author's inherited notion of femineity as inferior. Because of it, even Boccaccio's admirable heroines are viragolike, that is, atypical of their gender. In his dedication, for example, he praises Andrea Acciaiuoli for her achievements but also notes that her virile spirit is obvious from her very name, which derives from the Greek word for man. Her celebrated character ("celebres mores" [18]), her great honesty ("honestatem eximiam" [18]), her womanly dignity ("summum matronarum decus" [18]), her eloquence ("verborum elegantiam" [18]), her powers of intellect ("ingenii vires" [18]), and her generosity of soul

---

17. Ibid, "clarus."

18. Proof of this association is readily found in any of the twelfth-century *distinctiones verborum*, which list terms in sacred scripture and their varied metaphoric meanings. For example, in Alan de Lille, *Liber in distinctionibus dictionum theologicalium,* in vol. 210 of *Patrologiae latina,* ed. J. P. Migne (Paris: 1857–80), 844–45, light or "lux" is associated with faith, grace, knowledge, happiness, joy, justice, glory, illumination, eternal life, the converted soul, the word of God. The association of humans and rhetoric is also traditional in ancient rhetoricians who held that humans were essentially characterized by their powers of speech. See Seigel 1968, 3–30, for a discussion of the development of this idea.

("animi tui generositatem" [18]) are all the more remarkable for being found in a woman ("quibus longe femineas excedis" [18]). This conjunction of the satiric *rara avis* with the encomium's traditional strategy of praise by amplification and comparison becomes a reiterated technique in *De claris mulieribus;* pragmatically it enhances an individual's virtue by comparing her with an implicit history of feminine depravity. Such women do nothing to refute the long standing debasement of femineity; no matter how great their numbers or how impressive their achievements, they do not speak for their gender.

Within the catalog, misogynist dichotomies linking women with undesirable and men with desirable traits are also abundant. In fact, Boccaccio applies these truisms not only to individual women but to individual deeds of a single woman. Semiramis, an ancient queen of Babylon who was famous for prowess and infamous for incest, is a good case in point. The Middle Ages generally credited her with inventing the chastity belt, but only to frustrate rivals for her son's affections at court. Dante includes her in the circle of the lustful in the Inferno; Chaucer, as we shall see, invokes her similarly in the *Legend of Good Women.* Yet her accomplishments as general and ruler make her the equal of any virtuous virago. How to explain this apparent contradiction? Boccaccio resolves it by neatly separating Semiramis's "male" from her "female" side. When he speaks of her courage, her military prowess, or her judgment, he praises her manly spirit ("virili animo" [34]). When he discusses her greed, her self-indulgence, or her carnality ("quasi assidua libidnis prurigine" [36]), he deplores her feminine faults. The curiously bisexual figure he creates is perfectly expressed by the statue erected to honor her conquest of Babylon. Told of the city's revolt as her maids are doing her hair, Semiramis refuses to let them finish until she subdues the rebellion. The statue shows her as she appears in battle: braided hair on one side (feminine), flowing locks on the other (masculine).[19] Semiramis becomes, in these pages, both genders at once.

Besides isolating active virtue from femineity in this fashion, in the sketches where he adopts Jerome's virtuous models of femineity Boccaccio also perpetuates the tenet that feminine virtue lies in passive submission and self-effacement. While famous women without men (virgins or widows) are generally seen as "masculine" spirits in *De claris mulieribus,* married women

---

19. The division is even more obvious if seen within the context of Semiramis's interrupted activity in *De claris mulieribus.* Boccaccio presents the braiding of Semiramis's hair as a "feminine care" (6) ("feminea solertia" [34]) and a "womanly pursuit" (6) ("offitio muliebri" [34]) done while Semiramis is "resting at leisure" (6) ("ocio quiescente" [34]).

who submit to their husbands are both feminine and good. Both the good wife and the continent widow are present in the catalog, but the latter is usually merged with the Jeromian virago, a sign of the continuing problem society had in classifying widows. *De claris mulieribus* has four such examples. Three—Artemisia, Thamegris, and Zenobia—are viragolike warriors and rulers. The remaining one, Dido, is said to have killed herself because of her first husband's death. Boccaccio specifically chose this older version of the Dido myth (as did Jerome) to make a point about women's chastity; he uses Vergil's version in some of his other works.[20] The preference does not reflect a partiality for an older and more accurate version but rather springs from the need to prove an ethical point. Interestingly, however, Boccaccio is always aware of the narrative verve of his exempla. Since Vergil's version is more interesting, Boccaccio spends a disproportionate amount of time telling and refuting it. With the other widows, he emphasizes the active narrative of their deeds rather than the theme of widowed chastity.

Boccaccio's good wives are passive, nondescript, and not very numerous. Their fame rests on their allegiance to their husbands. Tertia Aemilia, for example, endures Cato's promiscuity in silence so she won't tarnish a great man's reputation. Pompeia Paulina tries to follow her husband Seneca into death. Sulpicia, wife of Cruscello, gives up her feminine love of ease and luxury to go with her husband into exile. Such self-effacement also marks Boccaccio's definition of chastity. Another Sulpicia, Fulvius's wife, is chaste not simply because she is faithful to her husband but because she makes herself unobtrusive. Silent and modest, she keeps her words brief, respectful, and "spoken only at the proper time" (147) ("verba non solum honesta, sed pauca et pro tempore effundere" [270]); she shuns feasts, dances, cosmetics, and perfumes and occupies herself with her husband's household. She carefully avoids the gossip of other women and curbs her "lustful and wandering" (147) ("cupidos vagosque . . . oculos" [270]) eyes by keeping them always on the fringe of her dress. She even submits to her husband's embrace only for the sake of procreation and then with "shame in her face and breast" (147) ("non absque frontis animique rubore" [270]). While the last description is Christian in sentiment, the other points are equally descriptive of Semonides's bee woman. In the social sphere, "feminine" virtue had moved little in fifteen hundred years. It still consisted principally of denial and restraint.

20. For a discussion of Boccaccio's use of Dido see Kallendorf 1985. For a different view of Dido see Jordan 1987.

Considering the impoverishment of poor Sulpicia's life, it is not surprising that very few similar figures appear in *De claris mulieribus*.[21] In
general, Boccaccio prefers either wicked wives, such as Sempronia, or
women who unite chastity with heroic action, such as Camilla. But he does
introduce heroines dissimilar to those found in earlier catalogs. Several seem
to excite his talents as a storyteller. Jocasta and Hypermenestra make for
tragic reading. Juno, Thisbe, and Polyxena are memorable because of a turn
of fortune rather than their deeds. Finally, Flora and Paulina provide entertainment in the manner of the *Decameron*.

Boccaccio's most striking innovation among his virtuous heroines is
his praise for women painters, writers, artists, sculptors, and scholars.[22]
Simply including such women is a novelty, for while Suetonius and Jerome
mention scholars as well as generals and kings in their collections of famous
men, no one before *De claris mulieribus* had thought of doing the same thing
in a catalog of women.[23] Boccaccio's own humanist interests may have
prompted this change, but whatever the reason, it makes a significant contribution to the catalog tradition. Heroines such as Minerva and Pamphile
(inventors); Nicostrata, Nicaula, and Hortensia (scholars); Thamaris, Irene,
and Marcia (artists); and Sappho, Cornificia, and Proba (writers) could open
new doors for women readers, who were encouraged to imitate them.

But perhaps the most important innovation of Boccaccio's catalog lies
less in whom he praises than in how he praises. *De claris mulieribus* differs
from misogynistic catalogs in that it often focuses on its heroines' deeds
rather than their nature. Though unfamiliar with *Mulierium virtutes,* Boccaccio frequently shaped his encomia as Plutarch had, by the standards of epideictic rhetoric.[24] Two specific themes traditionally functioned as the bases of

---

21. Of the 106 biographies in *De claris mulieribus,* only 17 focus upon the good wife. Among
these a considerable variety of portraits is found. Penelope, for example, is praised for being
loyal but also for being clever. Gaia Cyrilla's skills as a weaver are noted. Three wives combine
Jerome's portraits of the good wife and the virago: Hypsicratea followed her husband into battle;
the Cimbrans exchanged places with their imprisoned husbands that they might escape, and Turia
successfully hid her exiled husband in her apartments in Rome. Strictly speaking, Jerome's
pattern of passive feminine virtue is present in six sketches besides Sulpicia's: Lucretia, Tertia
Aemilia, Julia, Portia, Pompeia Paulina, and Turia. They make up approximately 6 per cent of
the biographies in *De claris mulieribus.*

22. Found in this group are Amalthea, Nicostrata, Sappho, Thamaris, Irene, Leontium,
Hortensia, Pope Joan, the Sempronia of chap. 77, Cornificia, and the Marcia of chap. 64.

23. Suetonius's addition comes in *On Grammarians and Rhetors;* St. Jerome's in *De viris
illustribus.*

24. Aristotle divided rhetoric into three branches: the judicial rhetoric of the courts, the
deliberative rhetoric of the political assemblies, and the epideictic rhetoric of ceremonial and

such praise: the goods of nature and fortune (the topics of *effictio*) and the goods of character (the topics of *notatio*). Cicero, Quintillian, and others had recommended using both but giving preeminence to the latter as the most likely to inspire virtue. *Notatio* was also thought more representative of character than *effictio* because it illustrated the actions taken under humans' free will. Boccaccio is the first cataloger after Plutarch to apply these principles to women. He does so inconsistently—he begins by praising Eve's beauty ironically—but the sketches that are marked by this change have a new orientation. Concomitantly, they attempt to relate the heroines to their societies.

The relationship described between Boccaccio's *mulier clara* and her community is not a simple one. In fact, it is as complex and inconsistent as the relationships between virtue and femineity that the catalog describes. At times Boccaccio's women are isolated from public life (Sulpicia); at others they aren't (Sempronia, Eve, Nicostrata). Sometimes their participation is beneficial (Nicaula); sometimes it is not (Sempronia). In portraying these options Boccaccio calls upon several traditional patterns. Two have already been examined. The good wife is a woman who remains at home and pledges her life to her husband; the manly and virtuous woman defends the male status quo. The first divorces feminine virtue from civic life; the second divorces femineity from civic virtue. Both consequently continue the catalog tradition that isolates women from public power.

Boccaccio also includes numerous wicked heroines who exemplify classical satiric patterns, most conspicuously the behaviors found in *Satire Six*. With these, *De claris mulieribus* suggests that integration of women within a community's public affairs can only spell disaster. Unlike *Satire Six*, however, *De claris mulieribus* advances this idea in a scholarly frame.

The sketches separating woman from society are among the most resonant in *De claris mulieribus*. They draw on a wide variety of material. Some simply reiterate the lessons of sermons. Europa's rape illustrates, for example, why parents shouldn't let young girls wander around alone, and Queen Iole, who makes Hercules her handmaiden, recalls the venerable examples of how women brought low David, Solomon, and Samson. Other heroines extend the ill effects of unchastity to the state. Clytemnestra murders not only her husband but also her king, Helen begins a war, and Athaliah butchers the entire royal family of Israel. These and other chapters use the three accusations found in satiric catalogs to justify the privatization of women's

---

occasional speaking. For how this latter kind of oratory developed in relationship to literature, see Hardison 1962 and Burgess 1902.

lives. Women can't be trusted with authority because they are either too greedy (Athaliah, Procris, Medusa), too wanton (Clytemnestra, Cleopatra, Agrippina, and Olympia), or too disobedient (Iole, Eve, and Sempronia). The first two complaints are voiced more frequently than the third, but each is an important motif in the catalog.

This preponderance of wanton, greedy, and contentious women makes it likely that *De claris mulieribus* was influenced, if only subliminally, by *Satire Six*. As an educated and avid reader, Boccaccio undoubtedly knew Juvenal well. Like any medieval reader, he knew him as a moralist. While *Satire Six* has never been directly identified as a source of *De claris mulieribus,* its echoes in the catalog are numerous. Oddly enough, Boccaccio's most impressive Juvenalian link occurs in his biography of Veturia, Coriolanus's mother, who saved Rome by persuading her son to halt his siege. For this action, Veturia gets a scant paragraph of praise before Boccaccio launches into a lengthy condemnation of the Roman Senate that honored her service by granting special privileges to women. Among other things, Boccaccio notes that a temple to Fortuna Muliebris was erected; men were commanded to rise and give way to women as they passed; women were allowed to wear gold jewelry and the purple dress; most disastrous, they were allowed to inherit property. All this unwise generosity ruined the world, Boccaccio laments. Women now deplete their husbands' fortunes to adorn themselves and have created a society where the "world belongs to women and men are womanish" (121) ("Muliebris est mundus, sic et homines muliebres" [226]). In tone and intent, the whole chapter bemoans social degeneracy in exactly the same terms as *Satire Six*. And just as in Juvenal's poem, social decline is linked to women's control of a society's financial resources that are then squandered on luxeries.

The combination of femineity, greed and sexual appetite is even more disastrous for civic stability. Nowhere is this effect more pronounced than in Boccaccio's sketch of Cleopatra, who often resembles Juvenal's Messalina of *Satire Six*. Boccaccio's sources for this sketch are the Roman historians who had wasted no possible opportunity to blacken Cleopatra's name and glorify Augustus Caesar's. But Boccaccio also invents incidents to portray Cleopatra as strikingly and purely depraved.[25] More than simply presumptuous, the Queen of the Nile is portrayed as the murderer of her brother, the seducer of Julius Caesar, and the whore of Mark Anthony. Once she acquires

---

25. Godman (1977) compares Cleopatra in *De claris mulieribus* to Cleopatra in *De casibus virorum illustrium* and Chaucer's *Legend of Good Women.* Hamer (1988) discusses the issues of sexuality, power, and domesticity in this portrait by Boccaccio.

her kingdom through crime, she gives herself over to pleasure and a feminine taste for *luxuria*. Like Juvenal's *matrona,* she is avid for gold, and this taste devastates both lovers and their kingdoms:

> Having become almost the prostitute of Oriental kings, and greedy for gold and jewels, she not only stripped her lovers of these things with her art, but it was also said that she emptied the temples and the sacred places of the Egyptians of their vases, statues, and other treasures. (193)

> (quasi scortum orientalium regum facta, auri et iocalium avida, non solum contubernales suos talium nudos arte sua liquit, verum et templa sacrasque Egyptiorum edes vasis statuis thesaurisque ceteris vacuas liquisse traditum est. [348])

Her crimes are political, not just personal. She tricks Anthony out of half of his possessions and then tries to seduce Herod Antipater to get more territory, a story entirely original with Boccaccio. Finally the "insatiable queen's craving for kingdoms" (195) ("cum insatiabilis mulieris in dies regnorum aviditas" [352]) grows so large that her eyes turn to Rome, a greed that proves her undoing, for at Actium she loses lover, kingdom, and life at a single stroke. As one critic has noted, "the inequity of Cleopatra is . . . an inexhaustible subject" for Boccaccio (Goodman 1977, 205). More important, she is his most vivid exemplum of women's corrupting influence on the state. In fact, the sketch virtually takes the threat women's sexuality posed for men and translates it into a threat against the state. Cleopatra's aggressive lust for sexual conquest is linked to her lust for territorial conquest. As a queen and as a woman, she exemplifies the destructive notion of femineity operating at full tilt.

Women's greed and lust were not new reasons for confining them to their homes; their cleverness was. Yet *De claris mulieribus* makes such a gesture. Several characters describe a feminine malignancy linked entirely to feminine *ingenium,* a word with specific application to the *Decameron* as well.

In his commentary on Dante's *Inferno* II.7, Boccaccio had defined *ingenium* as a quality of the mind which enables us to discover new things never taught us by others. His understanding of the term probably derives from Bernardus Silvestris, an important figure of the twelfth century School of Chartres, whose *Megacosmus et microcosmus* was transcribed by Boccaccio into his notebooks. Bernardus divided the brain into three parts: *ingenium* or *imaginatio, ratio,* and *memoria.* In the *Microcosmus,* Bernardus describes how Physis divided the human skull into three chambers, the front of which houses *ingenium,* the power of apprehension, so that it may receive the impression of things. These impressions are transmitted to *ratio,* which occupies the second chamber and which exercises governance over both *ingenium* and *memoria,* the faculty found in the last chamber. *Ingenium* thus has a specific relationship to the uniquely human intelligence that obtains knowledge from experiences. It was also especially associated with rhetoric. In *De institutio,* Quintillian names it as one of the great powers of the orator (X.2.12), and later Martianus Capella, one of the great teachers of the Latin West, reiterated the connection. While not a major theme in the catalog, *ingenium*'s appearance here, as in any Boccaccian work, deserves special attention. If Boccaccio did relate *ingenium* to empirical knowledge, it is an important index to Boccaccio's definition of femineity and perhaps a clue to why he included women artists and scholars.

Consistent with Boccaccio's use of older patterns, women's ingenuity is portrayed as both a positive and a negative social force. While *De claris mulieribus* does establish a new type of heroine—one whose worth is based on her mental acumen—it also condemns other women on precisely the same grounds. The most striking example of such condemnation occurs in the biography of Ceres, the Greek and Roman goddess of grain, whose *ingenium* Boccaccio links causally to the end of the Golden Age. As in the biography of Veturia, Boccaccio places the accusation in what should be a context of praise, another indication of the ambivalences of *De claris mulieribus.* Ceres's inventiveness and her discovery of agriculture made civilization possible. As Boccaccio himself asks, who could fault this? ("Quis enim damnet vagos silvestresque eductos in urbes e nemoribus homines?" [44]) Yet he abruptly switches tone almost immediately after the rhetorical question to charge that these very inventions opened the door "to vice" (12) and to corrupting luxuries that ruined the world. The new society thus created is clearly the world of *Satire Six,* a world characterized by

> the softening of the body and the swelling of the belly, ornament in dress, more elaborate dinner tables, more splendid banquets, laziness and leisure. And concupiscence began to rouse itself. (13)

> (hinc mollicies corporum sagina ventris, ornatus vestium, accuratiores mense, convivia splendida, torpor et otium advenere; et, que in dies usque illos friguerat, Venus calefieri cepit. [46])

To accuse women of guile is not unusual, nor is the association of women with civic malaise. But to identify the instrument of that malady as feminine ingenuity (as opposed to vice or unchastity) is striking. Not only does this portrait reverse usual associations made between mind and male, but it also reverses the great novelty of Boccaccio's praise for the scholarly, creative, and inventive heroine, and it does so within the context of civic virtue. In the same catalog where the Roman courtesan Sempronia, the philosopher Leontium, and the apocryphal Pope Joan ruin their societies by their wit, the *ingenium* of Minerva, the Sibyls, Sappho, Cornifica, Proba, Thamaris, and Irene enrich theirs. In fact, the chapter devoted to the scholarly inventor Nicostrata completely inverts implications of Ceres's biography, because Nicostrata's inventions of grammar and the Roman alphabet figure as the lavishly praised basis of Italian superiority. (This association between Latin and a new Italian nationalism was a frequent humanist commonplace but one not necessarily linked with women.)[26] Just as Boccaccio does not present femineity as either virtuous or vicious, then, so he comes to no clear position with respect to women's effect on society. But because one of the collection's most striking innovations includes women with *ingenium* among the heroines, the ambivalences in Boccaccio's treament of women's civic virtue invite a third question: does Boccaccio's catalog connect women to poetry or history and (by extension) are these two approaches linked or separate?

To approach this problem, we must consider the very complex subject of Boccaccio's attitude toward *poesis,* a subject he explicitly addresses in *De genealogia deorum gentilium* (Of the Geneology of the Gentile Gods). This work (also a text of Boccaccio's latter years) contains one of three defenses of poetry written by early Italian humanists. Boccaccio, however, goes further than Albertino Mussato or Petrarch's *Invective against a Physician,* answering apparent attacks on poetry raised by the Italian scholastics. If this work responds to such attacks, the debate mirrors an earlier French struggle between medieval humanists and scholastics, who had disagreed on poetry's placement among the arts.[27] The humanists favored applying an allegorical approach to pagan writers as well as to holy texts and often associated poetry with philosophy. The scholastics, however, following Aristotle and the Arabs, placed poetry in the study of logic (as in Aristotle's *Organon*) and saw it as a faculty, or technique for manipulating languages. Unlike the other

---

26. See Kristeller 1961. For another discussion of how Boccaccio treats the issue of civic virtue in *De claris mulieribus,* see Jordan 1987.

27. For a detailed history of this debate, see Henri d'Andeli, *The Battle of the Seven Arts,* ed. and trans. L. J. Paetons (Berkeley: University of California Press, 1914).

faculties—rhetoric, the study of persuasive speech, and dialectic, the study of probable demonstration—poetry's function was illusion, not truth, and it could therefore be seen as relatively valueless. While it is easy to overstate the opposition of the scholastics and the humanists (St. Thomas Aquinas, for instance, granted poetry's utility as a means to teach ethical truths), an opposition of sorts did exist and produced a humanist position that elevated poetry with a scholastic one that attacked it.

Boccaccio's defense is shaped by that attack. He lists seven main charges against poetry in *De genealogia deorum gentilium,* answering each in one or more chapters. His mentor, Petrarch, had responded to the attack rather conservatively, emphasizing poetry's utility as a means of instruction, a storehouse of eloquent speech, and a spur to patriotism. In comparison, Boccaccio made radical claims, allying poetry with theology and asserting that poets are inspired by God. He defended poetry's utility by defining it as a science and associating it with the truths of revelation as well as the truths of ethics and political science. He associated it with rhetoric as well, deriving the word from the Greek *poetes,* which he translated into Latin as *exquisita locutio.* Another etymology answered the scholastic complaint that poems are false and corrupt readers. *Fabula* (fiction), he says, derives from the verb *for, faris* (to speak or say, to sing, to celebrate) and is speech that "illustrates or proves an idea."[28] Fiction, he argues, can quell "minds aroused to a mad rage," restore "the strength and spirits of great men," "furnish consolation," and recall lazy spirits to "a state of better and more vigorous fruition" (463).

Boccaccio ends by declaring that to reject poetry is to reject the Bible, but he also says that even a fool would not confuse the old poets with Christian theology. This surprising statement in a treatise that equates sacred with secular allegory shows that despite the elevated definition of *poesis,* there are ambivalences in Boccaccio's defense. The ambivalences can be traced to a platonizing Christianity, but Giuseppe Mazzotta's (1986) analysis of Boccaccio's approach to literature suggests that another source may be Boccaccio's consciousness of literature as an aesthetic—and hence dangerous—experience.

Mazzotta proposes that Boccaccio saw literature in two distinct roles. The first—erotic mediation—predicates a break between history and literature, giving its readers "an intransitive aesthetic experience, which has been refined, preserved, and used to be enjoyed" (1972, 79). Such a role does not form (as *De genealogia deorum gentilium* proscribes) "a crucial nexus be-

---

28. Boccaccio, "Genealogy of the Gentile Gods," trans. Charles Osgood in Preminger (1974, 452). All further references to this work appear in the text.

tween God and man" (1972, 64), but literature as prophetic mediation does. Here the author uses literary myths as tools for cataloging and interpreting world history, often in the Augustinian vein as an advance to God. Mazzotta sees Boccaccio as retreating to prophetic mediation after experiencing the dangers associated with the aesthetic imagination in the *Decameron*. We know, however, that Boccaccio never rejected his earlier works and even *De genealogia deorum gentilium* demonstrates an attempt to find a valued place for *fabula*. I propose that the *mulier clara* shows signs of this endeavor as well. In *De claris mulieribus* Boccaccio usually treats his heroines with a mixture of historic and literary technique (that is, literature as prophetic mediation), but he also associates them with the dangers of literature as erotic mediation and so with a type of writing that threatens the defense in *De genealogia deorum gentilium*.

No one has attempted to link *De claris mulieribus* to Boccaccio's poetics in this fashion, but there are strong medieval precedents for identifying poetics as feminine. In speaking of Horace's *Ars Poetica*, for example, Conrad of Hirsau's *Didascalon* claims that *poetica* (or *poetria* in the medieval title) means a woman studious of poetry (*mulier carminis studens*). He adds that Horace's opening image of a mermaid shows he thought of poetry as feminine and that many of the poet's odes are immoral (*viciosa*). Closer to Boccaccio, Dante's description of Paolo and Francesca's meeting over a courtly romance takes advantage of the associations between literature and erotic ensnarement, a danger also associated with women. In *De genealogia deorum gentilium* itself, the attacks that have been made against poetry echo the misogynist attacks on women; both are thought of as trivial, false, lewd, corrupting, and sinful. And in *De genealogia deorum gentilium*, Boccaccio associates *poesis* with a feminine figure when he tries to defend poetry in its basest form:

> . . . there was never a grumbling old woman, sitting with others late of a winter's night at the home fireside, making up tales of hell, the fates, ghosts, and the like—much of it pure invention—that she did not feel beneath the surface of her tale, as far as her limited mind allowed, at least some meaning— sometimes ridiculous no doubt—with which she tries to scare the little ones, or divert the young ladies, or amuse the old, or at least show the power of fortune. (Preminger 465)

It seems quite possible that Boccaccio conceived of some types of writing as "feminine" and that traces of that understanding affect the presentations in *De claris mulieribus*.

The allegorical treatments of heroines in *De claris mulieribus* often suggests the conception of literature that lies behind Boccaccio's defense. The different chapters sometimes appear as allegories of virtues and vices, as etymological clues to truth, or as garbled accounts of historical incidents (euhemerism). Juno is treated euhemeristically. Circe is presented as an allegory of lust. And Medusa is described as skilled in agriculture because Gorgon (Boccaccio thought) means farmer in Greek. (It actually means fierce.) Both historical and literary figures are also used to convey ethical truths. Circe and Cleopatra speak to the issue of unchastity. Examples that we see as literary—Dido, Medea, Circe, and Minerva—are sometimes treated historically as real figures. And historical figures are sometimes treated literarily when Boccaccio invents incidents (Cleopatra), adds descriptive detail (Megulla Dotata) or interpolates invented speeches (as in the case of Dido, whom Boccaccio largely treats as a historical figure). When Boccaccio uses philological methods to compare versions of his heroines' lives, there are signs of a new and more historical approach to his sources, but these methods are inconsistently applied, and there is no sign of the *topoi* often associated with medieval historiography (such as the *translatii topoi*). The links to history are thus present but not dominant, and they always coexist with literary technique.

On the other hand, the heroines are sometimes and a bit surprisingly linked to a form of literature that does not fulfill the grandiose role of Boccaccio's defense. When an example loses its moral purpose, when it becomes a means of entertainment, then it becomes, in Mazzotta's words, "a degraded object of erotic mediation" (1986, 50). The tragic tales of Thisbe and Jocasta; the story of Flora, a prostitute turned goddess; and the narrative of Paulina, who is persuaded to sleep with a man who poses as the god Anubis, are cases in point. These last two stories obviously parallel tales from the *Decameron*. Flora suggests the tale of Ser Ciappelletto's confession (1.1) and Paulina resembles Lisabetta, who sleeps with a counterfeit Gabriel (4.2). Passages in *De claris mulieribus* also strongly echo passages in the *Decameron*, reinforcing the catalog's link to literature as pleasure. Both books are addressed to women, both espouse pleasure as a final effect, and both conclude with the author's defense of his work. Given woman's figurative connection with physical pleasure, the importance of women in the *Decameron*, and Boccaccio's reservations about the aesthetic experience, such vestiges of erotic mediation in *De claris mulieribus* may explain ambivalences in the heroines' portrayals. The importance of such vestiges and their effect on the catalog as a whole are best gauged, however, by comparing Boccaccio's catalog of heroines with his catalog of famous men, *De casibus virorum illustrium.*

De casibus virorum illustrium and *De claris mulieribus* were sometimes thought of as similar works.[29] Both deal with fame, were composed around the same time, and were valued as reference books in classical and historical studies. But if examined closely, the two works actually differ in almost every major respect. Boccaccio's catalog of women is very loosely organized as an episodic series of sketches. The heroines appear in chronological order, from Eve (at the beginning of the world) to Boccaccio's contemporary Queen Joanna of Sicily at the end. A preface attempts to explain, a conclusion to defend the book's structure and purpose. While such deprecations and apologies were standard medieval *formulae,* Boccaccio also explicitly emphasizes that *De claris mulieribus* is a new type of collection and thus one more prone to errors.

In contrast, *De casibus virorum illustrium* has a well articulated frame with a flawless medieval pedigree. Organized as a dream vision and governed by the single topic of the operations of fortune and providence,[30] it is modeled on both Boethius's *De Consolatione Philosophiae* (The Consolation of Philosophy, a major work in the medieval canon) and Macrobius's *Somnium Scipionis* (Scipio's Dream, a major work of literary criticism with continuing influence in the Middle Ages). It is also significant that while Boccaccio stretches the meaning of titular words from both collections, the larger meaning in *De claris mulieribus* invokes a moral ambiguity—"claris" as famous and infamous—while it indicates a universal viewpoint in *De casibus virorum illustrium*—"virorum" as mankind not man.[31] In plan and execution, then, *De casibus virorum illustrium* is more ordered, more unified, more

---

29. Antoine Vérard, for example, clearly confused the two books when he noted in his 1401 translation of *De claris mulieribus* that it speaks of ladies' "fortunes et infélicités." Fortune is the guiding theme of *De casibus virorum illustrium,* not *De claris mulieribus.* Often the two catalogs were translated together and by the same person, as was possibly the case with the French versions by Laurent de Premierfait. And there is some evidence, as Godman (1977, 150) notes, that Chaucer looked at Cleopatra in both *De claris mulieribus* and *De casibus virorum illustrium* for *Legend of Good Women,* another possible connection.

30. St. Augustine's *City of God,* which in many ways presents the model of a medieval universal history, sees history as the story of humankind's progression toward God, thus connecting the world of fortune with the operations of providence. Boccaccio's book seeks justice in fortune's patterns; in this, it touches upon providence and the medieval understanding of historical causality.

31. In fact, several chapters in *De casibus virorum illustrium* are devoted to women, such as Cleopatra.

conventional, and (most important) more linked to universal verities than *De claris mulieribus*, albeit within conservative terms. In Mazzotta's terms, it represents prophetic rather than erotic mediation because it provides a history of humankind seen from the intersection of fortune and providence, the two medieval agents of historical causality.

An analysis of the audience and methodology for each volume confirms this contrast. The dedication to *De claris mulieribus* specifies pleasure not service, as the reason for its composition. The preface notes that Boccaccio lengthens his sources to "please women no less than men" because women "are not acquainted with history . . . and need and enjoy a more lengthy digression" (xxxviii). In contrast, *De casibus virorum illustrium* will benefit the community. Boccaccio particularly directs this book to "our princes" so that they may recognize "God's power, the shiftiness of Fortune, and their own insecurity."[32] Since history was widely characterized as a school of politics in both medieval and Renaissance notions of historiography, this purpose confirms the greater historical and civic slant of *De casibus virorum illustrium* and its concern with the universal truths that should govern society. On the other hand, by associating itself with aesthetic pleasure and with women, *De claris mulieribus* is organized around two important means of erotic mediation. It is not surprising that despite its scholarly tones, *De claris mulieribus* does not connect its heroines to any universal standards (aside from, perhaps, chastity).

Boccaccio's catalog, then, vacillates between polarities. It includes virtuous and vicious women, women whose deeds contribute to society and women whose deeds destroy it. There are links to both history and literature in *De claris mulieribus*—hardly surprising in an age that didn't yet clearly distinguish between the two—but no continuous link to universal absolutes as in the collection of illustrious men and in Boccaccio's defense of poetry. Boccaccio's work makes some interesting deviations from the misogynistic pattern, but in general, it passes the tradition on.

In this respect, it is important to make one further observation concerning the catalog. Like most florilegia, it begins with an exposition of its methodology in a prologue that clarifies Boccaccio's presence and purpose. Within the catalog, Boccaccio is also visible as he distinguishes between sources, notes problems with the written record, and applies various principles of interpretation. In these moments, he is quite close to the compiler of *Mulierium virtutes*. But the *Adversus Jovinianum* is not completely dis-

---

32. Boccaccio, *The Fates of Illustrious Men*, trans. Louis B. Hall (New York: Ungar, 1965), 2.

placed; Boccaccio is very much implicated in the medieval attitude toward *auctoritas*, even if he is not slavishly addicted to any particular *auctor*. He often manipulates his presentations silently, as when he invents Cleopatra's seduction of Herod Antipater to emphasize the portrait he obtains from his sources. He also tends to use an authoritative and impersonal tone when delivering the morals derived from his exempla, the most important part of his sketches. Jerome's influence survives here. As with so many other facets of *De claris mulieribus*, the compiler has two faces. At times he is submerged within a call to tradition; at other times his presence is highlighted as Boccaccio calls attention to his sorting of sources. The humanist context of the catalog, however, tends to make the compiler more obvious than previously, for like any humanist, Boccaccio's role as writer often involves an ongoing revelation of his role as reader.

Like others of Boccaccio's works, *De claris mulieribus* is subject to many interpretations and is shaped by many forces. Given its ferment of impulses, one can hardly dismiss it because of its ambivalences. Indeed, its equivocations are precisely the source of its interest. While *De claris mulieribus* draws extensively on misogynistic traditions, it is one of the first catalogs of women since antiquity to posit feminine fame based on women's deeds. Aware of the uniqueness of his approach, Boccaccio also knew that he was finding it difficult to define his subject. *De claris mulieribus* finishes in an open-ended fashion, actually inviting revision:

> it is possible that some things have been improperly included . . . for it often happens that a writer is deceived not only by ignorance of the matter but by the excessive love he has for his work . . . if anyone has a charitable soul, let him correct what has been improperly written by adding to it or deleting and improve it so that the work will flourish for someone's benefit, rather than perish torn by the jaws of the malicious without being of service to anyone. (251)

> (possibile esse et contigisse facile credam non nulla minus recte consistere. Decipit enim persepe non solum ignorantia rerum, sed circa opus suum nimia laborantis affectio . . . et si quis illis pie caritatis spiritus est, minus debite scripta augentes minuentesque corrigant et emendent, ut potius alicuius in bonum vigeat opus, quam in nullius commodum laceratum dentibus invidorum depereat. [450])

Such an invitation was formulaic for a work's end, but Boccaccio's reservations agree perfectly with the hesitancies expressed in his preface and with some of the inconsistencies in the catalog itself. Whether or not Boccaccio was invoking the formula seriously, his ending certainly proved prophetic, for many catalogs followed Boccaccio's in the next three centuries, often citing him as a major source. If *De claris mulieribus* did not articulate a new definition of femineity, it nevertheless made others possible. It also revealed how a new attitude toward the *studia humanitatis* could invoke new meditations on how women and "feminine" qualities were valued. If the *mulier clara* was simply another mirror reflecting the concerns, agitations, and fears of her male creator, the pattern of ambivalence to be read there portended the compiler's more prominent role in the catalogs to come.

Chapter 4

Al of Another Tonne

As *De claris mulieribus* demonstrates, a new spirit of inquiry emerged in late medieval Europe, one that would eventually inaugurate profound changes in the way medieval men and women examined and understood the world around them. Various philosophical and cultural currents marked this change—nominalism, humanism, even a nascent nationalism among them— but most important for the catalog tradition, all placed a new importance on the value of empiricism in the search for epistemological verities. Writers such as Boccaccio approached the ancient *auctores* with a new inquisitiveness and with a willingness to examine their own readings of these *auctores* as interpretations.[1] Such new humanists also focused more persistently on earthly experiences and the dignity of the human being. Trust in an absolute and achievable Christian truth persisted, and literature remained a theological and ethical enterprise at heart; the peculiar authority of the written word continued. But writers and readers of the later medieval centuries sought empirical data to support the truths their texts espoused. They thus approached books with a new willingness to question and to express individual opinion.

The catalog came into its own in this atmosphere. As Judson Allen has noted, the fourteenth and fifteenth centuries are not the "era of the exemplum" (1982, 71) by accident. The catalog unites a "focused and very material approach to physical reality" with the belief in a "certain achievement of truth" (1982, 71). It thus answers the claims of both authority and experience—at times reconciling the two, at others placing them in conflict. In the

---

1. The Italian humanists were more uncertain about their abilities to read the ancients correctly than the twelfth-century humanists had been. Thus in his introduction to *De genealogia deorum gentilium* Boccaccio laments that "so many minds, so many opinions" have made it very difficult to interpret the old texts correctly.

Divine Comedy, for example, Dante's experiences and those of the shades in his catalogs clarify his understanding of authoritative truth. In the Wife of Bath's catalog of misogamous literature, however, the Wife, who is very much associated with experience, misuses, misquotes, and misconstrues what written authority has to say about marriage.

Because of their subjects and methodologies, catalogs of good women were more suited to illustrating conflict than reconciliation. As we've seen, medieval catalogs often depended upon *auctoritas* not only for their material but also for their persuasive powers. The subject of women, however, was traditionally linked with the natural world. If a catalog were to argue for the genuine worth of women, it would naturally pit content (experience) against form (authority); a writer could exploit this tension to dramatize the problem of how these two elements interacted when there was conflict between them. One of Boccaccio's readers, Geoffrey Chaucer, took just such an approach in his catalog, the *Legend of Good Women.*

Like Boccaccio, Chaucer compiled his catalog of women in the latter years of his life, possibly from 1386 to 1394.[2] His principal inspiration was Ovid's *Heroides,* but he also used Boccaccio's *De claris mulieribus* and Jean de Meun's *Roman de la Rose* for material and inspiration.[3] His reading of Boccaccio's vernacular works was doubtless important as well, for these defined the kinds of poetical problems explored in Chaucer's catalog—the value of pleasure, the purpose of *fabula,* and the position of poets in relation to their sources, texts, and readers.

When Chaucer wrote *Legend of Good Women,* he had already visited Italy and benefitted from his contact with Italian texts by such authors as Dante and Boccaccio. By the time he started the legends in 1316, he had already synthesized these forces into one masterpiece *(Troilus and Criseyde)*

---

2. These dates come from Howard 1987. Like so many other aspects of this poem, its date has been a problem for critics. Lowes (1905) dated the poem between 1372 and 1386. *Troilus and Criseyde* is now believed to have been completed in 1386. Since *Legend of Good Women* is its ironic palinode, most Chaucerians believe that Chaucer started his legends in 1386. Howard bases his completion date on the poem itself, claiming that when Chaucer commits himself to write the legends "year by year," he means he will write one legend a year (1987, 394–97). Since he wrote nine legends, that makes 1395 the last year for his work on the poem.

3. For Chaucer's relationship to his sources see Lowes 1904; Dodd 1913; Estrich 1939; Kisser 1983; Rowe 1988; Frank 1972; Godman 1977; Henry Keller, *Love and Marriage in the Age of Chaucer* (Ithaca, N.Y.: Cornell University Press, 1975); Windeatt 1982; Fyler 1979; Eleanor Wilson Leach, "A Study in the Sources and Rhetoric of Chaucer's *Legend of Good Women* and Ovid's *Heroides*" (Ph.D. diss., Yale University, 1963); and M. C. Edwards, "A Study of Six Characters in Chaucer's *Legend of Good Women* with Reference to Medieval Scholia on Ovid's *Heroides*" (Ph.D. diss., Oxford University, 1970).

and was beginning to write his second *(Canterbury Tales)*. *Legend of Good Women* talks about Chaucer's poetics in his most creative and interesting period. While critics have often received it coolly[4]—many Chaucerians still believe that he abandoned the series in boredom—there is a growing body of work attesting to the text's sophistication and self-reflexion. In 1963 Robert Payne demonstrated that the prologue presents a myth of poetic creation.[5] More recently, Alastair Minnis has shown Chaucer's prologue borrows terminology from the academic prologues to the *auctores*.[6] I would like to argue that the legends fail to fulfill the prologue's promises, and because of that, raise interesting questions about the narrator's role in the text. Because Chaucer poses as a compiler, these questions apply to a strategy firmly associated with the catalog of women—the use of authorities as a shield for personal opinion.

By Chaucer's time, the compiler's role was well understood not only in and of itself but as one of four graded levels of authorship. In his *Medieval Theory of Authorship: Scholastic Literary Attitudes in the Later Middle Ages*, Alastair Minnis has traced the emergence of these roles and shown that each was recognized by a number of important medieval sources, such as St. Bonaventure's commentary on Peter Lombard's *Libri sententiarum* (1250–52).[7] Each role implied different levels of authorial responsibility for the text,

---

4. This is not to say that the poem has failed to attract any critical attention. Although studied far less than Chaucer's other last works, *Legend of Good Women* has built up quite a bibliography. On its relationship to courtly literature see, for example, Lowes 1904; Dodd 1913; and Estrich 1939. Christian themes are discussed in Griffith 1923. For the poem's relationship to its historical milieu, see Jefferson 1914; Kittredge 1908–9; Moore 1912; Tupper 1922; and Galway 1938. Opposing readings of the legends are common. Goddard (1908 and 1909) first read the legend as a satire against women. Lowes (1909) refuted this position. Baum (1945) persisted in the satiric reading. Hansen (1983) recently revived the idea of a satire but from a different angle. She sees the misogynist narrator as the target. On the other hand, Overbeck (1967–68) argued that Chaucer is proposing a new model of feminine characterization in the legends.

In the last thirty years, commentaries have often emphasized the legends' metaliterary aspect. On this very involved topic, see, for example, Payne 1963; David 1976; Kisser 1983; Minnis 1981; and most recently, Rowe 1988, who argues that Boethius's *Consolation of Philosophy*, which Chaucer was translating, and Dante's *Divine Comedy*, which Chaucer might have encountered in Italy, lie behind the legends. Earlier, Frank (1972) sought to link the poem to the *Canterbury Tales* and defend its artistic worth. Other recent additions to this bibliography include Delany 1985 and 1987; Allen 1986–87; Cherniss 1986; Sanderlin 1986; and the essays by Ames, Peck, and Delaney in Wassermann and Blanch 1986.

5. See Payne 1963.

6. See Minnis 1981.

7. See Praoemii qu. 4, conclusion, *Bonaventurae opera*, vol. 1, 14–15. Minnis (1988) quotes from this description in his lengthy discussion of authorial roles.

the most onerous belonging to the *auctor*, who was fully accountable for what he wrote. Ralph Fitz Ralph, the chancellor of Oxford University in the 1300s, described the *auctor* as one who asserts something *(assertor, affirmator)*, words whose roots in dialectic imply juridic responsibility.[8] *Auctores* were generally dead—as Walter Map jokingly remarked in *De nugis curialium*—and thus removed from their detractors. The other three roles were also safe from censure. A scribe *(scriptor)* merely copied the words of others while the *commentator*, who explained the views of others, only added his own words when necessary. Ostensibly, the *compilator* also added little original material since he merely repeated *(recitatio)* or reported *(reportatio)* from other sources. Yet even medieval critics recognized that compilers controlled several ways of making meaning, the most important being the choice of excerpts and the order in which those excerpts were presented.[9] In fact, as Jean de Meun's defense in the *Roman de la Rose* shows, writers often posed as compilers to write with impunity on controversial subjects such as love and women.[10]

In *Legend of Good Women*, Chaucer implicitly explores this strategy by dramatizing its execution through the Chaucerian narrator. Like the persona of *Adversus Jovinianum*, this narrator claims to be following his sources. Fictionally, his writing seems rigidly controlled, for Cupid dictates the catalog's content and theme and also directs Chaucer to find his material in other books. Within the prologue, and in the relationship between prologue and legendary, however, Chaucer the writer shows that such control is impossible. Any act requiring writing also requires reading, which requires interpretation. And interpretation is always an implicit betrayal. A writer (such as Chaucer) can be betrayed by his reader (such as Cupid), or a subject (such as women) can be betrayed by an author (such as Chaucer). The fact that Chaucer writes the legends as an ironic palinode for Criseyde's treachery in *Troilus and Criseyde* gives the interlocking treasons both frame and potency. For our topic, the most fruitful question to ask is why Chaucer uses a catalog of good women to demonstrate these problems. Does the tradition

---

8. See *Summa in questionibus Armenorum*, found in the *Summa Ricardi*, fols. 2–3v. Minnis discusses this work at length in "'Authorial Intention' and 'Literal Sense' in the Exegetical Theories of Richard Fitz Ralph and John Wyclif," in *Proceedings of the Royal Institute* 75, Section C (Dublin, 1975).

9. Minnis discusses this aspect (1988, 192).

10. The *locus classicus* for such a defense is Jean de Meun's apology in the *Roman de la Rose*, lines 15195–234, quoted at the end of chap. 2 of this work. Chaucer used this passage for the narrator's self-defense in his poem's prologue, where the narrator also protests he is simply quoting from the authoritites.

enlighten our view of the legendary? Conversely, does Chaucer's excursus on authorship expand the tradition? To address these issues, we must begin with the prologue, where a conventional approach to art is outlined and imperiled.

The Prologue

The *Legend of Good Women*'s prologue exists in two separate versions, now called F and G. Although critics have never definitively resolved which came first, many Chaucerians now accept G as the later draft, thus following the lead of John Lowes, who wrote on the problem in 1905.[11] Since G occurs in only one extant manuscript, however, F, whether first or not, may well have been the version Chaucer circulated.[12]

Because neither draft is universally preferred, both will be considered in these comments. They are by and large quite similar, for they both follow the form of an academic prologue to the *auctores*,[13] and both resemble the prologues to florilegia, which gave readers a rather precise description of the collection to come. According to F and G, then, the subject of the *Legend of Good Women* (its *materia libri*) is women who remain faithful to their loves. The narrator will praise the heroines for their constancy as well as blame their lovers for abandoning them (a *modus agendi*). By Cupid's instruction, the narrator is to begin with Cleopatra and end with Alceste (the compilation's *ordo libri*). Finally, reading these stories will make men trust the authorities (*utilitas*). G identifies the compiler's intention (*intentio*) as evoking such trust. F, however, defers defining his intention until an unspecified "later," which never occurs. Since both versions purport to make the reader trust authority, this difference in *intentio* looms large in Chaucer's discussion of poetic method. For the moment, the deferral poses a significant question for the reader, for it relates directly to the compiler's relationship with his text.

---

11. See Lowes 1905.

12. There are two (unfortunately) dated books on the manuscript tradition of the two prologues: Bilderbeck 1902 and French 1905. Other work on the prologue includes Lowes 1904 and Lowes 1905, Estrich 1937, and most recently, Gardner 1968.

13. For a discussion of such prologues see Minnis 1988; J. Allen 1982; N. M. Haring, "Two Commentaries on Boethius by Thierry of Chartres," *Archives d'histoires doctrinale et littérature de moyên age* 26 (1960): 65–136; L. Jenaro-Maclennan, *The Trecento Commentaries on the Divina commedia and the Epistle to Cangrande* (Oxford: Clarendon, 1974); C. E. Lutz, "One Formula of *accessus* in Remigius' Works," *Latomus* 19 (1960): 774–80; G. Przychocki, "'Accessus Ovidiani,' *Rozprawy Akademii Umietjetnosci*, wydzial filologiczny, serya 3, tom. 4 (1911): 65–126; Quain 1945; E. M. Sanford, "The Manuscripts of Lucan: Accessus and Marginalia," *Speculum* 9 (1934): 278–95; and A. Stoelen, "Les Commentaries scripturaires attribués à Bruno le Chartreux," *Recherches de théologie ancienne et médiévale* 24 (1958): 177–247.

Such a question involves an understanding of the interaction between experience and authority, an interaction played out in the poet's legends and dramatized in the action of the prologue. In both F and G, the action neatly splits into two parts: the narrator's experience in the meadow and an ensuing dream vision. The meadow roughly corresponds to the natural world of experience while the dream relates to the world of written authority. The narrator begins by strongly affirming his love of books, but he deserts his studies early on to describe his love of the daisy, whose presence in the meadow proves an insurmountable temptation. After a day of daisy worship, he falls asleep in his garden and dreams of the meadow again, this time peopled by Cupid and the Lady Alceste (who is the daisy transformed). Much to his surprise, the god of love accuses him of heresy, of betraying the Lady Alceste. She defends him and saves him from exile but assigns him the penance of writing about "Cupides martyres," women faithful and true to love. The legends that follow are the narrator's fulfillment of that penance and also the continuance of his relationship with his love and muse. Interestingly, he awakes at the end of version G but in F remains asleep.

Critics have traced many differences between the two versions, but none has commented on the contrasting endings and the relation they create between the meadow and dream narrative. Interestingly, F leaves Chaucer in the world of books (often associated with dreams because of Macrobius's commentary on the *Somnium Scipionis,* where literary commentary is intermixed with a dream vision), but it also concentrates more heavily on the world of experience.[14] G leaves Chaucer awake (in the world of experience) but elaborates on the dream. Yet this variance reinforces other differences between the two texts. The experience in the meadow is much more fully developed in F than in G, where several lines describing the daisy are cut.[15] F also confines the daisy to the meadow and Alceste to the dream, but in G, the daisy appears in both. If one sees the dream as explicating the experience in the meadow (just as books make our experiences clear to us), G blurs a fundamental distinction roughly analogous to the two types of knowing posited by the nominalist philosopher William Ockham—intuitive knowledge (knowledge of the flower) and abstractive knowledge (knowledge of Alceste,

---

14. See especially Estrich 1937.

15. The first section is much larger in F than in G. F includes a detailed evocation of Chaucer's devotion to the daisy, couched in the language of courtly love, and a vivid description of the springtime meadow. In G, the courtly devotion is dropped, the springtime description curtailed, and the dream vision expanded, arriving some 105 lines earlier in the poem.

who allegorically presents what the flower "means").[16] (According to Ockham's works, intuitive knowledge is the knowledge by which we know if a thing exists or not; abstractive knowledge is the understanding of a thing's nature.) F thus draws a much clearer line between the narrator's meadow experience and his attempt to understand it in his dream. In nominalist terms, it develops the problematic connection between knowledge derived from experience (intuitive) and knowledge derived from authority (abstractive).

This bias makes the narrator's greater prominence in F extremely important. Both versions cast the Chaucerian narrator in roles traditionally ascribed to biblical authors such as David and Solomon; that is, he is both a compiler and a repentant sinner.[17] In F, unlike G, Alceste controls both because she is his muse and lady. Narrator F can speak of love not only from books but also from his own experience, unlike narrator G and unlike the Chaucerian narrator of *Troilus and Criseyde;* what he loves (as with Ovid's Sappho) is both his art and his lover. Prologue F intertwines these levels by implicating both in the narrator's legend-making, an action that is both an artistic enterprise and a loving atonement. Since the compiler's individuality, human character, and ways of knowing are squarely at the center of our interest, it is significant that F obscures the one factor in a medieval *accessus* that was most closely associated with the compiler himself, that is his *intentio*. This obfuscation forces the reader to ponder the compiler's relationship to this text and his intentions in writing it.

Because they change our understanding of the narrator's work, the different *intentiones* of G and F are worth examining in detail. While both versions of the prologue claim that the poem advises readers about authority, G makes this advice Chaucer's *intentio* as well as the collection's *utilitas:*

> But wherfore that I spak to yive credence
> To bokes olde and don hem reverence
> *Is* for men shulde autoritees beleve.[18]

> (81–83G, italics mine)

---

16. For an introduction to William Ockham, see P. Vignaux, *Le Nominalisme au XIVème siècle* (Montreal: Institute d'études mediaevales, 1948); L. Baudry, *Guillaume d'Occam* (Paris: J. Vrin, 1949); M. H. Carré, *Realists and Nominalists* (Oxford: Clarendon, 1946); and Leff 1958.

17. Minnis discusses these roles in relation to David and Solomon (1988, 103–17).

18. Chaucer (1961, 480–518). All further references to this work appear in the text.

In other words, the work's final effect and the author's intention are the same: to make the reader trust authority. F embraces the same *utilitas* but hedges on the writer's *intentio,* adding that the narrator will clarify this point later:

> But wherfore that I spak to yive credence
> To olde stories and doon hem reverence,
> And that men mosten more thyng beleve
> Then men may seen at eye or elles preve,—
> *That* shal I seyn, whanne that I see my tyme."
>
> (97–101F, italics mine)

The poem still aspires to make its readers trust authority, but the narrator's motives for doing so are left unclear, at least for the moment. Chaucer's choice of words here is suggestive. By saying he will make his intentions clear in "tyme," the narrator sets up important resonances in a text that claims its stories of temporal heroines are "legends," a word heretofore used in Middle English only for the stories of eternity's heroines (the saints). The word "tyme" also reinforces F's greater interest in experience, which occurs in the temporal world, and it highlights the reader's greater commitment to the experience of reading (which occurs and changes in time). Since narrator F never sees an appropriate moment to reveal his intentions, readers must infer these points for themselves by focusing closely on whatever clues the compiler has left behind him in the text. Paradoxically, then, the narrator in F makes his presence inescapable by not defining it.

For all these reasons, I contend that F introduces the poem more satisfactorily than G. The prologue's very opening announces an interest in the connections between experience and authority; F connects these two more crisply than G. Since both prologues also defend the Chaucerian narrator more than they defend women, it is safe to assume the compiler's experience will be an important factor in the legends to come. F's emphasis upon the narrator, his experience, and the reader's experience of the text more forcefully direct the audience's attention to the narrator, alerting us that in the work we are about to read, the difference between the authoritative text and our experience of reading it will not be easy to capture. Since all medieval writers, including and especially compilers, were readers before they were writers, this question addresses assumptions at the very heart of medieval poetics. As usual in Chaucer, the ramifications are not simple.

Chaucer's opening lines, practically identical in F and G, brilliantly infuse this problem in the very language of his poem, making readers immediately aware of linguistic aspects of the text. The first three words situate us in the temporal world; the confusion that follows confirms the implications of this position:

A thousand tymes have I herd men telle
That ther ys joy in hevene and peyne in helle,
And I acorde wel that it ys so;
But, natheles, yet wot I wel also
That ther nis noon dwellyng in this contree,
That eyther hath in hevene or helle ybe,
Ne may of hit noon other weyes witen,
But as he hath herd seyd, or founde it writen;
For by assay ther may no man it preve.
But God forbede but men shulde leve
Wel more thing then men han seen with ye!
Men shal not wenen every thing a lye
But yf himself yt seeth, or elles dooth;
For, Got wot, thing is never the lasse sooth,
Thogh every wight ne may it nat ysee.
Bernard the monk ne saugh nat all, pardee!

(1–16F)

On the surface, Chaucer appears to be making a simple point: there are things that people must accept on faith (like heaven and hell) because they cannot experience them ("assay"). The flood of conjunctions and adverbs—yf, but, yet, though, natheless—qualify that assertion, however, and actually compromise it. The first three lines insist that men claim there is a pleasant heaven and a painful hell; the next three add that the authority for this assertion is books, not experience; in the next seven, however, the reiterations of the word "sight" hopelessly confuse the issue of whether the narrator is advocating trust of books or trust of experience, because sight brings in many complex allusions.

In any medieval text, sight carried certain strong associations no matter what the context.[19] Philosophically, it often indicated a soul's intellectual and rational power.[20] Twelfth-century theologians (e.g., Alexander of Hales and John of Rochelle) often associated it with empirical knowledge and the

---

19. For other commentary on the prologue's use of sight see Smith 1981.
20. This metaphor goes back at least as far as St. Augustine's *Soliloquia*.

human sciences, which pursued wisdom.[21] But it was strongly associated as well with the universal truths dictated by *auctoritas*. Dante's vision of God was visual, as was the experience of many mystics such as Bernard of Clairvaux. And in Chaucer's time, contact with the *auctores* themselves was rapidly becoming a visual as well as an aural experience. Men not only "herd seyd" but "founde it written."

All these meanings are played upon by Chaucer's opening. What man "has seen with ye" and should not form the limit of his knowledge is left tantalizingly unclear. Lines 12–13, with the double emphasis on "seeth" or "dooth," suggest that it is empirical knowledge of the natural world that is being discussed. But the use of sight in reading is also suggested in line 8 (which translates the usual formulae of textual inceptions, *audimus* or "we hear" and *legimus* or "we read"). Finally, if Bernard the monk in line 16 is really Bernard the Clear-sighted (Clairvaux), then the last line denies the completeness of the mystic's vision of absolutes, thus asserting empirical claims to verity.[22] We are not sure if we are being advised to go beyond the sight of the natural world or the supernatural world or the written page. In fact, the only thing we are made to "see" clearly is a semantic confusion. From the very start, then, the reader comes alive not simply to the authoritative page but also to the less than authoritative reading of the page, to a mixture of experience and authority that will characterize the catalog to come.

The Chaucerian narrator himself also exemplifies this mixture, for he appears as a reader, a writer, and a lover. Compiler and repentant sinner, the narrator suggests that his two worlds impinge on one another. He loves books; he also loves the daisy. When he deserts the former for the latter at the beginning of the poem, he seems to suggest that the two are incompatible; but the poem itself insists on their connection. His springtime experience is charmingly lifelike but constructed of textual allusions from the French Mar-

---

21. See the "Tractus Introductoris quaestio 1 de doctrina theolgiae," in Alexander de Hales, *Summa Theologica* (Quaracchi: Collegium S. Bonaventurae, 1924–48). John of Richmond, Alexander's pupil, was also responsible for parts of this text.

22. In his commentary to the poem in his edition of Chaucer's works, Robinson notes that this line is an English translation of the Latin proverb "Bernardus moanchus non vidit omnia" (Chaucer 1961, 841). For identification with Bernard Clairvaux, see R. Smith 1946 and Marie Hamilton, "Bernard the Monk: Postscript," *Modern Language Notes* 62 (1947): 190–91. For dissenting views see *Notes and Queries*, 8th series, 3:433, where an E. S. A. suggests the monk might be Bernard of Morlaix. John Tatlock, "Chaucer's Bernard the Monk," *Modern Language Notes* 66 (1931): 21–22, suggests that it might be Bernard the Traveler. The very fact that so many Bernards might fit Chaucer's description shows how ambiguous the proverb reference is.

guerite poetry. Moreover, the narrator's use of this tradition shows he is not a careful or sensitive reader, for while the hymn is eloquent and beautiful on one level, it is ridiculous on another. The bumbling narrator addresses a literal flower rather than a woman. The arrival of Flora and Zephyrus is equally ambiguous. It represents the very experiential act of reproduction, which will become central to the poet's investigation of experience, but it also recalls scenes from two important books associated with the catalog tradition, the *Roman de la Rose* and *De claris mulieribus*. In the first, La Vielle uses the couple's entrance to describe the Golden Age of the satiric catalogs, whose portraits of women and love would certainly have offended Cupid. In *De claris mulieribus*, Flora exemplifies feminine deceit and trickery because she is, in fact, a prostitute turned goddess. These negative overtones complicate Chaucer's positive presentation of Flora and Zephyrus, and the propagation of meadow flowers engendered by their appearance. Again, experience and authority are so closely interwoven as to be inextricable. To understand the narrator's experience, we must know what he has read. Cupid's accusations against the narrator Chaucer and Alceste's defense also argue that to understand what he has written, we must know something of his personality. The god of love implicitly links personal experience with the handling of a text when he accuses the narrator of sexual and artistic impotence, of being "nothing able" (320F; 246G) as a writer and lover. He has hindered people's devotion to love by translating the *Roman de la Rose*, has slandered women and betrayed Alceste by describing the perfidious Criseyde, and has chosen inappropriate "matere" for his "makyng." All these accusations, but particularly the last, which speaks to a compiler's role in his collection, show that Cupid is more than willing to hold the Chaucerian narrator responsible for what he says and how he uses his sources.

While Cupid is a less than reliable critic (he is rather thick-headed and refuses to listen to the narrator's own protestations of innocence), his "relyke" (321F) Alceste also supports this stance in her defense of the narrator. She briefly suggests that Chaucer may be the victim of envious slanderers (thereby implying that personal bias can alter the way a reader reads). She goes on to the traditional argument of the compiler's distance from his text (he did not originate the material), but she uses it in a less than complimentary fashion. If Chaucer were "nyce" (362F; 340G)—a bit thick-headed and inattentive to his choice of "matere"—he did, after all, only "translaten that olde clerkes writen" (370F; 350G). Her next point reaffirms Cupid's charges and forecasts the narrator's penance. Perhaps Chaucer wrote these works under orders he could not disobey; perhaps he now repents his wrong. Her closing plea implies not only the narrator's guilt but also the corollary that a compiler *can* affect his work by bending his excerpts to a predetermined bias. By the end of her "defense," Alceste is tacitly pleading that the narrator is guilty and assuring Cupid that Chaucer wishes to do better.

As a penance for his sins, Alceste and Cupid direct the narrator to write the "legends" of faithful women betrayed by men. In doing so, they go to great lengths to control the order and choice of excerpts, textual aspects a compiler was thought free to manipulate. They also specify other incidentals. Cupid identifies the legends' heroines and in F names possible sources. He also tries to provide an order for the book which is to begin with Cleopatra and end with Alceste. The penance itself will have three parts. Chaucer is to write of faithful women, tell of their unfaithful lovers, and speak well of love. For the narrator as compiler, these commands identify a final cause *(utilitas)*, a style *(modus agendi)* and a subject matter *(materia libri)*. For the narrator as a penitent, they prescribe the three stages of a penance: confession (to speak of dishonest men), contrition (to speak well of love), and restitution (to speak of faithful women).

Ideally, the spiritual penance and literary program should converge and point to a single meaning, just as the story of David's repentance for adultery was held to point to the same meaning found in his psalms. Alceste as Chaucer's muse provides an image of such harmony[23] because while she is a heroine of pagan literature and a model of the good wife, she is also a type of Christ and a parallel of Mary. Like Christ, she died for another (her husband Admetus), descended to Hell, and rose again (when she was rescued by Hercules). Like the Virgin Mary, she intercedes for another—for the Chaucerian narrator with the god of love. As Admetus's faithful wife and Chaucer's piteous lady, she exemplifies perfect earthly love, as a type of the Virgin, perfect heavenly love. In her transformations, she also moves easily from the heavenly to the earthly. Jove changed her into a star, Cybele into a daisy. Her pagan character (connected as it is with earthly love) in no way contradicts a higher love that is the subject of authoritative texts.

Since she is the narrator's love and muse, she should guide his work, but the legendary reveals he often falls short of her exacting standard. Love (Cupid) demands a great deal, in fact everything. His parting commands indicate that the legends should do nothing less than unify earth and heaven, both rhetorically and thematically. Medieval rhetoricians such as Geoffrey

---

23. Kisser (1983, chap. 2) comments at length upon Alceste's unification of the various levels of meaning and relates this unity to her exemplification of a properly constituted metaphor.

of Vinsauf had advised writers to choose between the methods of abbrevia-
tion and amplification.[24] To follow Cupid, Chaucer must adopt both by
speaking of all the faithful women of Cupid's court but in abbreviated form.
He must "sey shortly" (577F) and, like any compiler of a florilegium, show
all of the important points—"reherce of al hir lyf the grete" (574F). How one
repeats the "grete" while saying "shortly" is not specified and will cause a
dilemma, as we shall see in the legends. In addition, these stylistic points
indicate a thematic dilemma between praising and blaming. Medieval rhetoricians often associated *amplificatio* with heightening and *abbreviatio* with
diminishing a subject. In like manner, Chaucer must praise (women), blame
(men), and yet make love appealing.[25] It seems an impossible task, but like
any penance, the legendary requires the narrator understand and reenact divine justice. The legends themselves chart his progress toward this goal.

Since the metaphor of penance governs the work as a whole, it is
appropriate that Chaucer builds his prologue around the image of resurrection, the reward for a successful penance and an appropriate metaphor for the
Boccaccian task of recovering neglected texts. (Many of the legends translate
these myths into English for the first time.) The ease with which resurrection
applies to spiritual, physical, and even authorial actions enables Chaucer to
connect the many layers of his work and suggest that a final resolution exists
between the three levels, even amid immediate confusion.

Again, Alceste exemplifies this resolution in her multiple resurrections
as daisy and heroine. As a daisy, she is reborn in the world of time (experience); as Alceste, she is reborn in the world of art (literature); as a figure of
Christ, she exemplifies rebirth into eternity (universal truth). Her own defense recognizes no conflict between Cupid's worship and "the other holynesse" (424F). She harmonizes all three levels. Her temporal resurrections
are also arranged within a hierarchical but interconnected series. The daisy
follows the sun, opening each day at dawn and closing each dusk. Its rebirth
in spring implies the seasonal resurrection after winter's death,[26] and in the

---

24. See Geoffrey of Vinsauf 1967, 4.202–736.

25. Vinsauf (1967) clearly implies this relationship between amplification and praise, abbre-
viation and censure. See the introduction to the chapter on Vinsauf in Preminger (1974, 387).

26. The prologue's language clearly connects this springtime rebirth to the eternal rebirth.
In his paean to spring, the narrator sings of how the "erthe" (his body) has forgotten his "poore
estate" of winter (life on earth) and has been clad anew by the "atempre sun" (an obvious
reference to Christ). In addition to the Easter service, the church also celebrated the feast of
Mary's Assumption in the spring. Assumption texts used the *Canticum Canticorum* for Christ's
words in calling Mary from the tomb, and usually mentioned the Canticles' references to birds
and flowers, which also appear here in the poem.

meadow where she flourishes, the propagation of bird and blossom represents the earthly rebirth of the species. The daisy and the good woman thus exemplify all possible cycles of time—night/day, winter/spring, decay/florescence, depletion/fecundity, rest/activity—all of which play upon the link made in past catalogs between women and temporality.

As Queen of Thrace and the narrator's lady, Alceste represents literature as well, and she ties that (pagan) art and the daisy's earthly manifestations to the eternal certitudes that *auctoritas* embodies.[27] While her rebirth as heroine is an instance of literary immortality, her story can also typify Christ's. Since she is Chaucer's muse—the "maistresse of my wit, and nothing I" (88F)—she should control his flow of talent, inspiring him to write texts that harmonize the heavenly and the earthly, the authorial and the experiental, much like the four-fold allegorical model Dante and others used. But the narrator is not always equal to his task. Although she is his "maistresse," Alceste and the narrator's penance are at the mercy of his interpretive skills. Both are the "matere" for his "makyng"; both are subject to his interpretation of "fyn lovyng." We already suspect that the narrator's "makyng" is faulty, and in fact, he will never get to Alceste's legend at all. For the reason why, we must again consider the human characteristics of the individual compiler. The text also insists upon this in its linguistic strategy. Of all the four levels of medieval allegory—literal, allegorical, topological, and anagogical—medieval exegetes held the human narrator most accessible on the first.[28] Commentaries often note that human motives are most clearly revealed here. Renewed attention to the literal had been a major outgrowth of the early humanist poetics, particularly in the material generated by the twelfth-century School of Chartres. Dante and Boccaccio had also endorsed this emphasis in both their own works and their critical writings.[29] For medieval readers, unlike modern ones, tropes and figures were part of the literal level. As Chaucer's prologue demonstrates, the *Legend of Good Women* will repeatedly draw our attention to this language. Although the narrator prom-

27. Chaucer says that books are the key of memory in the prologue (26F and G). These lines are the source of Payne's title *Key of Remembrance* (1963).

28. Minnis 1988 notes that the new type of exegesis that emerged in the thirteenth century focused on the human *auctor* of the scripture. Consequently, such commentaries became more attentive to the literal sense of the Bible, where human intention was believed to be expressed. On the inclusion of figurative language in the literal level, see Minnis 1988, 74.

29. Among others, Geoffrey of Vinsauf and Dante both stressed the importance of the literal story. Kisser discusses the prologue to the *Legend of Good Women* as an extended illustration of proper and improper metaphoric uses, that is metaphors in which the heavenly tenors do and do not accord with their earthly vehicles.

ises to tell his tales in "naked Engylish" (86), that is, without *figura*,[30] he loads his prologue and legendary with involved metaphoric language. These *translationes* (to use the medieval term for metaphor) force the reader to scrutinize the narrator's words carefully. Deciding when and if a word speaks figuratively can be vital to its meaning.

While the opening references to "sight" amply demonstrate the kinds of problems such metaphoric language produces, an even more significant example occurs in the narrator's disavowal of his intentions. The Chaucerian narrator does not tell us what he will do, but he does tell us what he will not. "I ne have nat undertake / As of the lef agayn the flour to make, / Ne of the flour to make ageyn the lef," (72–74F), he says. Rather this work is "of another tonne," (79F), narrating stories written long before such strife was instituted. Two key words in this disavowal—"lef" and "flour"—immeasurably enrich and complicate the statement, complex enough as it is. They could mean many things to a medieval reader and indeed suggest several things simultaneously. In the courtly sense, they name a popular love game of Chaucer's day, where parties of leaf and flower met in mock combat.[31] An associated biblical tradition identifies flower with transience and leaf with permanence, while some Marguerite poems reverse the values. Additionally, the word "flour" in middle English could mean several things besides "flower," among them inner virtue, elegant speech, or model.[32] One of the Virgin's titles (which is used by Alceste) is "flower of flowers." "Lef," on the other hand, could indicate several things besides "leaf," among them outward appearance, embellishment, a sheet of paper, or the beloved.[33] The narrator, then, may wish to avoid one or all of the following in his work: a courtly game, the old question of marriage versus virginity, the even older battle between the sexes, or an issue of rhetoric. Should a *figura* be an embellishment (leaf) or something more integral (a flower)? In any case, we are told—not very helpfully—that this work is different because it concerns old, old stories written before these conflicts began. That statement is at least literally true since Chaucer's legends revive antique tales that depicted sexuality frankly. On the other hand, however, his vow to avoid strife is ironic since this very disavowal embodies conflict. Amid such an abundance of meanings, different interpretations are inevitable, interpretations behind

---

30. The equation of figures with clothing is traditional. Vinsauf, for example, calls the *figura* "ornaments" and refers to them as a precious garment.

31. Pearsall discusses this game (1962, 56).

32. *The Middle English Dictionary*, 1956 ed., s.v. "flour."

33. *Ibid*, s.v. "lef."

which a reticent compiler treating the dangerous subject of love can hide or be lost.

The prologue, then, imitates academic prologues to the commentaries on the *auctores* and thus suggests a meaning and form for the legends to come. Interestingly, while the commentary's form is quite traditional, the prologue's language and its charges against the narrator suggest that the compiler *can* distort or destroy such interpretations. The legends elaborate on this point by showing the narrator in the process of authorship, an emphasis that makes these tales interesting as examples of creation in progress, not as gripping narratives. The legends themselves have never been precisely examined in this fashion; in fact, they are usually dismissed as inferior tales. W. W. Skeats set this tone in 1889 by taking the Chaucerian narrator's boredom for Chaucer the writer's and suggesting that Chaucer abandoned his work because he found it tedious (xiv). Other and more recent scholars have come closer to the poem's literary commentary by demonstrating how Chaucer treats his sources cavalierly, then thematizes the changes by pointing out his excisions.[34] (In fact, as will be shown, Chaucer changes the legends in other ways as well.) The poem focuses not so much on these changes, however, as on the motivation for them and thus on the author and his intention. To trace this motivation, the legends must be considered as an integrated whole, not as separate narratives. The story they develop is the same one begun in the prologue, the relationship between the narrator (as man and writer) and Alceste (as lady and muse).

Very little attention has been paid to this aspect of the legends, but its importance is clearly indicated when the narrator refers to Alceste not only as "love" and "maistresse" but also as "wyf" (520F; 508G). In many respects, he is like a husband who owes his wife the debt of his body, which is to say, sexual service. Misogamous literature made much of this debt as a threat to the husband's health—women were known to be insatiable and frequent intercourse was believed to shorten a man's life.[35] Just like the husband, the narrator stands in "dette" (541F) to Alceste for life, owing her his talent and time. His task may well be as threatening as the task of a husband with an insatiable spouse, for he must spend the rest of his life writing the legends. (Cupid suggests that he discuss all twenty thousand or so women in his

---

34. See especially Fyler 1979 and Eleanor Wilson Leach, "A Study in the Sources and Rhetoric of Chaucer's *Legend of Good Women* and Ovid's *Heroides*" (Ph.D. diss., Yale University, 1963).

35. The *locus classicus* for this definition of woman's sexuality is Aristotle's *Physics*, 1.9 (19a 22).

entourage.) Furthermore, like the wife in misogamous portraits, Alceste makes a demand that imperils the narrator's artistic potency, testing his devotion to both daisy and art. She requires his fidelity; the narrator should write only about her assigned theme. Eventually the narrator, like Criseyde, will flee, a treason that the legends narrate and motivate. This flight links the compiler to the penitent, for as the narrator's flagging taste for pornography modifies his legends, we witness at close range how the progress of a penance influences the shape of the Chaucerian catalog.

The Legendary

Since several critics have already explored the legends' selective editing of their sources, I will focus on two other ways the beleaguered narrator tries to control his text: the order he gives his legends (the *ordinatio partium* or *forma tractatus)* and the figurative language he uses in telling the story, especially the various metaphors or *translationes*. To medieval readers, as medieval commentaries and *accessus ad auctores* show, these processes were as important as selective editing. An author's *forma tractatus* was thought to dispose and arrange his material to a certain end; completely understanding this order clarified his intention.[36] Indeed, understanding the *ordinatio partium* was often the first task a medieval critic addressed, along with deciding when a writer was expressing his meaning properly speaking *(proprie dicta)* or figuratively *(figurate)*. A commonplace, repeated by William Ockham, was that *translationes* were used for three reasons: to keep the meter (as in poetry), to add ornament (as in rhetoric), and to preserve brevity or utility (as in philosophy). The last two utilities apply explicitly to Cupid's commissions to speak briefly and "well" (elegantly as well as in praise). In a sense, the narrator is thus licensed to use metaphors by Cupid himself. Indeed, we should expect them.

As we shall see, the legends' various *translationes* speak directly to the narrator's understanding of his penance, an understanding that is at first hopelessly literal-minded and restrictive. Given that the legends celebrate Cupid's love, a "trewe" heroine can be not only faithful to one man but devoted to sexual pleasure as well, just as medieval biology assumed women to be. The false hero deprives her not only of his presence but also of his person. Finally, the poet who speaks well of love may extol its virtues or tell the truth about it, eloquently and artfully.[37] Since satiric catalogs attribute

---

36. See J. Allen 1982, 117–18.

women's infidelity to a libidinous nature, these interpretations of Cupid's orders make it unclear whether the narrator will affirm or reverse the misogynistic portrait propagated by authoritative texts. At least initially, the ambiguity allows Chaucer to proceed along a path not very different from that of authoritative catalogs of the past.

The tales speak in two voices. On one hand, they often reproduce, sometimes word for word, Ovid's fabled pathos, but, on the other, their multiple *translationes* for sexual intercourse make them bawdy and frankly risque in the manner of Map and Jean de Meun. Chaucer draws these metaphors from traditional sources. Architectural and martial images come from the *Roman de la Rose,* which Cupid censors Chaucer for having translated. The *Heroides'* abundance of wayward sailors suggests traditional equations between the sea and passion.[38] Finally, references to the "beast" recall a favorite patristic euphemism for lust. Often the patterns merge. Maritime and martial metaphors, for example, make the opening description of Actium equally plausible as a battle or an orgy. When Cleopatra and Anthony happen to meet at sea, the "grete gone" (637) comes out; "from the top doun come the grete stones" (639), and "in with the polax preseth he and he . . . " (642) until "begyneth he to fle / And out ageyn" (643–44). In goes the anchor (a Middle English euphemism for penis).[39] The "speres ord" (645) begins to sting; the sail (a hymen) is ripped with "hokes" (also Middle English for penis),[40] and after participants have "gon togidere" (644) with pots of lime (mortar as well as potash), the cup is brought out in a conventional image of sexual excess—the linkage of Bacchus and Venus.[41] After a whole day of such combat, Anthony understandably begins to flag, and the insatiable queen flees with

> . . . al hir purpre sayl,
> For strokes which wente as thikke as hayl
> No wonder was she myghte it nat endure.

(654–56)

---

37. As Howard notes in his biography of Chaucer, "Talking about love was a great evening pastime, and talking about it well was a recognized skill" (1987, 104). In *Gawain and the Green Knight,* for example, the ladies approve of Gawain's abilities in this area.

38. See, for example, chap. 2 where I mention Map's reference to Jason's oars deflowering the seas.

39. *The Middle English Dictionary,* 1956 ed., s.v. "anchor."

40. *Ibid,* s.v. "hooke."

41. This linkage of gluttony and lust was traditional. The specific confluence of Bacchus (wine) and Venus (lust) goes back at least to Terence—"Sine Cere et Baccho amor moritur." St. Jerome quotes the line in *Adversus Jovininanum.*

Desperate at his failure to "serve" his queen, Anthony commits suicide with a sword. In other words, Cleopatra, true to her lover and to her needs, demands more than Anthony can give. He "deserts" her by not being able to perform, and she flees. Such a reading explains the long-standing problem of why Chaucer began his legends of good women with an infamous example of feminine vice.[42] Cleopatra may indeed be the incarnation of wickedness in *De claris mulieribus,* but a woman more faithful to physical love would be hard to find.

Over and over again, such teasing *translationes* foreground the language of the legends (their literal body) just as they also highlight the body of their heroines. Images of a wall or a narrow passage, for example, often imply the taking or traversing of a woman's sexual organs in libidinous combat. Minos's daughter (6) and Lucrece (5) both pray for the walls to fall in siege. To enter Lucrece's room, Tarquin traverses a narrow, private passage with a drawn sword, echoing the *Roman de la Rose*'s final rape, where the pilgrim's staff penetrates the tower room shielding the heroine. Ariadne's tale also features Theseus's famed threading of the labyrinth, a "hous . . . krynkeled to and fro," with "queynte weyes for to go" (2012–13). Naturally, in Pyramus and Thisbe's tale the wall plays a central part, which Chaucer heightens by making the young lovers Babylonians. The Babylonian Queen Semiramis (mentioned at the legend's beginning as the builder of Babylon's walls) was frequently cited as the inventor of the chastity belt, which Chaucer associates with the partition that separates the lovers— "walles . . . / Ful hye, of hard tiles wel ybake" (708–9).

References to cloth frequently indicate the hymen as well. Besides Cleopatra's purple sail, Thisbe's bloody wimple affords an amusing example. Pyramus picks up the cloth after she flees and, declaring "Wympel . . . thow shalt feele as wel the blod of me" (847–48), smites himself to the heart. The blood spurts out of the wound "as brode sterte / As water,

---

42. For an interesting interpretation of Cleopatra, see Aiken 1938; see also Godman 1977 and Taylor 1977. The alternative reading of the legends by *translationes* explains the strange manner of Cleopatra's death, which was invented by Chaucer and/or his friend John Gower. Chaucer's Cleopatra commits suicide by leaping naked into a pit of snakes. Anthony's death was the result of sexual excess. The sword, a common English *translatio* for penis, makes his suicide a metaphoric reproduction of the motivation for his death. Cleopatra had sworn, "That ryght swich as ye felten, wel or wo, / . . . The same wolde I fele, lyf or deth" (689; 692). Like Anthony, then, she meets her end in an atmosphere of sexual excess, amid a crowd of phallic fangs. For an interesting interpretation that links Cleopatra's death to the medieval view of the body as worm's meat, see V. A. Kolve 1981.

whan the conduit broken is" (851–52), and Thisbe finds him with his "heles on the grounde" (863)—the only man true to love. Since semen was thought to be thinned blood, the only loyal man in the catalog may well have chosen death by masturbation. Later in the collection, the cloth on which Philomene embroiders her story continues Chaucer's opening and teasing equations between sex and art. In other legends, the convergence of a cloth with a pole or a sword makes an icon of sexual union. Aeneas leaves Dido a cloth and "his swerd stondynge" (1332). Theseus abandons Ariadne on the island; "Hire coverchef on a pole up steked she" (2202).

References to the "beast," the church fathers' favorite *translatio* for lust, begin in the prologue where the sun is in Taurus, the "brest . . . of the beste" (113F) that bore Europa away.[43] In legend 3, Dido and Aeneas consummate their affair on a hunting expedition, and Venus appears as a huntress with her skirt hiked up. Thisbe and Pyramus's tragedy results from lions; with Medea's help, Jason slays a dragon and fire-spitting bulls. The beast references reach their logical climax in legend 6, where Theseus and Ariadne are joined by Phaedra to create an odd ménage à trois of Chaucer's invention. Not only does the beleaguered Theseus "slay" the Minotaur, but he escapes in a boat with two women, not one. He thus overloads his barge, a "loaded" term anyway since Chaucer had used this metaphor in legend 1 to refer to the narrator's taking on too much material (621). Poor Theseus, a man much tried, has to stop at Eunopyne to get a "newe barge" (2160) and soon after must abandon Ariadne on an island filled with wild beasts. After he leaves her for her sister Phaedra, the gods place Ariadne's crown (the horns of the cuckold) in the "signe of Taurus" (2223).[44] Appropriately for Chaucer's most populated tale of passion, this legend is surrounded by explicit and implicit beast images. Ariadne's mother, Pasiphaë, copulated with a bull, and Ariadne is later rescued by Bacchus, who has just escaped the beast-creating Circe.

After legend 6, however, beasts disappear from the legends altogether, along with portraits of abandoned sexuality. In their place Chaucer substitutes images of solitary bondage and imprisonment, often associated with both marriage and with hell, and here linked with what is becoming an

---

43. Rowe also sees this as an image of sexual passion (1988, 29–30).

44. As far as I know, no one has ever suggested this rather logical explanation of Ariadne's crown. For example, Robinson in his notes for *Legend of Good Women* suggests Chaucer is referring to the Corona Borealis (Chaucer 1961, 852); Rowe connects it with Alceste's "stellification" (1988, 70).

irksome task for the narrator.[45] All three concluding legends incorporate this image pattern by making their heroines victims. In legend 7, Philomene is locked away in a castle; in legend 8, Phyllis dies by the "corde" (2485) (an instrument of restraint as well as part of the celibate monastic garb), and in the last legend, Hypermnestra winds up in a dark dungeon. These images reflect the Chaucerian narrator's growing distaste for both his subject and his service to Alceste. They also touch upon themes of temporality, for in legend 9, we come to the end of various natural cycles. The prologue begins in day; legend 9 ends at night. The prologue occurs in spring; legend 9 ends in winter. In the prologue the narrator is fresh and enthusiastic; in legend 9, he is fatigued and discouraged. His taste for Alceste's task, as well as for Alceste's love, has obviously disappeared.

The whole poem must be read in light of this pattern. The *Legend of Good Women* ends abruptly in midsentence, but that abruptness indicates the narrator's, not the author's, desertion. As a contrived ending the desertion makes the point that time limits man's art, as it limits his earthly life and loves. The *Legend of Good Women* narrates that story with the male as faulty lover, thereby reversing and atoning for the pattern in *Troilus and Criseyde*. Legend 9, then, really ends the poem, whether or not Chaucer also intended a more lengthy and "finished" version.

The *ordinatio partium* of the legends supports the same point. Like any medieval work, *Legend of Good Women* is not haphazardly assembled. Most simply, it carries through Alceste's commands by structuring a list of unfaithful men along the same lines as a satiric catalog of women. The narrator begins with fairly innocuous heroes—Anthony, who despairs at his failing, and Pyramus, who mimics the virtuous rara avis—but it then goes on to increasingly brutal heroes, until it reaches Tereus, whose rape and mutilation of Philomene is unutterably foul. Three of the sources that Cupid recommends to the Chaucerian narrator in prologue G (Juvenal, Jerome, and Walter Map) arranged their exempla of heroines similarly, beginning with virtuous heroines or mild villains and ending with monsters of perversity. The order of the legends may also point to Ovid's *Heroides*.[46] Most medieval *accessus ad auctores* see the *Heroides* as presenting examples of proper and improper

---

45. See, for example, the *Quinze Joyes de Mariage* and the sermons discussed in chap. 2. The image also appears in the prologue. The birds celebrate their escape from the winter's fowler nets. B. B. Koone (1959) identifies the prologue's fowler with Satan.

46. This topic has been studied in an unpublished thesis by M. C. Edwards, "A Study of Six Characters in Chaucer's 'Legend of Good Women' with Reference to Medieval Scholia on Ovid's 'Heroides'" (Ph.D. diss., Oxford University, 1970). I have not seen this work.

love. In *Legend of Good Women,* Chaucer also mixes stories of fidelity (women) with stories of infidelity (men).

I would like to argue, however, that the most consistent pattern in *Legend of Good Women* develops the theme of experience, most notably the narrator's link to Alceste as lover and author. Plot, *figura,* and repeated shortcuts and complaints—instances of *abbreviatio* and *occupatio*—illustrate a changing attitude toward love that develops as the narrator tires of his lady and task.[47] This pattern of diminished interest mimics the natural cycle of birth and diminishing desire, connecting the text to the compiler's motivation in the richest, most literal, and most corporeal of manners. It is the narrator's footprint left in the text, the clue to his intentions.

As advised by Cupid, the narrator begins cautiously. In Cleopatra's legend, he omits the wedding feast not because he fears he cannot describe it but because he has a long task in front of him and must stick to incidents that "bereth more effect and charge" (620). He skips the courtship to get right to the battle, which does indeed bear more "effect," and is, in terms of carnal love, the "grete" part (574). He does the same thing in legend 2, where a timely *abbreviatio* lands us instantly at Ninus's tomb. By the third legend, however, he is more imprudent. His appetite whetted and foolishly over-confident, he proposes to tell Dido's story by following the greatest pagan *auctor* of all -- Vergil. "I coude folwe, word for word, Virgile," he says, "But it wolde lasten al to longe while" (1002–3). Indeed, he doesn't excise enough, for Dido's legend is the longest of the nine, and the most replete with coy insinuations. In fact, the narrator only reaches the "fruyt of all" (1160)—the love scene—after 236 lines of verse.

In legend 4 (Hypsipyle and Medea), the narrator is still overconfident, but also more introspective. He begins to speak not only about his stories but also about his art. The tale begins with a grand rhetorical flourish that questions Jason's "manere" of "feyned trouth" (1374). ("Manere" is Chaucer's customary translation of *modus agendi.*) Later in the legend he alludes to another technical term when he says that appetite always forms "matere" (1582), Chaucer's usual translation for *materia liberi* or content. The story itself insinuates that the narrator's "appetite" may indeed affect "manere" and "matere." Given the changes the narrator makes in his sources, one of the legends' obvious problems is the narrator's manner of "feyned trouth," the

---

47. Frank, in his book (1972) and in *"Legend of Good Women," Chaucer Review* 1 (1966): 110–33, first suggested that the narrator's comments were not to be confused with Chaucer's own, that the exclamations of distaste could be explained as incidents of *occupatio* and *abbreviatio.*

misappropriation of the *auctores*. In legend 4, for example, the narrator says nothing about Medea's famed excesses and deliberately excises crucial bits of the story to alter his characterizations. As for matter, although legend 4 gives its reader a gracious plenty of material—there are two betrayals, not one—it also hints that the narrator omits material because he is becoming tired of the project. After only eighty lines, Chaucer refers his reader to Ovid for more information. He also refuses to record Medea and Hypsipyle's complaints, for it "were to longe to wryten and to sen" (1565). If appetite forms matter, the narrator's stories must change in this way as his eagerness declines.

Lucrece's legend (5) reaffirms this fact. The narrator begins the legend with the blunt confession that this story he "wol but shortly trete" (1692). He also calls not only his gender but himself into question, affirming that the truest man "ys ful brotel for to triste" (1885). He manages to build up again for the ménage à trois in Ariadne's legends, but he tires more quickly. He starts with the story of Minos and Nysus's daughter but stops since that "tale were to long as now for me" (1921). He invokes *abbreviatio* three times while describing Ariadne, Phaedra, and Theseus's affair. He also refuses to tell Ariadne's complaint because "It is so long, it were an hevy thyng" (2219). Clearly, we and the narrator are on the downward path. We are also past the midpoint in terms of content, since the legendry treats of ten heroines.

Legend 7 (Philomene) affirms that the narrator is rethinking his attitude toward his subject. Chaucer begins by questioning God, "thow yevere of the formes," (2228) for creating "swich a thyng" (2233) as Tereus. "Formes" suggest both the human body and the literary genre. "Thyng" may refer to a phallus, a pen, or Tereus himself. What is a phallus, an author's talent, or this disgusting hero made for? The narrator exclaims:

> Why madest thow, unto the slaunder of man,
> Or, al be that it was nat thy doing,
> As for that fyn, to make swich a thyng,
> Whi sufferest thow that Tereus was bore.
>
> (2231–34)

Between the pauses at the ends of 2230 and 2233, the narrator is clearly working through a problem. Perhaps the phallus wasn't made for pleasurable sex alone; perhaps he should be expending his talent in other ways; perhaps Tereus was never intended to be such a criminal. Whichever way you take the outburst, the narrator is plotting a departure from his first interpretation of Cupid's commands. In fact, legend 7 reads like a repudiation of passion, for the concluding moral openly advises women "be war of men . . . / Ful lytel while shal ye trewe hem have" (2386; 2391).

At legend 8 (Phyllis), the narrator strengthens this rebellious tendency and seems to be reaching a decision. Authority as well as experience, he says, teaches us that only wicked fruit can come from a wicked tree. The proverb here clearly contradicts the opening statement that pits experience against authority. There are other implications as well: only trouble (wicked fruit) can come from passion (wicked tree); only carnal stories can come from Cupid; only heresy can come from the narrator; only flawed art can come from man. In midstory, the narrator rebels and protests he would like to change at least his emphasis because he is having difficulty "performing" his tasks:

> . . . I am agroted herebyforn
> To wryte of hem that ben in love forsworn,
> And ek to haste me in my legende,
> (Which to performe God me grace sende!)
> Therfore I passe shortly in this wyse.
>
> (2454–58)

He returns to the story, but just as in *Troilus and Criseyde,* dwells on the betrayed character (Phyllis) rather than the betrayer (Demophon). He also ends the legend by advising women to beware of men and to trust none but him, an ironic twist in light of what happens in legend 9, but also quite literally true since the narrator has been protesting man's brittleness with a rising urgency for two legends.

Legend 9, Hypermnestra's tale, is clearly intended as the narrator's last. Only one short *abbreviatio* occurs, and that during Hypermnestra's wedding night. This positioning starkly contrasts with the use of this style in earlier legends, where it functions to get the narrator *to* the sex scenes. Legend 9 also includes a natal chart that Chaucer apparently invented for Hypermnestra.[48] Long a puzzle to scholars, the chart emphasizes the heroine's total lack of carnality because Mars is badly aspected, Venus has repressed his "crewel craft" (2592), and his "venim is adoun" (2593). Since Mars and Venus were famous as lovers—Map, for example, uses their

---

48. Robinson in his notes to the poem notes that no source for this chart has been discovered (Chaucer 1961, 554).

story—the chart suggests not only timidity but an absence and depletion of carnal desire. (Venus has, after all, repressed Mars's craft.) This interpretation is reinforced by the narrator's next comment; poor Hypermnestra cannot "handel a knyf" (2594), the church's favorite euphemism for penis. The horoscope also mirrors the narrator's double fatigue with both penance and Alceste. Both deficiencies are depicted as natural, however; legend 9 is set in the season of old age and death, where endings occur. At Hypermnestra's feast, the flowers and leaves are torn up "by the rote" (2613). Chaucer focuses on the guests as they "taken leve, and hom they wende" (2621). Lyno is even discreetly drugged so that he can't perform on his wedding night, thereby removing the narrator's obligation to describe it. In fact, Chaucer's last picture of Lyno leaping from the wedding bed offers an interesting parallel not only to Sappho's Leucadian leap but also to the narrator's leap from the legendry as he forsakes both Alceste and his readers. The desertion is clearly part of the fiction of the narrator's involvement with the legends, even if his motivation for leaving is left unsaid. Perhaps the narrator stopped in midsentence because he woke up; perhaps he deserted because of boredom with the repetitive pornography; perhaps his creative juices had been used up by the legends; perhaps he died; or perhaps he felt he had completed his penance, since in the last legends, the heroines are clearly less carnal than in the first. Whatever interpretation one chooses, such an action is inevitable given the legends' subject. As Chaucer declares in his last line, "*This* tale is seyd for *this* conclusioun" (2723, italics mine), which the reader is characteristically left to draw.

To read *Legend of Good Women* this way contradicts a long critical tradition that holds Chaucer abandoned the legends in boredom, a charge seemingly confirmed by the *Canterbury Tales*' description of either twenty-five heroines (the Retraction) or nineteen (the Man of Law's Tale). Most critics, assuming that one of these numbers represents Chaucer's original (unfulfilled) plan, see the last legend as simply halted in midstride. Donald Howard (1988), for example, has suggested that the two numbers may refer to the Order of the Garter, which had nineteen ladies in 1386 and twenty-five in 1390. But the correspondence is not necessarily definitive proof that Chaucer abandoned this series. He was often careless with numbers—not in the medieval sense of numerology but in the modern sense of keeping an accurate count—perhaps because of the continuous "in progress" nature of his last two works. Moreover, the images, structure, and themes of the *Legend of Good Women* strongly argue that we have the final legend of the series even if we do not have a complete ensemble. Even the last qualification is not a certain one. If the tales were designed to look abandoned, what better way to perpetuate the fiction than to indicate in another fictional poem that Chaucer had intended to write more? If we read *Legend of Good Women* as I have suggested, we can answer such persistent and troubling questions as why Chaucer begins with Cleopatra, why the legends oscillate from pathos to comedy, why Hypermnestra has a natal chart, and why Ariadne's crown is "stellified." Assuming the importance of the poem's structure in this way also conforms to late medieval assumptions that order imparts meaning. Finally, the reading fulfills, even if ironically, the poem's stated *utilitas*. On the face of it, the *Legend of Good Women* agrees with the authorities. Love is a dangerous and treacherous art. The narrator's experience with Alceste tells him so.

But the author's intent is neither as lucid nor as simplistic as the narrator's. While the latter is concerned with women, Chaucer's "matere" is the compiler himself. As writer and reader, this agent is shown in the very act of manipulating his text. His tales are shaped by his excisions, his figurative language, and his imposed order. Most important, all of the above are subject to his appetite, as he himself notes. When his penance becomes tiresome, his service to Alceste weighty, his legends become less pornographic. Paradoxically, since this trend is also a sign that his penance is succeeding, the legends as well as his own story point to one meaning, just as medieval commentaries held that the life and works of David did. Both treat of the inevitable betrayal of human love, which can be used up and depleted like the body it focuses on.

The legends' heroes can serve to illustrate this progress as the compiler comes to some awareness of his sin. In the first stories, Anthony, Pyramus, and Aeneas are relatively innocent men, reflecting the narrator's sense of himself and his guilt. As Chaucer warms to the task, his repentance and self-knowledge deepen. Jason, Theseus, Tarquin, and Tereus are monsters whose iniquities are vividly painted. By the end of the legends, the last two heroes—Demophon and Lyno—hardly appear at all. Instead, Phyllis and Hypermnestra emerge as pictures of self-sacrifice. They are emblems of the temporal world, but like Alceste and the Virgin, they are also instruments of salvation. Phyllis saved Demophon, and Hypermnestra saved Lyno just as Alceste saved Admetus; furthermore, both, like Christ, are the sacrificial means for saving Chaucer from his "sin," his misapprehension of love. Their portraits illumine Chaucer's growing sense of error. Legends 1–3, then, narrate a dawning sense of contrition while legends 4–7 give a confession and legends 8 and 9 portray betrayed women in an act of restitution, however limited. If the narrator cannot live up to Alceste's demands or if he dies with the penance completed (we are not sure which happens), the reader can at least trace a dawning awareness of what the basest interpretation of carnal love actually means. By turning love into pornography, he has betrayed both his lady and his muse.

I think Payne (1974) is ultimately correct when he argues that the *Legend of Good Women* demonstrates a failed myth of the artist, but in light of this connection between the human hand and the authoritative page, the poem must also be seen as recording a tentative success as well. Chaucer's later work often flirts with the problem of an art grounded in earthly concerns. In *Canterbury Tales* as well as *Troilus and Criseyde* and the *Legend of Good Women,* Chaucer wrestles with this very problem. Just as it did for Ovid, a catalog of good women may well have struck Chaucer as a peculiarly appropriate place to investigate such problems because women were not associated with values embodied in authoritative poetics. Women, even virtuous ones, had often been sundered from communal contexts, whether those contexts be social, historical, or literary. Because Chaucer's myth of poetry portrays a poet with an identity crisis in a society undergoing vast changes, women may well have seemed the perfect emblems for a new way of looking at authorship. Additionally, equating women with poetry may have appealed to Chaucer because women were linked with the physical body, and hence with temporal experience and the literal text.

In this respect, the hagiographic overtones may well be significant. Chaucer chose to call his stories legends, a word used exclusively for saints' lives in middle English. He also emphasizes his choice by terming his heroines "Cupides Martyrs." His reason has never been fully explained, although one motive was undoubtedly parody. Fourteenth-century hagiography, such as the *Legenda aurea,* generally dwelt upon a saint's miraculous powers, usually manifested through his or her ability to withstand bodily pain. On one level, Chaucer is humorously mimicking this power with his heroines' "miraculous" appetite for sex. But even though the parodic element is present, I think there is a serious side to the play on hagiography as well. A number of christological features are found among the heroines. Alceste and Hypermnestra's self-sacrifices are Christlike. Philomene is reminiscent of Christ because of the nightingale's song (long considered an allegory of the Passion). Phyllis, Dido, Hypsipyle, Thisbe, and Ariadne are innocent victims as well. By modeling these tales of earthly love on the legends dealing with heavenly charity, Chaucer asserts the claims of his subject matter. If superseded by the "other holynesse" in time, if imperfect in many ways, earthly love is not without its own value. Concomitantly, the level of the text most concerned with earthly reality is also assigned a sure importance. The numerous *translationes* imperil any interpretation that ignores the literal level of the legends or overlooks the narrator's intentions and its effects on a text.

The poem's hagiographic echoes may also set up other resonances with this concern for the body. Medieval interest in empirical knowledge was not limited to nominalist philosophy or humanist thought; it also shaped various reform movements within the church, especially the penitential movements of the thirteenth century. These movements had insisted on the validity of the bodily penance. Such an assumption informs the legends of numerous women saints, for example Margaret of Cortona and Angela da Foligno, both of whom were involved in the penitential movements. The body is precisely what the narrator denies in his opening lines. Yet his own experience in the legendry (like the experience of these penitential saints) proves him wrong. His surfeit of sex stories brings him to a very precise experience of hell, one graphically mirrored in the images of confinement and sexual, moral, and artistic distaste. Such is the object of a penance, which seeks to make a sinner understand his sin and abandon it. The reader too comes to a similar point. We begin by surfeiting on the very pornographic stories authority would deny us and which we think we desire. But we, like the narrator, soon tire of the joke. The *Legend of Good Women* not only asserts a sort of union between experience and authority but makes the reader experience it as well. Its ability to oversatiate and bore us is a sign of its artistic power.

While this mimesis of experience—we feel what Chaucer the narrator feels—displays a new literary power, the legends also speak eloquently of Chaucer's reservations about what such art might accomplish. A dead end to both legendry and art occurs in legend 9, where winter weds the end of the poem with the end of life. In Lyno's leap from the marriage bed, we can legitimately read our eventual departure from the world. Chaucer does not attempt to describe what kind of world awaits us. He does not trust experience quite that far. Instead, he lets its unspoken presence give the natural world that is described shape, definition, and poignancy. Earlier, his narrator proclaimed his intentions by telling us what he would not do, by assuring us that his reasons would come clear in time. The time never comes, however, and at the end, the reader must infer what is not said from what is. For such a poetry of indirection, the good woman also provides an excellent emblem. Catalogs such as *De claris mulieribus* often defined a woman's virtue by what she did not do rather than by what she did (witness Boccaccio's definition of chastity). The *Legend of Good Women* takes the same approach, defining an author who makes his presence known by not explaining himself. In other words, it is what Chaucer does not dare say that is most tantalizing and revealing, just as it is what *De claris mulieribus*'s Sulpicia does not do that makes her worthy of virtue.

Like Ovid's *Heroides*, then, the *Legend of Good Women* finds artistic merit in the devalued. Chaucer uses the good woman to explore the problems and potentials of a changing notion of poetry. He also comments on past catalogs, specifically holding the compiler more responsible for his text's meaning. In terms of the catalog tradition, this commentary may well be Chaucer's major contribution. But despite Chaucer's reevaluation of technique, the poem neither grounds absolute authority in a personal voice nor voices a definition of the good woman. Chaucer never lays claim to the title of *auctor* or uses experience to debate authoritative commonplaces about femineity. The last major medieval catalog would go beyond this questioning. Unlike the *Legend of Good Women,* it would defend womankind rather than the qualities associated with her and, in the process, it would give the compiler not only prominence but importance as a source of reinterpretation.

Chapter 5

The Defense of Gender, the Citadel of Self

Chaucer's emphasis on the compiler's role and his experience introduced new strategies into the catalog tradition. Among other things, this change made the author's gender a potential factor in his or her collection and (by implication) authorship by a woman desirable. Yet for a fifteenth-century woman to take Chaucer's reflections one step further, she needed a diverse, even antithetical background: on the one hand, experience of life outside the cloister; on the other, an erudition almost exclusively found within it. Christine de Pizan met such requirements. A French writer of Italian birth, she was unusual among medieval women writers not only for her erudition, which was acquired outside of the convent walls, but also for her repeated efforts to defend the honor of her gender. Her catalog, *Le Livre de la cité des dames*, is usually dated only five years after the accepted date of Chaucer's death, but it moved the catalog tradition into the form it would most often assume in the Renaissance.

Christine's achievement in *Cité des dames* is both ground-breaking and pivotal. Written in 1405 during her most productive years, it responds to former catalogs through a judicious application of authority and individual judgment.[1] She not only produces the first collection since Plutarch's to argue

---

1. In 1405, Christine was arguably at the peak of her career and in the midst of an important change in style and subject matter. When she had begun to write in the late fourteenth century, she had worked primarily in verse and with courtly themes. By 1403, however, she was experimenting with prose and more erudite forms. The year of 1405 is associated with four of her other important works besides *Cité des dames:* the sequel to her catalog, *Le Livre des trois vertus;* her allegorical autobiography, *Avision-Christine;* her appeal to the queen, *Lettre à Isabeau de Bavière;* and a judgment poem entitled *Le Livre du duc des vrais amants.* For a full bibliography, see Kennedy 1984 and Yenal 1989.

that men and women's virtue are comparable, but she also structures her presentation as a rhetorical defense, making *Cité des dames* a natural bridge between the medieval catalog's exemplification by authority and the Renaissance catalog's assertion through debate.[2] At the same time, the treatise presents an incisive model of feminine self-definition, penned by a woman narrator who faces the antagonism of a misogynic *auctoritas*. The book recommends that its female readers follow a similar path of self-definition as a defense against detractors. This use of the catalog, Christine's alone, implicitly grounds her work's importance in the traditional utility of medieval letters—its effect on the reader.[3] But the effect on that woman reader would challenge traditional authority on several points.

Where Christine got the idea of compiling a catalog is uncertain. Her principal source was Boccaccio's *De claris mulieribus,*[4] which she might have known from copying its French translation in the Parisian manuscript houses where she is thought to have worked.[5] Wherever she encountered it, the Boccaccian catalog would have been sure to attract her attention. Her father, a graduate of the University of Bologna and a one-time official of the city of Venice, knew Boccaccio at least by reputation and possibly in person.[6] She herself was associated with the early humanists of France, for she was the wife of one and the friend of several others. A new humanist text by an Italian writer known to her father would have been recommendation enough, but this book, in addition to these charms, also addressed a subject

---

2. The Renaissance catalog appears most frequently in the literature of the *querelle des femmes*. Joan Kelly's thoughtful article (1982) argues that women's proponents in this debate laid the foundation for a feminist philosophy. For another view, i.e., that the *querelle* was a game and that women's opponents were not serious in their propositions, see Emile Telle, *L'Oeuvre de Marguerite d'Angoulême: reine de Navaree et la Querelle des Femmes* (1937; reprint, Geneva: Geneva Reprints, 1969); and Dow 1936.

3. In emphasizing the catalog's ability to teach its readers ethical lessons, Christine is conforming to a late medieval understanding of literature. See again J. Allen 1982 and Minnis 1988.

4. Jeanroy (1922) was the first person to establish this relationship between *De claris mulieribus* and *Cité des dames*. Whether Christine used the original Latin text or Laurent de Premierfait's French translation, *De cleres et nobles femmes,* is uncertain. Curnow (1975) argues for the latter; Richards (1982) suggests the former. For interesting evidence to support his claim, see Richards 1983, where he argues that Christine's prose displays a conscious attempt to reproduce Boccaccio's hypotactic Latin style.

5. Willard (1975) mentioned this connection between Christine and *De claris mulieribus*.

6. Christine's father, Thomas, was employed in the health services of Venice in 1363, when Petrarch, who was dividing his time between Padua and Venice, received a three-month visit from Boccaccio. It is likely that Thomas at least knew Petrarch. One of the laureate's friends, Guido da Bagnolo, was an eminent physician. For more information on Christine's father, see Willard 1984, 18–25.

dear to her heart—woman's reputation. By the time she wrote *Cité des dames*, she had already written one major defense of her gender *(L'Epitre au Dieu d'Amours)* supporting her contentions with a short catalog.[7] As a humanist, scholar, and defender of women, she would naturally have been curious to see a longer listing.

For many years, Christine's use of Boccaccio's material was thought to be largely derivative. While Alfred Jeanroy established *De claris mulieribus* as Christine's main source as early as 1922, he and many others assumed that she had merely translated Boccaccio, adding nothing of her own. She certainly mined *De claris mulieribus* for examples, but it was not her sole source, and we now realize that she did not merely translate it.[8] Liliane Dulac, Jeffrey Richards, Charity Willard, and most recently Patricia Phillipy have demonstrated that Christine fundamentally revised Boccaccio's arguments in her treatise.[9] Furthermore, the organization, imagery, use of persona, and allegorical frame of *Cité des dames* were new in the tradition of catalogs of women and possibly (as we shall see) influenced by Boccaccio's *De casibus virorum illustrium*. *Cité des dames* is quite like *Mulierum virtutes* in argument and quite like *Legend of Good Women* in its use of the narrator, but there is no evidence that Christine herself knew these works. Far from being derivative of another catalog, Christine's specific methods seem to have grown from her own early humanist leanings and from her desire to associate women with virtues missing in earlier collections.

Christine herself announces a revisionist slant at the very opening of *Cité des dames*. She terms her city (her text in the allegory) a "deffence" (or fort) for the gender that up to now has had none.[10] Indeed, the work is a generic defense in the same vein as Philip Sydney's *Defense of Poesy*. Like other Renaissance defenses, however, Christine's work is as aggressive as it is defensive. It attacks an older viewpoint to persuade its readers to a new and so uses the catalog's heroines quite innovatively. Christine does not so

---

7. *L'Epitre au Dieu d'Amours*, composed in 1399, is a playful and satiric attack on misogyny. It is one of the very few satiric pieces we have from a medieval woman writer. Thelma Fenster's translation of this poem appears in *"Epistre au dieu d'amours" and "Dit de la Rose" with Thomas Hoccleve's "Letter of Cupide"* (Leiden: Brill, 1990).

8. Jeanroy (1922), for example, suggested that Christine's book is a translation. In the first major study of Christine's work, Marie-Josèphe Pinet (1974) includes *Cité des dames* among "les traductions." For studies of Christine's other sources, see Bozzolo 1967 and Reno 1974. Curnow also lists several sources (1975, chap. 3).

9. See Willard 1984, Dulac 1978, Richards 1982, xix–li, and Phillipy 1986.

10. All French quotations are taken from Christine de Pizan 1975. English translations are from Richards 1982. The French reference to "deffence" occurs on page 632 of Curnow's edition. All further references to these works will appear in the text.

much present her exempla as truth as explore them for truth; that is, she doesn't transmit tradition but investigates and redefines it. She also assumes a number of stances more characteristic of Renaissance than medieval rhetoric. Her appropriation implicitly asserts that truth is discovered through debate, that wisdom can emerge from the exercise of words, that dialogue can generate insight (although unlike many Renaissance dialogues, Christine's is not open-ended.) In short, Christine's new purpose widens the catalog's applicability, and opens the door to new interpretations of heroines that are used to illustrate a woman's search for her identity. Her *Cité des dames* not only records the deeds of past heroines but thematizes a process of self-definition that occurs through conflicts with and about the past.

This new direction emerges most clearly in Christine's arrangement of her text, which, unlike Boccaccio's, is quite carefully organized. In many ways, the defense has a typically medieval structure. There are three books, three guides, and a controlling allegory that compares the writing of Christine's case to the construction of a city. The use of the number three may well reflect Christine's admiration for Dante; the comparison of text and city calls upon an old rhetorical commonplace linking writing and construction. (Geoffrey of Vinsauf, for example, opens his *Poetria Nuova* by comparing writing a text to building a house.)[11] Christine, however, turns to an interesting external source for her polemical structure—Cicero's *De inventione* provided her with the six-part organization used for arguing legal cases in classical Rome. Not only does this structure emphasize the technical nature of Christine's defense, but it also speaks to her Italian (and humanist) heritage. In contrast to the curriculum at the Sorbonne, *De inventione* was an important text in the Italian universities where her father had studied. Moreover *De inventione*'s claim that rhetoric is *civilis ratio,* or related to politics, is especially favorable to various aspects of Christine's defense, which attempts to link women with the political life of a community.

De Inventione 1.19 advised the orator to proceed through the *exordium,* to the *narratio, partitio, confirmatio, refutatio,* and *peroratio.* Christine not only has these parts in the proper order but in each section, she does precisely what Cicero prescribes.[12] The opening confrontation between the narrator

---

11. See Geoffrey of Vinsauf 1967, 16–17. Nims links this comparison to Plato's *Timaeus* and manuscript illuminations of the Creator (1974, 226).

12. I also discuss this aspect and the connection between late medieval literary criticism and Christine's critique of literary misogyny in my essay "Poetics and Anti-Misogynist Polemics in Christine de Pizan's *Livre de la cité des dames*" in *Reinterpreting Christine,* ed. Earl Jeffrey Richards et al. (Athens: University of Georgia Press, forthcoming).

and misogynic *auctoritas* furnishes the *exordium*, which, like all *exordia*, seeks to make the reader well-disposed *(benevolens)*, attentive *(attentus)*, and receptive *(docilis)*. A speaker could draw on four loci for good will; Christine calls upon two—her narrator's integrity and the wickedness of her misogynistic opponents. The *narratio* opens with the visit of the three crowned ladies. Raison (reason), Droitture (rectitude), and Justice set forth Christine's case by analyzing her mistaken reactions and by criticizing the methods of literary misogyny. As Cicero had prescribed, they relate their objections clearly, briefly, and with probability. In the remainder of book 1, Raison's *partitio*—wittily presented as the raising of city walls—introduces the points Christine will seek to prove, namely that women are capable of virtuous action and that misogynists are misguided or worse. The building of the city in book 1, the construction of its houses and the introduction of its common citizens in book 2, furnish the *confirmatio*, where Christine marshals her arguments to lend credit, authority, and support to her case. Here too she calls upon the accepted modes of persuasion, for her proof derives from the evidence of women's actions. The *refutatio* also appears in book 2, where Droitture explicitly attacks misogyny by exposing inconsistencies in its arguments. Book 3, where Christine calls upon hagiographic tradition, gives readers an ethical digression of the kind recommended by the Greek rhetor Hermagoras. It implicitly compares the repression of women with the repression of Christianity, thereby amplifying Christine's subject in the approved fashion. Finally, Christine's address to her women readers at the conclusion of the book includes all three elements of a *peroratio*. It sums up her conclusions, excites indignation against the slanderers *(indignatio)*, and arouses sympathy for the speaker and her case *(conquestio)*.

Christine's use of this schema alone does not represent a break with tradition. *De inventione* was a noted medieval rhetoric, especially in Italy where its influence on the *ars dictaminis* (the art of letter-writing) was pervasive and important. The Ciceronian format occurs in other medieval works as well as in Renaissance texts such as Sydney's. But there are important departures in the way Christine moves her arguments through this organization. In addition to the Ciceronian overlay, Christine orders her book by her response to authority, which had played such a crucial role in traditional catalog strategy. The allegory of the three crowned ladies—each of whom dominates one of the three books of the *Cité*—carries the narrator/reader through a formidable process, from reason (book 1) to rectitude (book 2) to justice (book 3). It is worth noting that reason at one extreme invokes individual judgment while justice at the other calls on authority. While medieval

texts often juggled these two sources of knowledge and sometimes situated
them in this order, Christine adds a new note in how she relates the two. In
her catalog, authority is questioned but revised, and then adapted to the
narrator's objections. Usually, as in Chaucer's legendry, where the burdens
of *cupiditas* are explored and confirmed, medieval texts upheld authority.
Christine does not emphasize this revisionist element because her attempt to
redefine *auctoritas* is (by definition) subversive. Indeed, as Jeffrey Richards
has pointed out, her principal point is that misogynists, not women, speak
from the margins of Christian tradition (1983, 23). Naturally, such a conclusion does not quite represent the consensus of the church over its long
history, yet it is in the interests of Christine's argument to persuade her
readers that it does.

A second important departure implemented by Christine's organization
is her use of the catalog to structure the narrator's quest for identity. Originat-
ing as it does in individual reason, Christine's mimesis of that process reverses the usual order of self-defining found in medieval texts. Works from
Christine's period generally fashioned a character's "self" only after situating
him (or her) within heavenly and earthly societies. Christine, the narrator,
must begin with the individual because women have traditionally been isolated from these larger communities or associated with them only in negative
ways. By its very organization, then, *Cité des dames* inextricably unites the
narrator with her text and the defense of women. As we shall see, the city
functions as a powerful allegory for all three enterprises: authorship, self-
definition, and the defense of womankind.

The governing metaphor of the city has a historical dimension as well,
based in part on its echo of St. Augustine's *City of God,* Christianity's most
important universal history. *Cité des dames* has other links to the universal
history, however, and for good reasons. To authenticate narrator and gender,
Christine de Pizan must associate the good woman with the universal rather
than the particular. Past catalogs had fragmented the image of woman, isolating her from her virtue or gender, from her society, and from history.
Christine's refashioning will reassemble these pieces into a total definition.
In respect to history, she achieves her transformation by manipulating her
Boccaccian model. To the best of my knowledge, no one has pointed out
that *Cité des dames* responds to both of Boccaccio's catalogs: While its
content obviously comes from *De claris mulieribus,* its structure is much
closer to that of *De casibus virorum illustrium.* Both Boccaccio's male catalog and Christine's defense open with emissaries of Providence who come
to rescue the narrators in their studies. Boccaccio's visitor (Lady Fortune)
and Christine's crowned ladies (Raison, Droitture, and Justice) go on to

explain the ways of Providence by means of the exempla in their catalogs. These opening rescues parallel important scenes in other medieval texts, in Boccaccio's case, Boethius's *Consolation of Philosophy* and in Christine's, Dante's *Divine Comedy*. Finally, since both books link these catalogs with the recognized source of historical causality (providence) both explicitly set their catalog members within an understanding of history. As we shall see in *Cité des dames*, these changes remake the contexts in which Christine's cataloger discusses the *topos* of femineity.

At this point in the discussion, it is customary to address the problem of Christine's feminism. Granted that her catalog aspires to the higher genres and presents a positive definition of femineity, can we claim it as the work of a feminist? Answers have varied greatly, and discussion, particularly in the last ten years, has sometimes been heated.[13] The issue is, of course, largely an anachronistic one since the word feminist only entered the English language some 464 years after Christine died.[14] But given that caveat, the problem of characterizing Christine's polemic remains. I would like to argue that *Cité des dames* is not feminist but does play a significant, unique role in the history of feminist thought. It seeks to give women a recognized share of earthly fame and a place within a social and historical order. It also examines how a woman can refute misogynistic authorities that deny her a positive self-image. Such revisions may not constitute feminism in the late twentieth century, but in 1405 they were quite radical. In addition, what Christine tries to do in her catalog, i.e., accumulate examples of women "worthies," sounds very much like what feminist historians now call compensatory history, the first stage in the inclusion of women within the story of a culture.[15] This gesture acquires additional importance in light of Christine's own decision to write her catalog as a history. Here she is breaking new ground. Finally, the narrator's dramatized internalization and defeat of misogyny touches upon an early issue of feminism, the recognition of culturally inherited notions of inferiority in women's self-definitions.

All cultural and social movements must have roots somewhere, and since *Cité des dames* presents the first clear portrayal of a woman's confron-

---

13. See, for example, Kelly 1982; F. D. Kelly 1972; Bell 1976; Huot 1985; Ignatius 1978; Gottlieb 1985; Delany 1986; and Quilligan 1988. For older, more enthusiastic, and generally less trustworthy estimates, see Richardson 1929 and Rigaud 1911.

14. *Oxford English Dictionary*, 1971 ed., s.v. "feminism." The *OED* locates the earliest reference to the word in an 1894 newspaper article.

15. See Gerda Lerner, *The Majority Finds its Past* (New York: Oxford University Press, 1975), for remarks upon this point.

tation with misogyny, Christine's book seems a logical place to locate some of feminism's roots. It is important to remember, however, that some of Christine's assertions are more characteristic of modern antifeminists than of feminists. She was, after all, a woman of the fifteenth century and as such accepted many things now repugnant to many modern women, things such as female submission in marriage, patient suffering in the face of abusive husbands, and the absence of a political program for social reform. But Christine did work in her own cultural context to make ideological standards more equitable.

Perhaps the best way to describe *Cité des dames,* then, is to return to another anachronistic phrase and say it tries to raise its readers' consciousness by making them aware of alternative viewpoints, of how authoritative misogyny can destroy women's self-images, and of how misogyny introduces inequities into their culture's most cherished ideals. Christine's catalog takes an important first step toward creating new ways for women to think of themselves within a tradition. This first step logically involves an encounter with the written record, which embodies and perpetuates ideology. In *Cité des dames,* the encounter occurs in the narrator's study, where an opening scene gives the reader much the same introduction to Christine's catalog as he or she would have from a florilegium's prologue. This confrontation is also, however, a refashioning, and in that sense, it marks the beginning of a woman's, if not a feminist's, definition of femineity.

The Prologue

The opening scene of *Cité des dames,* like the prologue of a florilegium, explains Christine's methodology and purpose. It also introduces her readers to her sources and narrator, who is dramatized, as in *Legend of Good Women,* under the author's real name. In medieval poetics, this fictive element would not have seemed out of keeping with Christine's ethical purpose. As Allen and others have argued, medieval commentators commonly classified poetry as ethics, and medieval audiences were accustomed to looking for ethical truths in fictional stories.[16] In fact, Christine's catalog conforms to this understanding of literature, which supplies her main weapon against misogynistic tracts.

---

16. J. Allen notes, for example, that medieval commentaries often claim the *Heroides* teaches its readers how to love women chastely (1982, 10). See also Minnis 1988 for his discussion of medieval commentaries on the *Heroides.*

The opening scene begins with questions concerning genre—the forms genres of literary misogyny take and the association of less authoritative genres with femineity. The narrator is a scholar, but her critical encounter with misogynistic literature begins in her light reading, not her serious work. It is in looking for a book to relax with that she encounters Matheolus's *Liber lamentationum* (The Book of Lamentations), a particularly bad-tempered attack on marriage and women from the thirteenth century.[17] Christine goes to great lengths to stress this link between leisure and the misogynistic texts. In coming upon Matheolus, the narrator wishes to "to leave such subtle questions in peace" (13) ("laisser en paix choses soubtilles" [616]) and "read some light poetry" (13) ("regarder a une joyeusté des dist *[sic]* des pouettes" [616]). Traditionally, women such as Christine, not clerks such as Matheolus, were associated with literature for pleasure. Indeed, such an assertion reflects the conventional definition of "worthy" literature as edifying rather than pleasurable. The narrator's initial rejection of Matheolus's book also makes this connection between ethics and genre, but it reverses the traditional equation between misogyny and edification. *Liber lamentationum* offers nothing to people who do not delight in slander. It fails to improve the reader's virtues or habits and uses obscene words and material (one of Christine's complaints against another prestigious and misogynic book, the *Roman de la Rose*).

The narrator's reaction to the treatise makes the same points more dramatically. Like any medieval reader, she seeks patterns of behavior in her reading. Matheolus's patterns, while of "no authority" (3) ("de nulle auttorité" [617]) correspond to a gushing fountain" (4) ("fontaine resourdant" [619]) of male authors. These men convince her by their numbers that what they say must be true. Their books offer her no hope, for, according to them, woman is a naturally depraved creature, inferior by nature and doomed to malice. Crushed by this picture of her inevitable perversion, Christine's narrator almost despairs. She utters a prayer to God that voices her distress and suggests her doubts concerning providence:

> But since Your kindness has not been extended to me, then forgive my negligence in Your service, most fair Lord God, and may it not displease You, for the servant who receives fewer gifts from his lord is less obliged in his service. (5)

---

17. Matheolus's book was written in Latin and published at the beginning of the thirteenth century; Jean le Fèvre des Ressons produced a translation in 1370 with an ironic palinode. Curnow (1975) argues that Christine used this translation with palinode for *Cité des dames*.

(Mais puisque ainsi est que ta debonnaireté ne se est de tant estandue vers moy, espargnes doncques ma negligence en ton service, biaux sire Dieux, et ne te desplaise: car le servant qui moins reçoit de guerdons de son seigneur moins est oubligié a son service. [621])

In a system where literary value is measured by ethical effect, this reaction perforce denies misogyny's claim to literary (and authoritative) status. Clearly, leading one's reader to doubt God's mercy is no way to inspire proper behavior; by extension it is no way to write "ethically," that is, "poetically," either.

The narrator's rescue comes at the hands of God, who sends the three crowned ladies to her aid. As Raison upbraids the narrator for accepting these texts, she elaborates on Christine's association between misogyny and false authority. Specifically, she reminds the narrator of differences between kinds of writing. The only infallible authority is the Holy Word, whose sources and materials misogynists have avoided. Literary misogyny relies on fallible genres, philosophy and poetry, which should be read critically to be understood. Thus, philosophical principles are uncertain and open to debate, as Aquinas's rebuttals of Aristotle and Aristotle's rebuttals of Plato indicate. Just as misleading, poetry's distinctive use of words makes the literal meaning unclear since poets often employ antiphrasis, a figure of speech "which means . . . if you call something bad, in fact it is good and vica versa" (7) ("qui s'entant, si comme tu sces, si comme on diroit tel est mauvais, c'est a dire que il est bon, et aussi a l'opposite" [624]). In making such distinctions between the authority of pagan and Christian texts, Christine is partly responding to the paucity of Christian and Hebrew heroines in Boccaccio's catalog; however, this distinction between Holy Scripture and pagan *auctores* is also a commonplace of medieval criticism.[18] In any case, the charge announces an important change in sources—Christine will rely not merely upon pagan texts but also upon biblical and hagiographic material. Raison's appeal to genre thus does two things: attack the authority of misogyny by defining its generic (and hence methodological) limits and establish the "higher" authority by which Christine will justify her arguments.

Raison's assertions illustrate how important it is to read and respond "critically" to texts, that is, to use one's judgment to critique authority. She thus prepares the reader for *Cité des dames'* dominant technique—its *modus*

---

18. This distinction arose naturally in the scholastic community of the thirteenth and fourteenth centuries as all kinds of *auctores*—pagan and Christian—were examined in terms of moral relevance.

agendi—which involves the use of experience and personal judgment to validate (or change) authority. The narrator's rescue is a case in point since the three crowned ladies announce God's will (authority) and illustrate Christine's resilience (experience).[19] Raison's special mirror, which reveals an entity's true nature, also indicates this process of revision.[20] When Raison orders Christine to gaze into her glass, the narrator appeals directly to her experience of herself as a test of truth. Iconographically, however, the mirror itself refutes other feminine allegories of sin, such as the figure of Vanitas, who often appears as a woman with a mirror. In Christine's catalog, Vanitas's association between women and exterior, physical, transient beauty gives way to Raison's quest for the internal, moral, eternal beauty of truth. Authority, though invoked, is transformed. Similar revisions will occur repeatedly in the text.

Personal experience plays a key role in this opening scene when Raison examines the misogynistic writer's intent and motivations, that is, his human character. Like others before her, Christine indicts misogynists for their self-serving and unsavory motives.[21] Raison claims misogynists attack women to protect themselves. They often project their own sexual desires and fears onto the catalog's heroines, for some "with deformed and impotent bodies . . . sharp and malicious minds" (19) ("aucuns impotens et diffourmez de leur membres, qui ont l'entendement agu et malicieux" [645]) ease their misery by attacking the women they can't have. Others are impotent and old. They seek to spoil women for the young men who can have them. Still others, having met women more noble than themselves, slander the gender from jealousy. Finally, some do it in the mistaken notion that it is "poetic"— a reference to the projections of Ovidian catalogs.[22] In each case, to interpret a text, the reader must consider not simply the page but the human behind it.

---

19. The three ladies were sent by God; they also exhibit the inner character of the narrator, who begins her revision of misogyny by examining her own personality and the personalities of women she has known. Also Raison orders Christine "reviens a toy meismes" (625) as the three ladies appear to her.

20. Raison's mirror, as Willard (1984) points out, may have been inspired by Vincent of Beauvais's *Speculum Historiale*, which was also a source for *Cité des dames*.

21. Christine's allegory clearly characterizes these motives as unsavory. Raison's refutation corresponds to hauling away basketfuls of dirt to prepare the city's ground.

22. Christine classifies this poetry as insincere and therefore faulty. They are "poems of water without salt" (20) ("dittiez de eaue sans sel" [647]) or "ballads without feeling" (20) ("balades sans sentement" [647]). Earlier, in *L'Epitre au Dieu d'Amours*, Christine went to great pains to characterize misogyny as deceit, playing upon the image of an empty form that becomes a trap. In the poetics of the late Middle Ages, when writing was supposed to lead a reader to a greater appreciation of the normative and the truthful, this charge reduced the value of such literature considerably.

Fortunately, the process also works in the opposite direction; women can use their own experiences to correct what they read. Anatomical non-sense found in books like the *Secreta Mulierium* (The Secrets of Women) is quickly refuted by a woman's experience of her own body.[23] The overwhelmingly male clientele of taverns testifies that women are not more gluttonous than men. Finally, the narrator's own knowledge of abused wives contradicts the frequent portrait of wives as wicked and deadly. Again, this appeal to the narrator's experience establishes important precedents for the argumentation ahead. The examples of the catalog will always appear in the light of the narrator's background.

In making this kind of argument, Christine de Pizan obviously relies on our trust of her narrator "Christine," whose virtue she is at pains to prove. The final function of the *exordium* is to introduce us to this trustworthy "Christine," whose virtue is vindicated by her actions and the allegory of the three virtues. If read on the four conventional levels of interpretation, Raison, Droitture, and Justice allegorically stand for the narrator's inner nature, just as Vergil in the *Divine Comedy* is an allegory of Dante's reason. Their presence and control of the polemic assure readers of Christine's suitability as a speaker, an important point in an age when women writers often met with bitter opposition.[24] As the catalog progresses, the narrator Christine will exemplify Christine de Pizan's model of womankind. On occasion, she will join the historical exempla of the catalog.[25] Indeed, Christine de Pizan centers Christine's quest for gender identity in a personal crisis. By meeting her narrator during this crisis in her study, by accepting her commitment to ethics and to probity, by tracing her nascent opposition to misogyny, we come to like and sympathize with her. Her moral itinerary through *Cité des dames* becomes ours, her education ours. Indeed, education is the purpose

---

23. The *Secreta Mulierium* was a gynecology text erroneously attributed to Albertus Magnus. Supposedly, the pope found it so provocative that he forbade it to women, a rather extraordinary idea on the face of it since a text on feminine anatomy should more logically inflame men.

24. A good example of this opposition can be found in the assembled letters of the *querelle de la rose*. One of Christine's opponents in this debate, Pierre Col, suggested that it was ridiculous for a woman to question the judgment of so learned a man as Jean de Meun. He advised her, "if you have been praised because you have shot a bullet over the towers of Notre Dame, don't try to hit the moon for that reason with an oversized arrow; take care not to resemble the crow who, when his singing was praised, began to sing louder than usual and let the morsel he was holding fall from his mouth" (*Le Débat sur le Roman De la Rose*, ed. and trans. Eric Hicks [Paris: Champion, 1967], 109– 10). Christine quite naturally resented the patronizing tone.

25. She figures most prominently in book 2, where her education by her father supports examples of other women similarly educated. See Christine de Pizan 1975, 2.36. There are also parallels, however, in books 1 and 3.

of the book. Like Dante in the *Divine Comedy*, Christine grows in her meetings with the catalog's heroines. The author's assumption that her narrator's growth will parallel the growth of the female reader is an important part of her poetical program.

In Christine, then, Christine de Pizan perfects a narrator intensely and visibly involved with both audience and text; subjectivity is not only highlighted, as in *Legend of Good Women*, but valorized as well. Having established her purpose (to defend women), her structure (the three crowned ladies), and her sources (the genres of faith as well as genres of poetry and philosophy), Christine de Pizan also gives us a narrator who measures the progress of her defense by her growing self-awareness. With these points established, the construction of the *defense* can begin with the catalog proper.

The Catalog

The remainder of book 1 is under the guidance of Raison, whose mission is to define women as mental and physical beings.[26] To complete her task, Raison contests two of the most persistent assertions found in past catalogs: that a virtuous woman cannot be feminine and that femineity is most properly associated with the body, not the mind. In the process, she remodels two popular "types" of women—the traditional virago who is virile in character and Boccaccio's new type of the woman scholar. She also makes impressive claims for women's natural talents.

Like St. Jerome and Boccaccio, Christine begins her list with the viragoes. However, these women and their initial placement serve very different purposes in *Cité des dames* than in *Adversus Jovinianum* or *De claris mulieribus*.[27] Rather than illustrating woman's highest achievements, they begin Christine's argument on a sound basis, as the allegory emphasizes. Their stories are the base of the city walls, the first line of defense. The distortions they correct are equally fundamental to revising essential assertions made from Aristotle to Aquinas, namely that good women are unfeminine, that woman are by nature "imperfect" men, and that women are therefore unfit for power. Christine's opening question to Raison—why are women barred

---

26. The division is quite clear; 1.8–26 concentrates on physical courage and leadership; 1.27–48 exemplifies women's learning and skills.

27. I use the term virago to indicate not merely a virgin but a "manly" woman who engages in traditionally "manly" occupations, i.e., war, politics, and (later) scholarship. For more work on the virago, see Heisch 1980 and Margaret King, "Book-Lined Cells," in Patricia Labalme 1980, 66–90.

from the seats of legal counsel—implies all these issues and links the fact of woman's disfranchisement with the one visible difference between the genders, that is, physical strength. On the whole, the viragoes prove that women are not necessarily weak, nor unequal to public trust. Christine never advocates that women should seek public offices, but she suggests that men occupy them simply because they are more physically robust.

Because of her concern for defending womankind, Christine, unlike St. Jerome or Boccaccio, emphasizes that the virago is a woman. Nowhere does she suggest that their courage is unfeminine, nor does she use the traditional epithet of manly, an omission all the more striking since she occasionally uses it in her other works.[28] Instead, Raison emphasizes what a medieval audience would have seen as the heroine's femineity. Camilla is a loyal daughter as well as a warrior; Queen Berenice is an enraged mother; many of the contemporary French rulers—Queen Jeanne and the countesses of La Marche, Vendôme, and Chastres—are shown as loving wives. Viragoes did not traditionally appear in roles that required interaction with men. Not all of Boccaccio's viragoes are virgins either, but most of those who aren't and who fit the virago patterns are widows, who live without men.[29] Boccaccio does not stress feminine aspects of the virago's life as Christine does when she motivates Boccaccio's Queen Berenice more specifically and more logically by maternal love. Although the traditional virgin is present (Camilla and the various Amazons are examples), she is not alone among her sex nor is she a spiritual "man."

Christine's second important change reflects her focus upon women's deeds rather than a predefined conception of their nature, perhaps an adaptation and extension of changes in some of Boccaccio's sketches. She also emphasizes the social benefits of these women's rule, a change of focus that will be repeated throughout the catalog.[30] Queen Nicaula is remembered because she instituted rule by law. Queen Fredegund of France saved the crown for her son. Artemisia, Thamiris, and Zenobia successfully defended

---

28. In *La mutacion de fortune,* for example, Christine is pictured on a sea voyage with her husband. When he is washed overboard by a wave, Fortune changes Christine into a man so that she can pilot the boat to safety.

29. The only virago in Boccaccio's catalog who is also presented in a feminine role is Hypsicratea, who followed her husband into battle. In contrast, Christine includes Lilia, the mother of Theodoric, and Queen Fredegund, the widow of Chilperic of France and the mother of King Clotaire. She also discusses Zenobia and Artemisia as mothers and wives (as opposed to widows); Boccaccio does not.

30. One of the most important changes in *Cité des dames* is the addition of a social context. Willard especially stresses this point (1984, chap.8).

their realms from invaders, a situation doubtless impressive to Christine, who lived in France during an epoch of crippling civil and foreign wars.[31]

Finally, Christine strenuously avoids any reference to the virago's rarity. While she admits that her heroines are unusual, she never describes their abilities as exceptional nor uses them, as do Boccaccio and Jerome, to chastise her women readers. The viragoes exemplify a gender's, not an individual's, worth. They connect the catalog's examples to its female readers and argue for women's natural virtue. This change appears not only in individual histories but also in Christine's arrangement of feminine communities. The Amazons, for example, appear together in Christine's catalog rather than scattered through the narrative as in *De claris mulieribus*. Raison also uses Amazonia's long existence and production of heroines as an implicit argument for feminine potential and a historical precursor for the city of ladies itself.

Such changes may appear simple responses to a long tradition of typecasting, but the understated nature of Christine's change does not erase its fundamental importance. Raison's very first virago, the city's "cornerstone," is Semiramis, whose portrait issues a defiant challenge to past catalogs. Arguably, Semiramis is the most flawed of the traditional viragoes—a woman who was brave but libidinous and therefore linked to woman's characteristic failing of lust.[32] By reforming her, Christine debunks many misogynistic charges at one blow. Yet her changes passed unnoticed until Liliane Dulac demonstrated that Christine significantly revises Boccaccio's Semiramis by taking a different approach.[33] Where Boccaccio links the Babylonian queen with vice *and* virtue, emphasizing her affair with her son and describing her as a male/female anomaly, Christine, Dulac argued, presents her queen as virtuous, excusing her incestuous affair with the plea that standards were different in Semiramis's time and making the queen's achievements an emblem of her womanly nature.

In addition to these charges, however, Christine also adds a subtle shift in context that Dulac does not mention. She cites Semiramis's courage and military prowess, but appends references to her wisdom and justice. Semiramis's reconquest of Babylon is portrayed as a blow against open rebellion, one of the greatest crimes against the medieval ideal of political

---

31. For example, Christine de Pizan's *L'Epître sur la prison de vie humaine* was inspired by the French defeat at Agincourt.

32. Dante, for example, places her in the circle of lust in his *Inferno*.

33. Dulac (1978) was the first scholar to present evidence in print of Christine's refashioning.

order.[34] Moreover, Semiramis's affair with her son is explained by politics
as well as history. The queen very sensibly wants no crowned rivals to
jeopardize the realm's security. All these changes integrate Semiramis into
her society as well. Finally, Semiramis's placement also responds to Boccaccio's opening chapter. As the first example of the city—indeed, its cornerstone—Semiramis occupies the place granted Eve in *De claris mulieribus,*
where the first mother associated women with all the qualities traditional to
the heroines of past catalogs—physical beauty, fickleness, and instability.
Semiramis replaces these ontological debasements with a picture of a
woman who acts prudently and effectively as a ruler. She begins the work
not only with an argument for women's civic virtue, but with an argument
against their victimization in the record.

After the viragoes, Christine turns to a more lengthy refashioning of
Boccaccio's scholarly, inventive, and artistic exempla. Here she elaborates
at much greater length, possibly for strategic as well as personal reasons.
As she was a scholarly woman herself, these past women scholars would
have appealed to her as important precedents for her act of authorship.
Overemphasizing the virago's associations between women and the body,
moreover, would have been unfortunate when refuting a tradition that had
often worked this association to women's disadvantage. Accordingly,
Christine spends more time on women's mental than physical natures, and
yields no ground. In fact, if any assertion in *Cité des dames* is rash or
hyperbolic, it is Raison's claim that if women are less physically powerful
than men, God gave women, in compensation, "minds that are freer and
sharper wherever they apply themselves" (63) ("de tant ont elles l'entendement plus a delivre et plus agu ou elles s'applicquent" [721]).

These examples of women's mental acumen—and the very idea of
including them—probably come from Boccaccio. Unlike Boccaccio, however, Christine treats her scholars and sages as she treats her viragoes, making them examples of woman's general potential. She also accepts their
achievements without reservation. Women's ingenuity is never vicious,
never inferior, never questioned as in *De claris mulieribus.* While Christine
often quotes Boccaccio, she chooses her citations carefully. For example,
she includes *De claris mulieribus*'s enthusiastic praise of Proba (a woman
writer) but omits its use to chastise the woman reader's sloth. Raison also

---

34. Christine de Pizan was certainly aware of the threat of civil war in the summer of 1405.
That threat inspired her *Epître à Isabeau de Bavièr,* which was written at this time and which
warns of the civil strife that was eventually to overtake France.

sanitizes Boccaccio's references to Sappho, who is no longer the singer of erotic songs but an erudite scholar "learned in several arts and sciences" (67) ("car en plusieurs ars et sciences fu tres experte et parfonde" [728]). She even enlarges the definition of praiseworthy learning to include traditionally "evil" knowledge associated with women. Sorceresses such as Medea or Circe are praised for their sagacity, a clear rehabilitation of women's learning. The context of these achievements is always social. Nicostrata's invention of the Latin alphabet is a gift to the Latins. While Boccaccio had taken this slant with Nicostrata, he did not (as Christine does) take the same view of Minerva, who invented armor; Arachne, who first dyed wool; and Pamphile, who invented silk cultivation. The closing section on prudence—women's ability to apply their learning to the wise management of their lives—also stresses this social aspect while associating women with an ethical use of intelligence that philosophers such as Aristotle had long thought of as particularly male.[35]

In terms of mental prowess, Christine's most important revision of Boccaccio occurs in her sketch of Ceres, whose biography had occasioned *De claris mulieribus*'s link between women's inventiveness and social degeneration. We can sense how this treatment must have infuriated Christine, for she responds not once but four times to Bocccaccio's sketch.[36] She also piles up an outraged defense of Ceres's accomplishment. Agriculture gives men "more beautiful and radiant bodies" (79) ("le corps plus bel, plus clers" [749]); helps them "beautify the land" (79) ("de l'embellir" [749]); and eventually leads them from the "caverns of ignorance" (79) ("cavernes d'ignorance" [750]) to the heights of civilization. In her last reference, she explicitly refutes Boccaccio by name (a most unusual gesture in the *Cité*) because he suggested that "the world was better off when people lived only from haws and acorns" (82) ("le siecle valoit mieulx quand la gent ne vivoyent fors de cenelles et de glans" [754]). Her crowning refutation—that Christ himself honored Ceres's gift by bestowing his body in the communion wafer—attacks Boccaccio's source also. While he relies on pagan conventions, such as the Golden Age, Christine turns to Christian ones, such as the Last Supper. This change is consistent with Raison's examination of genre in book 1.

---

35. Maclean notes that prudence was traditionally considered the most important of the moral virtues (1983, 49–50). Both Plato and Aristotle agreed that men are generally more prudent than women, older men more prudent than younger. This distinction corresponded to differences in humors, the formative fluids of the body.

36. See Christine de Pizan 1975, 1.35.1, 1.38.1, 1.38.5, 1.39.3.

In terms of other strategies, the praise in book 1 sets many important precedents for *Cité des dames,* often by appropriating and perfecting techniques from *De claris mulieribus.* Christine avoids praise by topics of *effictio* (fame by beauty, birth, or a turn of fortune) for a consistent policy of praise by the topics of *notatio* (deeds). In book 2, Droitture will explicitly comment on this policy. Within the sketches, Christine also changes how amplification and comparison establish the limits of her praise. Boccaccio heightens a woman's virtue by comparing her with a history of feminine depravity; Christine amplifies a woman's virtue by comparing her with a less or equally impressive male. Amazonia measures up quite nicely to Troy in the chapter on Penthesilea. As independent warriors, Hippolyta and Menalippe compare favorably with Hercules and Theseus, and the Roman scholar Cornificia surpasses her brother in her scholarship, even though she could not attend school. Such comparisons stress the excellence of the feminine gender as well as the excellence of individual women, but that is the basis of Raison's argument. The first crowned lady's point is that women are virtuous, even heroic by nature. How that potential is used, and how women have been judged for it, are the subjects of her sister's discussion.

As implied by her name, Droitture is concerned not with women's potential but with their rectitude, which is demonstrated in their day-to-day life. Consequently, as her scepter (a ruler) implies, she is interested in how that rectitude has been measured.[37] She brings us more mundane but more pervasive examples of service by focusing on women in the home. She also places that domesticity within a communal and public context. Her speeches consistently attack the eroticization of women in past catalogs, questioning why marriage is linked with sexual content rather than social value and noting how the courtly heroine propagates an inappropriate and even dangerous social model. In all these comments, Droitture illustrates how catalogs have confined woman to the sexual areas of human existence. If book 1 (and Raison) unite the active good woman to her gender, book 2 (and Droitture) reform the traditional "feminine" good woman by uniting her with her society's civic life.

Three of Droitture's targets are images from past catalogs—the good but passive wife, the sexually active but morally reprehensible wife, and the sexually victimized but patiently suffering lover. As we shall see, this wholesale questioning of specifically feminine role models eventually makes for a

---

37. According to Willard, Dame Rectitude was possibly inspired by a similar figure in Phillipe de Mézières's *Songe du Vieil Pèlerin* (Willard 1984, 137).

major refashioning of the model of femineity itself. While the value of chastity does not change, the relationship between home and the community does, and so does the perceived interdependence of men and women. Book 2 argues that the removal of women from the community is as undesirable as the segregation of men and women, or the separation of public from private life, a separation that had begun to emerge in Christine's century and that would have important consequences for women's life in the Renaissance.[38]

While the first examples of book 2 do not deal with the home, they do illustrate women's probity and provide a clear transition between books 1 and 2. Richards, Christine's translator, describes these women as "ladies of vision and prophecy" (1982, xxxix); their gift of prophecy implies divine favor, however, for as Charity Willard has noted, Christine always equates prophecy with "a special sensitivity to God's thought" (1984, 141). In catalogs such as *Adversus Jovinianum,* these women appear with the viragoes. Here they not only give book 2 some continuity with book 1 but also underline the historical continuity of women's rectitude. Book 1 had begun with Semiramis, queen of one of the world's first kingdoms. Book 2 opens with three sets of exempla that connect the Hebrews (Deborah, Elizabeth, and the Queen of Sheba) to the Romans (Nicostrata, Cassandra, and Antonia) to the French (Queen Basine). The last two exempla, Antonia and Basine, also indicate the forthcoming themes of book 2, for their prophecies concern their husbands.

Droitture first mentions examples of filial piety such as Drypetina, Hypsipyle, and Claudia, but the majority of her heroines of the hearth exemplify marital excellence. Once again, Christine uses her experience as well as her studies to shape her interpretation of the heroines' lives. For example, in examining charges made against wives, she compares the misogynistic accusations with her knowledge of abused women and verifies this impression with historical examples of good wives. Queen Hypsicratea accompanied her husband into battle and exile; Sulpitia followed hers into poverty.[39] Caesar's daughter Julia loved an aged man, Xantippe a wise one. In place of the murderous wives who kill their mates, Christine lists women who try to save their husbands' lives, often with good advice. These include even antithetical pairings such as the wives of Brutus and Julius Caesar, who took

---

38. For a commentary on this change to a public/private schema and how it limited women's actions and opportunities, see Kelly 1977.

39. This is not the Sulpicia who provided Boccaccio with the occasion for his digression on chastity. That heroine is absent from *Cité des dames.*

opposing sides in Rome's civil wars. Christine's methodology in this is straightforward and clear. Misogynists charge that women are fickle, disdainful, contentious, and murderous. Droitture shows they aren't.

More important is how Christine handles the standard of chastity, the *sine qua non* of the good wife and (at least since St. Jerome) the leading catalog index of feminine conduct. She begins by simply denying misogyny's charges. Earlier catalogs had attacked women's chastity; Christine defends it. Chaste women are not rare, nor are beautiful women unchaste, as the stories of Susanna, Sarah, Rebecca, Ruth, Penelope, and Sulpitia prove. Boccaccio's insinuation that many women "want to be raped" (161) ("se veullent efforcier" [885]) is met with resentment. Christine assembles five examples to the contrary, argues in Lucretia's story that rape is "the greatest possible sorrow" (161) ("douleur sur toutes autres" [885]), and shows that many women have preferred death. Hyppo drowned herself, and the Sicambians committed mass suicide.

In addition to denying the charges, however, Droitture also redefines chastity and its application. She claims it is a double standard. Men expect more constancy from women than they themselves can muster. Heroines who exemplify this trend include Griselda, Florence of Rome, and Bernabo the Genovean (taken from, respectively, Boccaccio's *Decameron,* Philippe de Mézières' translation of Petrarch's translation of Boccaccio's story of Griselda, and the *Miracles of the Virgin*). Droitture also takes issue with the chaste woman's passivity, voicing her opposition in single and grouped exempla. Boccaccio's exemplum for self-effacing chastity (Sulpicia) is dropped, and a cluster of women whose education and learning benefits their community are added (Hortensia, Novella, Christine herself). (Christine's argument for women's education is her only specific call for social reform; it later became a standard *topos* in the pro-feminine tracts of the *querelle des femmes*.)[40] Finally, wives' loyalty to their husbands is also weighed as a contribution to society.

Most important for the civic themes of book 2, however, Droitture changes the context in which chastity is defined. Past catalogs used it to separate the good woman from public commerce because the chaste woman remained at home and tended her household silently. Droitture dramatizes her objection to this notion with the same satiric inversion that Chaucer uses in *Legend of Good Women.* She constructs a catalog of inconstant males,

---

40. Thomas More, Juan Vives, Erasmus, Laura Cetera, and later Marie de Gournay, Anna von Schurmann, and Bathsheba Matkin all made similar arguments for women's education.

treating its members and structuring its form as catalogs of wicked women had been treated and structured. In the male catalog, however, unchastity's synonym is treason. The crux of the comparison resides in the contrast between men's public virtue—a virtue that associates men with power and politics—and women's private one—which gags and silences her. All Droitture's male exempla are berated for disloyalty, just as the unfaithful wife is. But their disloyalties occur in a political or ecclesiastical office, not in a marriage. Claudius, Nero, Galba, Vitellius, Judas, Julian the Apostate, and Otho are thus public counterparts to the wicked wife.[41] The last of these even epitomizes her failings, since his vices include thievery, gluttony, weakness, self-indulgence, arrogance, and depravity. These men also contrast with an earlier list in book 2 detailing the stories of Thermutis and Esther (Israel), the Sabine women and Veturia (Rome), and Clotilda (France), women who had saved their nations as wives, mothers, daughters, or viragoes. The reader thus confronts two, interlocking points. If unchastity is comparable to treachery, then men have not been properly judged. Likewise, if public treason harms the community, the private chastity of wives must help it. Chastity becomes an instrument for feminine participation rather than exclusion. Its associations with sexuality are replaced by ties to public welfare in a manner completely in accord with humanist sentiments.

Such assertions attack the use of chastity in catalogs such as *De claris mulieribus* and *Satire Six;* in closing, Droitture censors catalogs such as the *Heroides* and *Legend of Good Women* for their unsuitable appropriation of "feminine" virtue. Portraits such as we've seen in the Ovidian and Chaucerian catalog were poetic staples of courtly literature and a long-standing irritation to Christine; she voiced her objections to them throughout her career, in the main protesting that they give women a dangerous and inappropriate model of behavior.[42] In *Cité des dames,* Dido, Medea, and Thisbe (from Ovid's *Heroides*), and Ghismonda and Lisabetta (from Boccaccio's *Decameron*) doubtless serve as examples of feminine fidelity. But they also reiterate Christine's warning against "the dangerous and damnable sea of foolish love" (202) ("celle mer tres perilleuse et dampnable de folle amour" [951–52]) where voyages are "always detrimental and harmful to . . . [women's] bodies, their property, their honor, and—most importantly of all—their souls" (202) ("tousjours . . . a leur grant prejudice et grief en corps, en bien et en honneur et a l'ame, qui plus est" [952]). To celebrate

---

41. It appears that Christine drew many of these exempla from *De casibus virorum illustrium*.

42. *L'Epitre au Dieu d'Amours,* her first defense of womankind, makes women's portrait in courtly literature its major target.

such abused women is yet another misapplication of the chaste standard, Droitture implies, and an especially dangerous one since it encourages an inappropriate role model for women. This heroine type also propagates the misuse of epideictic technique, for elegiac portraits often concentrate on women's beauty, not their achievements. Heroines such as Europa, Jocasta, Medusa, Helen, and Polyxena are only famous by "coincidence rather than their own virtue" (203) ("par divers accidens plus que par grans vertus" [952]). Women's integrity and honesty are their true sources of attraction, says Droitture; their actions make the most urgent claims on our memory.

With this emphasis upon women's deeds, book 2 attempts to place women within the context of the community, to argue that women's lives cannot and should not be separated from men's. In making this argument, Christine seems to draw on a passage from the source of her title, St. Augustine's *City of God*. There Augustine claims that pagan Rome had never been a true republic because it had neglected the good of the whole for the benefit of the few.[43] The catalogers of old similarly erred because women "are not another species or dissimilar race, for which they should be excluded from moral teachings" (187) ("non mie une autre espece ne de dessemblable generacion par quoy elles doyent estre forcloses des enseigne[me]ns moraux" [928]). In eliminating them from their lessons, past catalogers harmed the community. Book 2 tries to redress that wrong by integrating Christine's city into the *res publica*. Book 3 will show that the *Cité des dames* is a *civitas dei* as well.

Book 3 concludes Christine's defense with what has often struck modern readers as an anticlimactic summary of saints' tales, a disappointing ending to a book begun in such a forward-looking fashion under Dame Raison. Yet these concluding stories play an important part in Christine's plan. They forge links between the pagan past and the Christian present, they confirm the arguments of books 1 and 2, and they set all that went before within a vision of history. The last of these revisions is probably the most important, but its presence and import intrinsically depend upon the arguments of earlier sections. In his English translation, Richards mentions several ways that Christine establishes her work as a universal history (1982, xxviii–xxx). Some are confined to book 3; most appear throughout the commentary. The title draws upon the Augustinian metaphor for history as a tale of two cities. The path traced by the universal history as power moved from East to West frequently governs how Christine arranges exempla, as we saw

---

43. For this argument, see *The City of God* 5.20.

in book 2's opening. But the confirmation of Christine's use of historical patterns really depends on her organization of book 3.

Associating *Cité des dames* with the universal history has many important consequences. Richards points out that it gives the book a "universality" that "sets it apart" (1982, xxx). This observation is both just and perceptive, but it is important to note that Christine's earlier arguments impart a new secularity to universal history as well. In *The City of God,* St. Augustine separates pagan from Christian. Christine's Justice unites the two. Since the lives of Christian saints correspond to patterns of Christine's other heroines, Justice also reverses the direction of exemplification. In Augustine, human history moves toward God's heavenly city, which is earth's sole source of meaning. Although the city of ladies ultimately derives its authority from God, its significance is earthly. The usual climax to the martyr's story—the ascent to heaven—never occurs in book 3, even though many of its exempla are Christian martyrs. This change emphasizes that the saint's importance lies not in heavenly saintliness but in her resistance to oppression on earth. Furthermore, the pattern of history that emerges from such resistance runs in cycles, not in the Augustinian straight line. We encounter oppression-resistance-oppression rather than the traditional Christian fall-redemption-transcendence. Such a vision of history, far more characteristic of Renaissance than of medieval thought, demonstrates how forward-looking Christine's overall plan is.[44] Book 3 provides not the triumph, but the appropriation, of tradition, its redefinition by a woman speaker who seeks authentication. In this section, Christine makes history, and Christian dogma, her own.[45] As we shall see, the gesture gives final shape not only to a view of history but also to the narrator's and her gender's new identities.

We can see this appropriation at work in the very first passages of book 3, where Justice welcomes the Virgin Mary as the leader of the city. In her address, Justice uses two types of titles. The first is conventional and christocentric. Mary is the Temple of God, the Cell and Cloister of the Holy Spirit, the Vessel of the Trinity, the Joy of Angels, Star, Guide, Hope of the True Creation. But the Virgin is also welcomed with the titles of an earthly prince. She is womankind's "defender, protector, and guard against all assaults of enemies and of the world" (218) ("leur deffenderresse, protectarresse, et

---

44. The cyclic interpretation of history is, of course, implicit in the name we give to the Renaissance (rebirth). For a brief but enlightening commentary on Renaissance historiography, see Baker (1967).

45. In his introduction to the *City of Ladies,* Richards compares this appropriation to Martin Luther King's (1982, xxvix).

garde contre tous assaulx d'annemis et du monde" [976]). With Mary, two hemispheres of meaning meet in a new whole. This union of secular and sacred is also reflected in other reconciliations in book 3.

Christine's saints summarize and vindicate the arguments found in books 1 and 2. On the broadest level, they authenticate the analysis of misogyny. They also struggle against a false and repressive authority. That male authority also masks its prejudice under self-serving claims of patriotism or probity. Some of the pagan judges envy their victim's achievements; others lust for their bodies; still others feel insecure or take a sadistic delight in pain.[46] In all cases, the motive is self-serving and destructive. The body of the female saint, abused and battered, incarnates the condition of her gender; her resistance sets an example for feminine conduct. Finally, God's support extends His approval to the individual saint and by analogy to Christine's analysis, which sees this pattern as the principal plot of feminine history.

Within this larger model, the saints themselves reiterate Christine's specific claims for women's virtue. Mary and Mary Magdalene uphold the dignity of women's love. The learned St. Catherine exemplifies the scholarly woman's worth. Numerous martyred virgins exhibit the virago's courage. Women saints who see their children martyred recall book 2's defense of wives and daughters. Saints Marina and Euphrosyne support the refutation of the "manly" woman. (They live disguised as men but reveal their identities upon death.) Saints Natalia, Anastasia, and Theodota, who minister to Christian martyrs, exemplify women's conventional services to the weak. St. Afra, a prostitute who embraced chastity, parallels the reform of the courtly heroine. Finally, the various women who minister to the apostles exemplify the worth of traditionally feminine services—preparing food, providing clothing, and burying the dead. Book 3's last example, Basillisa, finishes the catalog with the example of a woman priest, ending the list with an ecclesiastical counterpoint to the women rulers who open book 1 and Mary's appearance at the beginning of book 3.

The saints also close many circles that other catalogs had left broken

---

46. St. Catherine's judge lusts for her and is enraged by Catherine's posing of a question he cannot answer. The long list of torments designed for St. Martina can only be described as sadistic. Her body is slashed, drawn, staked down and broken with chains, set on fire with burning oil, and ripped with iron hooks. She is also thrown to the lions, and walled up in a pagan temple. Finally, her throat is cut. The detailed and graphic description of physical torments was traditional to hagiography; here Christine's point seems to be that women's bodies, despite the attempts to degrade them, cannot be soiled.

or incomplete. By evoking the Christian heroine, they unite pagan with Christian. By invoking God's authority to confirm Christine's experience, they reconcile both sources of knowing. Finally, by uniting the narrator and her narrative, they bring together the woman reader/writer and her text. While implicit throughout *Cité des dames,* this last closure is most prominent in parallels between the narrator and her namesake, St. Christine. Like Christine, St. Christine struggles against a wrong-headed and repressive authority that has two male faces: fierce father (roughly parallel to the misogynistic philosophy that failed to nurture the narrator in book 1) and faithless lover (parallel to the courtly poets who misuse women's sexuality in their poems). Imprisoned by her father while still only a child, St. Christine refuses to give up her vocation. She is put to various tortures and persuasions but remains firm. Eventually she exhausts all his efforts and the efforts of two other male judges. The erotic motives of one of these suggests the misappropriation of the poets. St. Christine's father represents the misappropriation of the learned tradition. Their targets also mirror the misogynistic attacks since one judge singles out emblems of the saint's gender (her breasts) and her means of defense (her tongue). Like the narrator, however, St. Christine will not be silenced or debased. Although her tongue is twice cut out, she spits the stump in her judge's face and continues to speak. In like fashion, the narrator overcomes the objections of a false authority to speak the truth. Both women are finally vindicated in God—St. Christine is martyred; Justice holds Christine's arguments to be sound. The parallels between the narrator's experience and the authoritative *vita* of St. Christine is one of book 3's most impressive images of historical continuity. It authenticates Christine's task and gives the reader a pattern for relating the book's examples to her own life. In St. Christine as well, authority is vindicated, for here the narrator finds a written confirmation of what her judgment and her experience have told her, the completion of her own sense of identity.

This delicate meshing of detail in the final section of in *Cité des dames* unites many levels of the text. The narrator Christine's historically based sense of identity is linked to the author Christine's defense of femineity, which is connected in turn to a series of virtues (in book 1) that service the community (in book 2) and are commemorated in history (book 3). The image of the city governs all of these enterprises, linking the community of women, the community of humankind, and the community of saints to a personal identity. Each city, implicit in and dependent on the others, answers to one of the four levels of traditional allegorical interpretation. Literally, of course, the city is the text; allegorically, it is the narrator's sense of herself;

topologically, it is the female gender; and anagogically, it is the feminine portion of the city of God.

In the links between these levels, we see an interaction of traditional associations with Christine's special genius. She is unique in connecting the historical city of God (taken so clearly from St. Augustine) with not only a gender identity but also a presentation of the self that, as Danielle Régnier-Bohler recently noted, "took on spatial attributes" at the close of the medieval period (1988, 377). The link was possibly suggested by rhetoric as well, as the city's connection with the text implies. One of the five traditional divisions of rhetoric was memory. *Cité des dames* refers to this connection by accusing its narrator, as Philosophy had accused Boethius, of a faulty memory. The narrator Christine corrects this failing by writing a book that connects personal memory (identity) to social memory (history). Making the image for all three a city not only echoes Augustine and late medieval images of subjectivity but also calls upon the ancient art of artificial memory, which taught the student of rhetoric to memorize moral and theological exempla by placing them in imaginary and well-lit buildings, *loci illustres*. The city thus continues three traditions and unites them into one: the Augustinian city merges with these imaginary buildings filled with illustrious figures from the past; both are integral to the metaphoric spatialization of the self that represents the building of a personal identity; finally, all are contained within the city that is Christine's text. Moreover, Christine makes these traditions her own by using the city to present a metaphorically valid conception of self-consciousness. As the manuscript illuminations of the *Cité des dames* show, her community is circular and enclosed, like any medieval city. It is both complete and apart, just as the narrator's sense of self is. Yet through its gates, a free interchange flows between inner and outer world, between the individual and her readings. Most significant, the gates can be closed at Christine's will, for Justice gives the narrator the keys at the end of book 3. By thus assuming control of her identity, the narrator, as a woman, is left free to choose what influences she will accept and what models and interpretations from her readings she will take. In the catalog tradition, this control carves a new and important place for the compiler while defining a mental process that other women are encouraged to imitate as their surest line of defense.

The city is a notion of surprising complexity in the catalog tradition, but its very integration and intricacy, its orchestration of a typical florilegean richness, succinctly answers the inequities of past catalogs. Women had been presented as isolated and incomplete, cut off from other women and/or from virtue and the sources of political and historical meaning. The identities projected by these catalogs were often fragmented and confused. Book 1 openly protests this confusion by dramatizing its effect on a woman reader and holding that effect inadmissible by standards common to medieval commentaries and *accessus ad auctores*. In place of fragmentation, *Cité des dames* offers the woman reader integration and numerous virtuous role models, the most important being the narrator herself, whose moral education *Cité des dames* plots with great detail. Women, Christine asserts, can structure their own natures by the selective use and interpretation of authority. Paradoxically, then, while *Cité des dames* attempts to define femineity, it is also one of the first documents to balance the parts played by culture and individual will in shaping an understanding of "feminine" nature. Women, the book thus implies, can make themselves, the basic point of Christine's sequel to *Cité des dames, Le Livre des trois vertus* (The Book of the Three Virtues, also referred to as The Treasury of the City of Ladies).

In the catalog tradition, *Cité des dames* marks a number of firsts. The first catalog since Plutarch's to defend womankind, the first to associate the good woman with the community, and the first to integrate her within history, it is also the first to use past heroines to oppose the misogynistic concept of femineity. Christine grounds her defense in some of the most important issues of her day—the importance of history, the desirability of fame, and the renaissance of interest in civic virtue—and she forecasts Renaissance forms by presenting her arguments in an abbreviated dialogue with the misogynistic canon. For all these reasons, *Cité des dames* is an important book that foreshadows the catalog's use in the Renaissance *querelle des femmes*.

The catalog, as we've seen, was remarkably useful for defining the present in terms of the past. But Christine de Pizan, like the Renaissance catalogers who followed her, was interested in the past because it illuminated the present. Her refashioning sought to change the cultural patrimony and give authority a less forbidding face for the next woman who confronted its legacy in a library. Chaucer indicated and Christine knew that the catalog, like a mirror, gave back a reflection not of tradition but of the compiler confronting tradition. In the past, the mirror had been turned to a male compiler, but with Christine, the compiler became a female. This new reflection not only transformed the monologue on femineity into a true dialogue but also illuminated the unspoken ways we use the past to shape our culture, our society, and, ultimately, ourselves.

Conclusion

The catalog of women tradition did not end with Christine de Pizan's work. Indeed, its greatest florescence occurred in the Renaissance, when catalogs were almost universally incorporated into the texts of the *querelle des femmes*. The late medieval catalog did, however, set the model for Renaissance catalogs, which introduced very few significant changes in content or methodology. For this reason, *Cité des dames* is an appropriate place to conclude our survey. The material reviewed so far gives rise to three further questions: Why do catalogs present a sporadic, as opposed to continuous, tradition? Why did womankind's apologists and detractors not only use the same device (the catalog) but many of the same exempla? Finally, why were Christine's innovations largely unrecognized for so long?

All three questions lead back to the catalog's social and historical dimensions, but the first particularly pertains to the catalog's development as a florilegium. The history of the catalog of women can be summarized very briefly. Chapter 1 documents the development of the catalog (in and out of literary forms) during the eighth, seventh, and first centuries B.C. as well as the first and third centuries A.D. The dominant medieval catalog strategy was established relatively early, by the fifth century A.D. Yet aside from *Adversus Jovinianum*, neither the early Fathers nor early medieval writers produced catalogs. Why?

Both cultural and literary conditions lay behind this lack. For the catalog to flourish, certain preconditions had to be met. Writers needed a well-stocked library and a modicum of education. In medieval Europe, such libraries did not coexist with a professional class of scholars until the thirteenth century, when the clerical class developed within the new university systems. At that point, catalogs began to be produced again. Moreover, defining femineity within a historical context is more likely to be a pressing issue at times when the historical legacy is subject to reinterpretation on a large scale. Both Boccaccio and Jerome, for example, lived in eras especially self-conscious about their inherited traditions. Christian Rome was trying to break with the pagan past; humanists in Italy were trying to reestablish that lost connection. Both Jerome and Boccaccio used the catalog to give continuity in the midst of change and, paradoxically, to validate change as a continuation of the "lost" past. Such periods occur sporadically.

Finally, catalogers such as Ovid and Chaucer also struggled with the past, but in the form of literary, not historical, precedents. Their catalogs, engaged in a dialogue with their sources, express the artist's desire to escape a literary tradition that has become oppressive. The aesthetic self-awareness of such catalogs flourishes later rather than earlier in a cultural period, when a body of work and a theory of poetics have been erected.

This interaction between the past and the present also accounts for the evolution of the compiler's central role and the catalog's later popularity with both sides of the *querelle des femmes*. Ancient writers often thought in terms of works in a literary tradition. Support from one's authorities was established very early on as a prerequisite for any piece of persuasive writing. *Adversus Jovinianum*'s catalogs capitalize on this strategy by emphasizing the call to tradition, a method pariculary apt in refuting Jovinian's claims that Christianity's love of chastity was a new and unique standard. Yet as *Adversus Jovinianum* itself demonstrates, a catalog's excerpts never remain unaffected by the act of compilation. Jerome changed as well as reported his examples. Medieval catalogers often adopted the same masking technique (sometimes intentionally, sometimes not), making the compiler's presence in his own catalog problematic. Evidence that this aspect was understood by medieval writers can be found in the medieval discussions of a compiler's role in commentaries and *accessus ad auctores*. Additionally, Jean de Meun and Chaucer both refer to the strategy (albeit playfully) in their own work. They can do so because a whole scholastic theory of authorship sanctioned divorcing the compiler from what his collection said, giving his sources ultimate responsibility for the text. This strategy was so pervasive as to be adopted practically without reflection at times. Boccaccio's historical methods in *De claris mulieribus* were somewhat enlightened for his time, but he nevertheless changed some of his material without explanation or notification to the reader.

Chaucer's fictional florilegium demonstrates both how compilers impart meaning and how personal experience can influence the way a compiler shapes his or her collection. This commentary is locked in a literary text; but

Christine takes the process a logical step further, making the compiler not only visible but a legitimate source of meaning. While she still relies on the authority of tradition to authenticate her arguments, she makes the compiler, her reason, and her experience important and very visible factors behind her collection. She not only opens her interpretations to the reader's attention but also supports them with references to her experiences. Renaissance compilers on both sides of the controversy on woman's nature would do the same thing. The catalog's authoritative assembly of information gave weight to its argument, but the cataloger's reinterpretations were also clearly visible. In the catalogs of *The Courtier,* for example, there are open debates about the meanings of exempla. Semiramis's interpretation by Boccaccio and her reinterpretation at the hands of Christine is a perfect precursor of this debate. As Christine's work demonstrates, compilers could have it both ways: they could introduce reinterpretation (and their personal opinion) while also invoking tradition.

Perhaps the most puzzling aspect of the Renaissance catalogs, then, is why Christine's work seems to have had such little influence. She was not totally ignored. Among the later catalogs that acknowledged her work are Symporien Champion's *Nef des Dames* (1503), Pierre de Lesnaudiere's *La Louange de mariage et des femmes vertueuses* (1534), Martin le Franc's *Le Champion des Dames* (1440–42) (which cites Christine as a model woman), and François de Billon's *Le Fort inexpugnable de l'honneur du sexe feminin* (1555). Brian Ansley translated *Cité des dames* into English in 1521, and there is an incomplete Flemish translation still in manuscript that was made around 1518. But when translations of *De claris mulieribus* became widely available, *Cité des dames* ceased to be copied, a signal that many saw it (as many modern scholars did later) as essentially derivative.

One obvious reason for the lack of interest may be Christine's argument; she spoke for the minority. The Western notion of femineity changed very little during the Renaissance, as Maclean (1983) and Kelso (1956) have demonstrated. Men continued to write most of the catalogs produced, and they continued to focus on women's sexuality, even if contexts were social or artistic. The catalog heroine—like femineity itself—was most often associated with passion. She either used it as a weapon, was portrayed as its victim, or worked its effects on the male. When Renaissance compilers focused on woman's social place, her sexuality often became an important excuse for relegating her to domestic duties, for keeping her, as the "weaker vessel," under man's guidance.

This (sometimes unconscious) bias toward women as objects of desire necessarily distorted the compilers' views. It was a stance as characteristic of Renaissance as of medieval thought. Viragoes capable of action continued to be seen as virile. Married women who exemplified moral or intellectual virtue were encouraged to limit their practice to the home. Finally, the education of women, the one concern of Christine most reiterated in the later catalogs, was advocated only if it encouraged a woman's more efficient fulfillment of her domestic chores. Women's limitation to the private life was arguably even more pervasive in the Renaissance than in the Middle Ages. The French writer Agrippa d'Aubigné, for example, educated his daughters but also warned them that education should not lead to the neglect of household duties or their husbands' needs. Sir Thomas Elyot in *The Defense of the Good Woman* likewise argued for women's education but saw women's proper sphere as the home. And in Christine's homeland, Francesco Barbaro began book 2 of *De re uxoria* with a very conservative discussion of wifely obedience.

To note this conservatism is not to say that fifteenth-, sixteenth-, and even seventeenth-century treatises on femineity are totally barren of innovation or positive reflections of women. The scholarly heroine introduced by Boccaccio and Christine had many Renaissance incarnations. Indeed, one baroque catalog by Johann Ebberti—*Eröffnetes Cabinet dess Gehlehrten Frauen-Zimmers* (1706)—was devoted entirely to such exempla. So too was Jean de la Forge's *Circle of Learned Women*. Less resonant, perhaps, was Christine's attempt to view traditional women's roles in a social context, but even here, the Protestant valorization of the wife encouraged some revisions similar to those in *Cité des dames*. The most fertile area for a Renaissance redefinition of feminine sexuality—Neoplatonism—built on an understanding of male and female desire entirely foreign to Christine's collection. In this endeavor, *Cité des dames* could not have been influential even if it had been known.

The most plausible explanation for the dismissal or misreading of Christine's most important revision—her association of the good woman with history—is that the notion of historiography changed greatly between the early and late fifteenth century. *Cité des dames'* most conspicuous ties to history recall the Augustinian universal history, which was out of favor with later Renaissance historians who were inspired by new, nationalistic fervors. One sympathetic reader of Christine, Françoise Billon, imitated her pun on "deffence" in his catalog, but chose the word "fort" rather than "cité" (*Le Fort inexpugnable de l'honneur du sexe feminin*). Such a substitution suggests an eagerness to avoid dated nuances.

In addition to the changing culture, two other factors might have contributed to the dead-end that *Cité des dames* seems to have reached by the end of the sixteenth century. The first was its author's scholarly reputation, the second her intended audience. Christine's use of *De claris mulieribus* was well-known. Indeed, later scholars assumed she had merely translated Boccaccio's work. As stated above, when vernacular translations of *De claris mulieribus* became widely available, *Cité des dames* ceased to be copied. In contrast, Christine's *Le Livre des trois vertus* enjoyed a longer and much broader popularity. Why this difference? One reason might be that *Cité des dames* is a more scholarly work than its sequel, and women spoke with less authority in scholarly genres. Readers seeking a learned compendium would naturally have turned to Boccaccio, who simply had a more prestigious reputation for erudition. Moreover, Christine's female audience—*Cité des dames* manuscripts were usually owned by daughters of the aristocracy or the mercantile elite—was hardly the readership likely to enlarge her reputation as a scholar, since they themselves had so little authority in this area. When men did read *Cité des dames,* they often found it alarming. Ansley translated it into English, for example, but expressed misgivings about its subject and altered Christine's treatment of chastity. It seems likely, then, that many later scholars simply had not read Christine's catalog attentively or at all. Consequently, it was not even the most influential of her own works, let alone among the medieval catalogs of women.

The catalog of women did develop an early polemic in defense of women, but also perpetuated a very ancient misogynistic tradition. The catalog's legacy was largely conservative because misogynistic thought continued to dominate. The minority opinion voiced by a woman was heard but forgotten, abruptly arrested in time.

Yet even though Christine's collection was forgotten by mid-Renaissance, recent scholars have taken up many of its aims. Feminist scholars have made important such issues as reclaiming the lost history of women, reopening the discussion on femineity, examining the male canon, and refuting literary misogyny. Many anthologies, dictionaries of famous women, and compilations of compensatory history have been assembled in the last two decades, material it is possible to view as the last ripple of this ancient catalog legacy. Arguably and ironically, then, *Cité des dames*'s model for linking femineity with the problems of community and cultural identity is bearing late but important fruit. And the catalog tradition, albeit in different forms, is still exercising some authority in the life of letters.

Works Consulted

I. Primary Sources

Augustine of Hippo. *Concerning the City of God against the Pagans.* Trans. Henry Bettenson. London: Penguin, 1972.

Andreas Capellanus. *The Art of Courtly Love.* Trans. John J. Parry. 1941. Reprint. New York: Norton, 1979.

Bede. *Libellus de Muliere Forti.* Vol. 91 of *Patrologiae cura completus ser. Latina,* ed. J. P. Migne. cols. 1039–54. Paris, 1844–64.

Bernardus Silvestris. *The Cosmography of Bernardus Silvestris.* Trans. W. Wetherbee. New York: Columbia University Press, 1973.

Boccaccio, Giovanni. *Boccaccio on Poetry.* Trans. Charles G. Osgood. Princeton: Princeton University Press, 1930.

———. *De casibus virorum illustrium.* Vol. 9 of *Tutte le Opere di Giovanni Boccaccio,* ed. Vittore Branca. Florence: Arnolado Mondadori, 1967–70.

———. *De mulieribus claris.* Vol. 10 of *Tutte le Opere di Giovanni Boccaccio,* ed. Vittore Branca. Florence: Arnolado Mondadori, 1967–70.

Chaucer, Geoffrey. "The Legend of Good Women." In *The Works of Geoffrey Chaucer,* ed. F. N. Robinson, 480–518. 2d ed. Boston: Houghton Mifflin, 1961.

Christine de Pizan. *Le Livre de la Cité des Dames.* In Vol. 2 of "The *Livre de la Cité des Dames* of Christine de Pizan: A Critical Edition," ed. Maureen Curnow. Ph.D. diss., Vanderbilt University, 1975.

———. *A Medieval Woman's Mirror of Honor: The Treasury of the City of Ladies.* Trans. Charity Willard. New York: Persea Books, 1989.

Geoffrey of Vinsauf. *Poetria Nova.* Trans. Margaret Nims. Toronto: Pontifical Institute of Medieval Studies, 1967.

Guillaume de Lorris and Jean de Meun. *Le Roman de la Rose.* Ed. Daniel Poirion. Paris: Garnier-Flammard, 1974.

Hesiod. "Eoiae." In *Homeric Hymns and Homerica,* trans. Hugh Evelyn-White, 154–220. Cambridge, Masss.: Harvard University Press, 1959.

Higden, Ralph. *Polychronicon Ranulphi Higden: together with the English translations of John Trevisa and of an unknown writer of the fifteenth century.* Ed. C. Babington and J. R. Lumby. London, 1865–86.

Homer. *The Odyssey.* Trans. Robert Fitzgerald. New York: Anchor, 1963.

Isidore of Seville. *Etymologiarum sive Originem Libri xx.* Ed. W. M. Lindsay. 2 vols. Oxford: Clarendon, 1911.

Jacobus de Vitrus. *The Exempla or Illustrative Stories from the Sermones vulgares of Jacques de Vitry.* Ed. Thomas Crane. 1890. Reprint. New York: Burt Franklin, 1971.

Jerome, Saint. *Epistola Adversus Jovinianum.* In vol. 23 of *Patrologiae cura completus ser. Latina,* ed. J. P. Migne. cols. 211–337. Paris: 1844–64.

Juvenal. "Satire Six." *Juvenal and Perseus,* ed. G. G. Ramsay, 82–135. Cambridge, Mass.: Harvard University Press, 1956.

Map, Walter. *De nugis curialium.* Oxford: Clarendon, 1983.

Matheolus. *Les lamentations de Matheolus et le livre de léese de Jehann Le Fèvre de Ressous.* Paris, 1905.

Ovid. *Heroides.* Ed. Arthur Palmer. Hildesheim: Georg Olms Verlagsbuchhandlung, 1967.

Plutarch. "Mulierum Virtutes." In vol. 3 of *Plutarch's Moralia,* trans. Frank C. Babbitt, 474–583. Cambridge, Mass.: Harvard University Press, 1949.

Semonides of Amorgos. *Women of the Species: Semonides on Women.* Ed. and trans. Hugh Lloyd-Jones and Marcelle Quinton. Park Ridge, N. J.: Noyes Press, 1975.

Virgil. *Eclogues, Georgics, and Aeneid: Books 1–6.* Cambridge, Mass.: Harvard University Press, 1956.

II. Secondary Sources

Aiken, P. "Chaucer's *Legend of Cleopatra* and the *Speculum Historiale.*" *Speculum* 13 (1938): 232–36.

Allen, Judson. *The Ethical Poetic of the Latter Middle Ages: A Decorum of Convenient Distinction.* Toronto: University of Toronto Press, 1982.

Allen, Peter. "Reading Chaucer's Good Women." *Chaucer Review* 21 (1986–87): 419–34.

Altman, Leslie. "Christine de Pizan: Professional Woman of Letters." In *Women Scholars: A Tradition of Learned Women Before 1800,* ed. J. R. Brink, 7–23. Montreal: Eden Press, 1980.

Ames, Ruth. "The Feminist Connections of Chaucer's *Legend of Good Women.*" In *Chaucer in the Eighties,* ed. Julian Wasserman and Robert Blanch, 57–74. Syracuse: Syracuse University Press, 1986.

Amy, Ernest F. *The Text of Chaucer's "Legend of Good Women."* New York: Haskell, 1965.

Anderson, W. S. "Juvenal 6: A Problem in Structure." *Classical Philology* 51 (1956): 73–94.

———. "Juvenal and Quintilian." *Yale Classical Studies* 17 (1961): 3–96.

———. "*Lascivia* vs. *ira:* Martial and Juvenal." *California Studies in Classical Antiquity* 3 (1970): 1–34.

———. "The 'Heroides.'" In *Ovid,* ed. J. W. Binns, 49–83. London: Routledge and Kegan Paul, 1973.

Arthur, Marilyn. "Early Greece: The Origins of the Western Attitude toward Women."

In *Women in the Ancient World: The Arethusa Papers*, ed. John Peradotto and J. P. Sullivan, 7–58. Albany: State University of New York Press, 1984.

Baird, J. L. "*Secte* and *Suite* Again: Chaucer and Langland." *Chaucer Review* 6 (1971): 117–19.

Baird-Lange, Lorrayne Y. *A Bibliography of Chaucer, 1974–85*. Hamden, Conn.: Archon Books, 1988.

Baker, Herschel. *The Race of Time: Three Lectures on Renaissance Historiography*. Toronto: University of Toronto Press, 1967.

Barolini, Teodelina. "Giovanni Boccaccio." In *European Writers*, ed. W. T. H. Jackson and George Stade, 509–34. New York: Scribners, 1983.

Barricelli, Jean-Pierre. "Satire of Satires: Boccaccio's 'Corbaccio.'" *Italian Quarterly* 18 (1975): 95–111.

Baugh, Albert. *Chaucer*. Arlington Heights, Ill.: AHM, 1977.

Baum, Paull. "Chaucer's 'Glorious Legende.'" *Modern Language Notes* 60 (1945): 377–380.

Becker, P.A. "Christine de Pizan." *Zeitschrift für Französische Sprache und Literatur* 54 (1930–31): 129–64.

Bell, Susan Groag. "Christine de Pizan (1364–1430): Humanism and the Problem of a Studious Woman." *Feminist Studies* 3 (1976): 173–84.

Bergin, Thomas. *Boccaccio*. New York: Viking, 1981.

Bickel, Ernst. *Diatribe in Seneca philosophi fragmenta*. Leipzig: B. G. Teubneri, 1915.

Bilderbeck, James Bourdillon. *Chaucer's* Legend of Good Women: *The Character and Relations of the Manuscripts, the Prologues, Some Doubtful Readings*. London: Hazell, Watson and Viney, 1902.

Bloomfield, Morton. "Chaucer's Sense of History." *Journal of English and Germanic Philology* 51 (1952): 301–13.

Boitani, Piero. *Chaucer and Boccaccio*. Medium Aevum Monographs, n.s., 8. Oxford: Clarendon, 1977.

Bono, Barbara. *Literary Transvaluation: From the Vergilian Epic to Shakesperean Tragicomedy*. Berkeley: University of California Press, 1984.

Bornstein, Diane. "An Analogue to Chaucer's *Clerk's Tale*." *Chaucer Review* 15 (1980–81): 322–31.

———, ed. *Ideals for Women in the Works of Christine de Pizan*. Michigan Consortium for Medieval and Early Modern Studies 1. Ann Arbor, 1981.

Bozzolo, Carla. "Il *Decameron* come fonte del *Livre de la cité des dames* de Christine de Pisan." In *Miscellanea di studi e ricerche sul Quattrocento francese*, ed. F. Simone, 3–24. Turin: Giappichelli, 1967.

———. *Manuscrits des traductions françaises d'oeuvres de Boccace XVe siècle*. Medioevo e Umanesimo, 15. Padua: Antenore, 1973.

———. "Manuscrits des traductions françaises d'oeuvres de Boccace dans les bibliothèques de France." *Italia Medioevale e Umanistica* 11 (1968): 1–69.

Branca, Vittore. *Boccaccio: The Man and His Works*. Trans. Richard Morges and Denise J. McAuliffe. New York: New York University Press, 1976.

Brandt, W. J. *The Shape of Medieval History: Studies in Modes of Perception*. New Haven: Yale University Press, 1966.

Breisach, Ernst, ed. *Classical Rhetoric and Medieval Historiography*. Studies in Medieval Culture 19. Kalamazoo, Mich.: Medieval Institute Publications, 1985.

Bremmond, Claude, and Jacques LeGoff. *L' "exemplum."* Typologie des Sources du Moyen Age Occidental, 40. Turnhout, Belgium: Brepols, 1982.

Brewer, Derek. *Tradition and Innovation in Chaucer*. London: MacMillan, 1982.

———. *An Introduction to Chaucer*. New York: Longman, 1984.

Brown, Marshall. "In the Valley of the Ladies." *Italian Quarterly* 18 (1972): 33–52.

Brownlee, Kevin. "Discourse of the Self: Christine de Pizan and the *Rose*." *Romanic Review* 79 (1988): 199–221.

Brucker, Gene. *Florentine Politics and Society 1343–1378*. Princeton: Princeton University Press, 1962.

Bühler, C.F. "The *Fleurs de Toutes Vertus* and Christine de Pizan's *L'Epître d'Othéa*." *PMLA* 62 (1947): 32–44.

Bumgardner, George H. "Tradition and Modernity, 1380–1405: Christine de Pizan." Ph.D. diss., Yale University, 1970.

Burgess, Theodore. *Epideictic Literature*. Chicago: University of Chicago Press, 1902.

Campbell, P. G. C. L'Epître d'Othéa: *étude sur les sources de Christine de Pizan*. Paris: Champion, 1924.

———. "Christine de Pisan en Angleterre." *Revue de Littérature Comparée* 5 (1925): 659–70.

Canon, Harold. Introduction to *Ovid's Heroides*, trans. Canon, 7–14. New York: Dutton, 1971.

Cerbo, Anna. "Il 'De mulieribus claris' di Giovanni Boccaccio." *Arcadia, Accademia Letteraria Italiana, Attie e Memorie*. 7 (1974): 51–75.

———. "Didone in Boccaccio." *Annali Istituto Universitario Orientale, Napoli, Sezione Romanza* 21 (1979): 177–219.

Cherniss, Michael. "Chaucer's Last Dream Vision: The Prologue to the *Legend of Good Women*." *Chaucer Review* 20 (1986): 183–99.

Child, C. G. "Chaucer's 'Legend of Good Women' and Boccaccio's 'De Genealogia Deorum.'" *Modern Language Notes* 11 (1896): 475–87.

Clasby, Eugene. "Chaucer's Constance: Womanly Virtue and the Heroic Life." *Chaucer Review* 13 (1979): 221–33.

Clogan, Paul M. "Chaucer's 'Legend of Good Women.'" *Explicator* 23 (1964), item 61.

Clubb, Louise George. "Boccaccio and the Boundaries of Love." *Italica* 37 (1960): 188–96.

Cowen, Janet M. "Chaucer's *Legend of Good Women*: Structure and Tone." *Studies in Philology* 82 (Fall 1985): 416–36.

Cropp, Glynnis M. "Boèce et Christine de Pizan." *Le Moyen Age* 87 (1981): 387–417.

Cummings, Hubertis M. *The Indebtedness of Chaucer's Work to the Italian Works of Boccaccio: A Review and Summary*. New York: Haskell, 1965.

Curnow, Maureen. "The Boke of the Cyte of Ladyes, an English Translation of Christine de Pisan's *Le Livre de la Cité des dames*." *Les Bonnes Feuilles* 3 (1974): 116–37.

———. "The *Livre de la cité des dames* of Christine de Pisan: A Critical Edition." 2 vols. Ph.D. diss., Vanderbilt University, 1975.

Curtius, E. R. *European Literature and the Latin Middle Ages.* Trans. Willard Trask. Bolligen Series, no. 36. Princeton: Princeton University Press, 1973.

David, Alfred. *The Strumpet Muse: Art and Morals in Chaucer's Poetry.* Bloomington: Indiana University. Press, 1976.

Davis, Natalie Z. "Gender and Genre: Women as Historical Writers 1400–1820." In *Beyond their Sex: Learned Women of the European Past,* ed. P. H. Labalme, 153–82. New York: New York University Press, 1980.

Delany, Sheila. "The Logic of Obscenity in Chaucer's *Legend of Good Women.*" *Florilegium* 7 (1985): 189–205.

———. "Rewriting Women Good: Gender and the Anxiety of Influence in Two Late Medieval Texts." In *Chaucer in the Eighties,* ed. J. Wasserman and Robert Blanch, 75–92. Syracuse: Syracuse University Press, 1986.

———. "Geoffrey of Monmouth and Chaucer's *Legend of Good Women.*" *Chaucer Review* 22 (1987): 170–175.

———. "Mothers to Think Back Through: Who Are They? The Ambiguous Example of Christine de Pizan." In *Medieval Texts and Contemproary Readers.* Ed. Laurie Finke and Martin Shichtman, 77–97. Ithaca, N.Y.: Cornell University Press, 1987.

———. "The Naked Text: Chaucer's 'Thisbe,' the Ovide Moralisee, and the Problem of Translatio Studii in the *Legend of Good Women.*" *Mediaevalia: A Journal of Mediaeval Studies* 13 (1987) 275–94.

Delhaye, Phillipe. "Le Dossier anti-matrimonial de l'*Adversus Jovinianum* et son influence sur quelques écrits latins du XIIe siècle." *Mediaeval Studies* 13 (1951): 65–86.

Dodd, William G. *Courtly Love in Chaucer and Gower.* Boston: Ginn, 1913.

Dow, Blanche H. *The Varying Attitudes toward Women in French Literature of the Fifteenth Century: the Opening Years.* New York: Publications of the Institute for French Studies, 1936.

Duby, Georges, and Philippe Braunstein. "The Emergence of the Individual." In *Revelations of the Medieval World.* 507–633. Vol. 2 of *The History of Private Life.* Cambridge, Mass.: Harvard University Press, 1988.

Dulac, Lillian. "Un mythe didactique chez Christine de Pizan: Sémiramis ou la veuve héroique." In *Mélanges de philologie romane offerts à Charles Camproux,* 315–43. Montpellier: Centre d'Etudes Occitanes de l'Université Paul Valéry, 1978.

Ecker, Gisela, ed. *Feminist Aesthetics.* Trans. Harriet Anderson. Boston: Beacon Press, 1985.

Edmonds, B. D. "Aspects of Christine de Pizan's Political and Social Ideas." Ph.D. diss., University of Maryland, 1972.

Erickson, Carolly. *The Medieval Vision.* New York: Oxford University Press, 1976.

Estrich, Robert N. "Chaucer's Maturing Art in the Prologues to the *Legend of Good Women.*" *Journal of English and Germanic Philology* 36 (1937): 326–37.

———. "Chaucer's Prologue to the *Legend of Good Women* and Marchaut's *Le Jugement dou Roy de Navarre.*" *Studies in Philology* 36 (1939): 20–39.

————. "A Study of Sources and Influences of Chaucer's 'Legend of Good Women.'" Ph.D. diss., Ohio State University, 1945.

Ferrante, Joan. *Woman as Image in Medieval Literature from the Twelfth Century to Dante.* New York: Columbia University Press, 1973.

Ferrier, J. M. *French Prose Writers of the Fourteenth and Fifteenth Centuries.* Oxford: Pergamon, 1966.

Finkel, Helen R. "The Portrait of Woman in the Works of Christine de Pisan." Ph.D. diss., Rice University, 1972.

————. "The Portrait of the Woman in the Works of Christine de Pisan." *Les Bonnes Feuilles* 3 (Fall 1974): 138–51.

Finley, John. *Homer's Odyssey.* Cambridge, Mass.: Harvard University Press, 1978.

Fisher, John H. "The Revision of the Prologue to the *Legend of Good Women:* An Occasional Explanation." *South Atlantic Review* 43 (1978): 75–84.

Foster, Judith. *Chaucer on Interpretation.* Cambridge: Cambridge University Press, 1985.

Frank, Robert. "The Legend of the *Legend of Good Women.*" *Chaucer Review* 1 (1966): 110–133.

————. *Chaucer and the Legend of Good Women.* Cambridge, Mass.: Harvard University Press, 1972.

French, John C. *The Problem of the Two Prologues to Chaucer's* Legend of Good Women. 1905. Reprint. New York: AMS, 1973.

Fyler, John M. *Chaucer and Ovid.* New Haven: Yale University Press, 1979.

Gabriel, Astrik L. "The Educational Ideals of Christine de Pisan." *Journal of the History of Ideas* 16 (1955): 3–21.

Galway, Margaret. "Chaucer's Sovereign Lady: A Study of the Prologue to the *Legend* and Related Poems." *Modern Language Review* 33 (1938): 145–99.

Gardner, John. "The Two Prologues to the 'Legend of Good Women'." *Journal of English and Germanic Philology* (1967): 594–611.

————. *The Poetry of Chaucer.* Carbondale: Southern Illinois Press, 1977.

Garrett, Robert Max. "'Cleopatra the Martyr' and Her Sisters." *Journal of English and Germanic Philology* 22 (1923): 64–74.

Gathercole, Patricia. "A Frenchman's Praise of Boccaccio." *Italica* 40 (1963): 225–230.

————. "Paintings on Manuscripts of Laurent de Premierfait." *Studi sul Boccaccio* 4 (1967): 296–316.

————. "Boccaccio in French." *Studi sul Boccaccio* 5 (1969): 275–97.

————. "The French Translators of Boccaccio." *Italica* 46 (1969): 300–309.

————. "Boccaccio in English." *Studi sul Boccaccio* 7 (1973): 353–68.

Gauvard, Christine. "Christine de Pisan, a-t-elle eu une pensée politique? A propos d'ouvrages récents." *Revue Historique* 250 (1973): 417–30.

Gaylord, Alan. "Dido at Hunt, Chaucer at Work." *Chaucer Review* 17 (1983): 300–315.

Gellrich, Jessie. *The Idea of the Book in the Middle Ages: Language, Theory, Mythology, and Fiction.* Ithaca, N.Y.: Cornell University Press, 1985.

Ghosh, P. C. "Cleopatra's Death in Chaucer's 'Legende of Gode Women.'" *Modern Language Review* 26 (1931): 332–36.

Gilmore, M. A. "The Renaissance Concept of the Lessons of History." In *Humanists and Jurists: Six Studies in the Renaissance,* ed. Gilmore, 1–37. Cambridge, Mass.: Harvard University Press, 1963.

Goddard, H. C. "Chaucer's *Legend of Good Women.*" *Journal of English and Germanic Philology* 7 (1908): 87–129.

———. "Chaucer's *Legend of Good Women* II." *Journal of English and Germanic Philology* 8 (1909): 47–111.

Godman, Peter. "Chaucer and Boccaccio's Latin Work." In *Chaucer and Boccaccio,* ed. Piero Boitani, 269–95. Medium Aevum Monograms, N. S., 8. Oxford: Clarendon, 1977.

Golenistcheff-Koutouzoff, E. *L'Histoire de Griseldis en France au XIVe et XVe Siècle.* 1933. Reprint. Geneva: Slatkine, 1975.

Gottlieb, Beatrice. "The Problem of Feminism in the Fifteenth Century." In *Women of the Medieval World: Essays In Honor of John Mundy,* ed. Suzanne F. Wemple and Julius Kirstina, 337–62. London: Blackwell, 1985.

Green, Richard H. "Nature and Love in the Late Middle Ages." *Modern Language Notes* 79 (1964): 58–70.

Green, V. H. H. *Medieval Civilization in Western Europe.* London: Edward Arnold, 1971.

Griffith, D. D. "An Interpretation of Chaucer's *Legend of Good Women.*" In *Manly Anniversary Studies,* ed. J. Manly, 32–41. Chicago: University of Chicago Press, 1923.

Grimal, P., ed. *Histoire mondiale de la femme.* Paris: Nouvelle Libraire de France, 1974.

———, ed. *The Dictionary of Classical Mythology.* Trans. A. R. Maxwell-Hyslop. London: Blackwell, 1986.

Guarino, Guido. Introduction to *Concerning Famous Women,* by Giovanni Boccaccio, trans. Guarino. New Brunswick, N.J.: Rutgers University Press, 1963.

Hadas, Moses. *A History of Greek Literature.* New York: Columbia University Press, 1962.

Hagendahl, H. *Augustine and the Latin Classics.* Studia Graeca et Latina Gothoburgensis, 21. Göteborg: Flanders Boklryskeri Altiebolga, 1967.

Hall, Louis Brewer. "Chaucer and the Dido and Aeneas Story." *Mediaeval Studies* 25 (1963): 148–59.

Hamer, Mary. "Cleopatra: Housewife." *Textual Practice* 2 (1988): 159–79.

Hansen, Elaine Tuttle. "Irony and the Antifeminist Narrator in Chaucer's *Legend of Good Women.*" *Journal of English and Germanic Philology* 82 (1983): 11–31.

Harder, Henry L. "Livy in Gower's and Chaucer's Lucrece Story." *Publications of the Missouri Philological Association* 2 (1977): 1–7.

Hardison, O. B. Jr. *The Enduring Monument: A Study of the Idea of Praise in Renaissance Literary Theory and Practice.* Chapel Hill, North Carolina: University of North Carolina Press, 1962.

Haskell, Ann S. "The Portrayl of Women by Chaucer and His Age." In *What Manner of Woman: Essays on English Literature and American Life and History,* ed. Marlene Springer, 1–14. New York: New York University Press, 1977.

Hauvette, H. *Les plus anciennes traductions françaises de Boccacce (XIVe–VIIe siècles)*. Bordeaux: Feret, 1909.

Hay, Denys. *The Italian Renaissance in Its Historical Background*. 2d. ed. Cambridge: Cambridge University Press, 1961.

Heisch, Allison. "Queen Elizabeth I and the Persistence of Patriarchy." *Feminist Review* 4 (1980): 45–56.

Hentsch, A. A. *De la littérature didactique du moyen âge s'addressant spécialement aux femmes*. Cahors: A. Couestant, 1903.

Herlihy, David. "Land, Family, and Women in Continental Europe, 701–1200." In *Women in Medieval Society*, ed. Susan Stuard, 13–46. Philadelphia: University of Pennsylvania Press, 1976.

Hieatt, Constance B. *The Realism of the Dream Vision: The Poetic Exploration of the Dream-Experience in Chaucer and His Contemporaries*. The Hague: Mouton and Co., 1967.

Highet, Gilbert. *Juvenal the Satirist*. Oxford: Clarendon, 1954.

Hindman, Sandra. "With Ink and Mortar: Christine de Pizan's *Cité des Dames*: An Art Essay." *French Studies* 10 (Fall 1984): 457–84.

Howard, Donald. *Chaucer: His Life, His Works, His World*. New York: Dutton, 1987.

Huot, Sylvia. "Seduction and Sublimation: Christine de Pizan, Jean de Meun, and Dante." *Romance Notes* 25 (Spring 1985): 361–73.

Huppé, Bernard F. "Chaucer: A Criticism and a Reply." *Modern Language Review* 43 (1948): 393–99.

Ignatius, Mary Ann. "A Look at the Feminism of Christine de Pizan." *Proceedings of the Pacific Northwest Conference on Foreign Languages* 29 (1978): 18–21.

Jacobson, Howard. *Ovid's 'Heroides.'* Princeton: Princeton University Press, 1974.

Jeanroy, Alfred. "Boccace et Christine de Pizan: le *De claris mulieribus* principale source du *Livre de la cité des dames*." *Romania* 48 (1922): 93–105.

Jefferson, Bernard L. "Queen Anne and Queen Alcestis." *Journal of English and Germanic Philology* 13 (1914): 434–43.

Johnson, W. R. *Darkness Visible: A Study of Vergil's Aeneid*. Berkeley: University of California Press, 1976.

Jones, Christopher. *Plutarch and Rome*. Oxford: Clarendon, 1971.

Jordan, Constance. "Boccaccio's In-famous Women: Gender and Civic Virtue in *De mulieribus claris*." In *Ambiguous Realities: Women in the Middle Ages and Renaissance*, ed. Carole Levin and Jeanie Watson, 25–47. Detroit: Wayne State University Press, 1987.

Joukovsky-Micha. F. "La Notion de vaine gloire de Simund de Freine à Martin Le Franc." *Romania* 87 (1968): 1–30; 210–39.

Kallendorf, Creg. "Boccaccio's Dido and the Rhetorical Art of Virgil's *Aeneid*." *Studies in Philology* 82 (Fall 1985): 401–415.

Kelly, F. D. "Reflections on the Role of Christine de Pisan as a Feminist Writer." *Sub-Stance* 2 (Winter 1972): 63–71.

Kelly, Henry. *Love and Marriage in the Age of Chaucer*. Ithaca, N.Y.: Cornell University Press, 1975.

Kelly, J. N. D. *Jerome: His Life, Writings, and Controversies*. New York: Harper and Row, 1975.

Kelly, Joan. "Did Women Have a Renaissance?" In *Becoming Visible: Women in European History*, ed., Renate Bridenthal and Claudia Koonz, 139–64. Boston: Houghton Mifflin, 1977.

——. "Early Feminist Theory and Querelle des Femmes, 1400–1789." *Signs* 8 (1982): 4–28.

Kelso, Ruth. *The Doctrine of the Lady of the Renaissance*. Urbana: University of Illinois Press, 1956.

Kemp-Welch, A. *Of Six Mediaeval Women*. London: Macmillan, 1913.

Kennedy, Angus. *Christine de Pizan*. London: Grant and Cutler, 1984.

Kennedy, G. A. *Classical Rhetoric and Its Secular Tradition from Ancient to Medieval Time*. Chapel Hill: University of North Carolina Press, 1980.

Kisser, Lisa. *Telling Classical Tales*. Ithaca, N.Y.: Cornell University Press, 1983.

Kittredge, George L. "Chaucer's Alceste." *Modern Philology* 6 (1908–9): 435–49.

Knopp, Sharon. "Chaucer and Jean de Meun as Self-Conscious Narrators: The Prologue to the *Legend of Good Women* and the *Roman de la Rose* 10307–680." *Comitatus* 4 (1973): 25–39.

Kökeritz, Helge. "Rhetorical Word Play in Chaucer." *PMLA* 69 (1954): 937–52.

Kolve, V. A. "From Cleopatra to Alceste: An Iconographic Study of the *Legend of Good Women*." In *Signs and Symbols in Chaucer's Poetry*, ed. John Burke, Jr, 130–78. Birmingham, Ala.: University of Alabama Press, 1981.

Koonce, B. G. *Chaucer and the Tradition of Fame: Symbolism in the House of Fame*. Princeton: Princeton University Press, 1966.

Koone, B. "Satan the Fowler." *Mediaeval Studies* 21 (1959): 176–84.

Kristeller, Paul Oskar. *Renaissance Thought: The Classical, Scholastic, and Humanist Strains*. New York: Harper and Row, 1961.

Labalme, Particia, ed. *Beyond their Sex: Learned Women of the European Past*. New York: State University of New York Press, 1980.

La Hoed, Marvin J. "Chaucer's Cybele and the *Liber Imaginum Deorum*." *Philological Quarterly* 43 (1964): 272–76.

Laidlaw, J. C. "Christine de Pizan—An Author's Progress." *Modern Language Review* 78 (1983): 532–50.

Laigle, M. *Le Livre des trois vertus de Christine de Pisan et son milieu historique et littéraire*, Bibliothéque du XVe Siècle, 16. Paris: Champion, 1912.

Larner, John. *Italy in the Age of Dante and Petrarch, 1216–1300*. New York: Longman, 1980.

Lattimore, R. Introduction to *Hesiod*, by Hesiod, trans. Lattimore. Ann Arbor: University of Michigan Press, 1959.

Layman, Beverly J. "Boccaccio's Paradigm of the Artist and His Art." *Italian Quarterly* 13 (1970): 19–36.

Leach, Eleanor W. "Morwe of May: A Season of Feminine Ambiguity." In *Acts of Interpretation: The Text in its Contexts*, ed. Mary J. Carruthers and Elizabeth D. Kirk, 299–310. Norman, Ok.: Pilgrim, 1982.

Lecoy de la Marche, Albert. *La chaire française au moyen âge, spécialement au XIII siècle*. Paris: Libraire Renouard, 1886.

Leff, Gordon. *Medieval Thought: Augustine to Ockham*. Baltimore: Penguin, 1958.

Le Goff, Jacques. *Medieval Civilization 400–1604*. Trans. Julia Barrow. London: Blackwell, 1988.

Lightman, Margorie and William Zeisal. *"Univira:* An Example of Change and Continuity in Roman Society." *Church History* 46 (1977): 19–23.

Lipschy, Anna Laura. "Boccaccio Studies in English 1945–69." *Studi sul Boccaccio* 6 (1971): 211–29.

Lloyd, G. E. *Polarity and Analogy: Two Types of Argumentation in Early Greek Thought*. Cambridge: Cambridge University Press, 1971.

Loukopoulos, H. D. "Classical Myths in the Works of Christine de Pizan with an edition of *L'Epistre d'Othea* from the Manuscript Harley 4431." Ph.D. diss., Wayne State University, 1977.

Lowes, John L. "The Prologue to the *Legend of Good Women* as Related to the French Marguerite Poems and the *'Filostrato.'*" *PMLA* 19 (1904): 593–683.

———. "The Prologue to the *Legend of Good Women* Considered in Its Chronological Relations." *PMLA* 20 (1905): 749–864.

———. "Is Chaucer's *Legend of Good Women* A Travesty?" *Journal of English and Germanic Philology* 8 (1909): 513–65.

McCall, John P. *Chaucer among the Gods*. University Park, Pa.: Pennsylvania State University Press, 1979.

McCall, John. "Chaucer and the Pseudo-Origen *De Maria Magdalena: A Preliminary Study*." *Speculum* 46 (1971): 491–509.

McLaughlin, Eleanor. "Equality of Souls, Inequality of Sexes: Women in Medieval Theology." In *Religion and Sexism,* ed. Rosemary Reuther, 213–66. New York: Simon and Schuster, 1974.

McLaughlin, John C. "The Honour and the Humble Obeysance: Prologue to the 'Legend of Good Women' L135 G Text." *Philological Quarterly* 38 (1959): 515–16.

Maclean, Ian. *The Renaissance Notion of Woman: A Study in the Fortunes of Scholasticism and Medical Science in European Intellectual Life*. Cambridge: Cambridge University Press, 1983.

McLeod, Enid. *The Order of the Rose: The Life and Ideas of Christine de Pizan*. London: Chatto and Windus, 1976.

McMillan, Anne. "Ever an Hundred Good Ageyn Oon Badde." Ph.D. diss., Indiana University, 1979.

———. Introduction to *The Legend of Good Women* by Geoffrey Chaucer, trans. A. McMillan. Houston: Rice University, 1987.

McNamara, Jo Ann. "Sexual Equality and the Cult of the Virgin in Early Christian Thought." *Feminist Studies* 3 (1976): 145–58.

———. *A New Song: Celibate Women in the First Three Christian Centuries*. New York: Haworth Press, 1983.

Massimo, Miglio. "Boccaccio biografia." In *Boccaccio in Europe,* ed. Gilbert Tournoy, 149–63. Proceedings of the Boccaccio Conference, Louvain. December 1975. Louvain: Leuven University Press, 1977.

Mazzotta, Giuseppe. *"The Decameron:* The Marginality of Literature." *University of Toronto Quarterly* 42 (Fall 1972): 64–81.

————. *The World at Play in Boccaccio's "Decameron."* Princeton: Princeton University Press, 1986.

Meech, Sanford B. "Chaucer and an Italian Translation of the *Heroides*." *PMLA* 45 (1930): 110–28.

————. "Chaucer and the *Ovide Moralisé*." *PMLA* (1931): 182–204.

Meyer, Paul. "Plaidoyer en faveur des femmes." *Romania* 6 (1817): 499–503.

————. "Les Prémières Compilations Françaises d'Histoire Ancienne." *Romania* 14 (1885): 1–81.

Mikhailov, A. D. "Deux Etapes de l'utopisme au temps de la Renaissance." In vol. 2 of *Mélanges à la Memoire de Franco Simone: France et Italie dans la culture européene*, 251–59. Geneva: Slatkine, 1980–84.

Minnis, A. J. "The Influences of Academic Prologues on the Prologues and Literary Attitudes of Late-Medieval English Writers." *Mediaeval Studies* 43 (1981): 342–83.

————. *Chaucer and Pagan Antiquity.* Cambridge: Cambridge University Press, 1982.

————. *Medieval Theory of Authorship.* 2d ed. Philadelphia: University of Pennsylvania Press, 1988.

Mombello, G. *La tradizione manoscritta dell' 'Epistre Othea' di Christine de Pizan: Prolegomeni all'edizione del testo.* Torino: Accademia delle Scienze, 1967.

————. "Quelques aspects de la pensée politique de Christine de Pizan d'après ses oeuvres publiées." In *Culture et Politique en France à l'époque de l'humanisme et de la Renaissance*, ed. F. Simone, 43–153. Torino: Accademia delle Scienze, 1974.

Moore, Samuel. "The Prologue to Chaucer's *Legend of Good Women* in Relation to Queen Anne and Richard." *Modern Language Review* 7 (1912): 488–93.

Morris, Lynn King. *Chaucer: Source and Analogue Criticism: A Cross-Referenced Guide.* New York: Garland, 1985.

Mosher, Joseph A. *The Exemplum in the Early Religious and Didactic Literature of England.* New York: Columbia University Press, 1911.

Murlaugh, Daniel M. "Women and Geoffrey Chaucer." *ELH* 38: 473–92.

Murphy, James. *Rhetoric in the Middle Ages: A History of Rhetorical Theory from St. Augustine to the Renaissance.* Berkeley: University of California Press, 1974.

Nepaulsingh, Colbert. "Juan Ruiz, Boccacio and the Antifeminist Tradition." *Coronica* 9 (1971): 13–18.

Nims, Margaret. "*Translatio:* 'Difficult Statement' in Medieval Poetic Theory." *University of Toronto Quarterly* 43 (Spring 1974): 215–30.

Nys, Ernest. *Christine de Pisan et ses principales oeuvres.* La Haye: Martinus Nijhoff, 1914.

Ouy, G. "Paris l'un des principaux foyers de l'humanisme en Europe au début du XVe siècle." *Bulletin de la Societé de l'Histoire de Paris et de l'Ile de France* 70 (1967–68): 71–98.

————. "Le dialecte des rapports intellectuels franco-italiens et l'humanisme en France aux XIVè et XVè siècles." In *Rapporti culturali ed economici fra Italia e Francia nei secoli dal XIV al XVI: Atti del Colloquio Italo-Francese, Roma 18—20 Febbraio, 1978*, 137–56. Rome: Giunta Centrale, 1979.

Overbeck, Pat Trefzgar. "Chaucer's Good Woman." *Chaucer Review* 2 (1967–68): 75–94.

Owst, G. R. *Preaching in Medieval England: An Introduction to Sermon Manuscripts of the Period, c. 1350–1450.* Cambridge: Cambridge University Press, 1926.

———. *Literature and the Pulpit in Medieval England: A Neglected Chapter in the History of English Letters and the English People.* New York: Barnes and Noble, 1961.

Page, Denys. *The Homeric Odyssey.* Oxford: Clarendon, 1955.

Pagel, Elaine. *Adam, Eve, and the Serpent.* New York: Random House, 1988.

Parr, Johnstone. "Chaucer's Semiramis." *Chaucer Review* 5 (1970): 57–61.

Payne, Robert. *The Key of Remembrance: A Study of Chaucer's Poetics.* New Haven: Yale University Press, 1963.

———. "Making His Own Myth: The Prologue to Chaucer's *Legend of Good Women.*" *Chaucer Review* 9 (1974): 197–211.

Pearsall, Derek. Introduction to *The Floure and the Leafe and the Assembly of Ladies.* London: Nelson, 1962.

Peck, Russell. "Chaucer's Poetical Prologue to the *Legend of Good Women.*" In *Chaucer in the Eighties,* ed. Julian Wasserman and Robert Blanch, 39–55. Syracuse: Syracuse University Press, 1986.

Perkell, Christine G. "On Creusa, Dido, and the Quality of Victory in Virgil's 'Aeneid.'" In *Reflections of Women in Antiquity,* ed. Helene Foley, 355–77. New York: New York University Press, 1981.

Pernoud, Régine. *Christine de Pisan.* Paris: Calmann-Lévy, 1982.

Perret, Jacques. "Les Compagnes de Didon aux enfers." *Revues des études latines* 42 (1964): 247–61.

Phillippy, Patricia. "'Establishing Authority': Boccaccio's De Claris Mulieribus and Christine de Pizan's Le Livre de la Cité des Dames." *Romanic Review* 77 (1986): 167–195.

Pinet, Marie-Josèphe. *Christine de Pisan 1364–1430: étude biographique et littéraire.* 1927. Reprint. Geneva: Slatkine, 1974.

Pomeroy, Sarah. *Goddesses, Whores, Wives, and Slaves.* New York: Schocken Press, 1975.

Poschl, Viktor. *The Art of Virgil: Image and Symbol in the "Aeneid."* Trans. Gerda Seligson. Ann Arbor: University of Michigan Press, 1962.

Pratt, Robert. "Chaucer and Isidore on Why Men Marry." *Modern Language Notes* 74 (1959): 293–94.

Pullan, Brian. *A History of Early Renaissance Italy: From the Mid-Thirteenth to Mid-Fifteenth Centuries.* London: Allen Lane, 1973.

Quain, E. A. "The Medieval *Accessus ad auctores.*" *Traditio* 3 (1945): 215–64.

Quilligan, Maureen. "Allegory and the Textual Body: Women's Authority in Christine de Pizan's *Livre de la Cité des Dames.*" *Romanic Review* 79 (1988): 222–48.

Rand, E. K. *Founders of the Middle Ages.* New York: Dover, 1957.

Régnier-Bohler, Danielle. "Imagining the Self." In *Revelations of the Medieval World,* 311–95. Vol. 2 of *A History of Private Life,* ed. Georges Duby, trans. Arthur Goldhammer. Cambridge, Mass.: Harvard University Press, 1988.

Reno, Christine. *Self and Society in "L'Avision—Christine" of Christine de Pizan.* Ph.D. diss., Yale University, 1972.

———. "Christine de Pizan's Use of the *Golden Legend* in the *Cité des Dames.*" *Bonnes Feuilles* 3 (Fall 1974): 89–99.

———. "Christine de Pizan: Feminism and Irony." In *Seconda Miscellanea di Studie Ricerche sul Quattrocento Francese,* ed. Franco Simone, Jonathan Beck, and Gianni Mombello, 129–32. Chambéry/Torino: Centre d'Etudes Franco-Italien, 1981.

Rice, J. P. "A Note on Christine de Pisan and Cecco d'Ascoli." *Italica* 15 (1938): 149–51.

Richards, Earl Jeffrey. Introduction to *The Book of the City of Ladies,* by Christine de Pizan, trans. Richards. New York: Persea, 1982.

———. "Christine de Pizan and the Question of Feminist Rhetoric." *Teaching Literature through Language* 22, no. 2 (1983): 15–24.

Richardson, Lula. *The Forerunners of Feminism in French Literature of the Renaissance. Part I: From Christine de Pisan to Marie de Gournay.* Baltimore: John Hopkins University Press, 1929.

Rigaud, Rose. *Les Idées feministes de Christine de Pisan.* Neuchâtel: Attinger, 1911.

Robertson, D. W., Jr. *A Preface to Chaucer: Studies in Medieval Perspectives.* Princeton: Princeton University Press, 1962.

Romilly, Jacqueline de. *Précis de littérature Grecque.* Paris: Presses Universitaires de France, 1980.

Root, Robert W. "Chaucer's Legend of Medea." *PMLA* 24 (1909): 124–153.

Rosier, M. F. "Christine de Pisan as a Moralist." Ph.D. diss., University of Toronto, 1945.

Rouse, Richard and Mary. *Preachers, Florilegia, and Sermons.* Toronto: Pontifical Institute of Medieval Studies, 1979.

Rowe, Donald. *Through Nature to Eternity.* Lincoln: University of Nebraska Press, 1988.

Rowland, Beryl. *Companion to Chaucer Studies.* Oxford: Clarendon, 1968.

———. *Chaucer and Middle English Studies in Honor of Rossell Hope Robbins.* London: Allen and Unwin, 1974.

Ruether, Rosemary. "Misogynism and Virginal Feminism in the Fathers of the Church." In *Religion and Sexism,* ed. Rosemary Ruether, 150–83. New York: Simon and Schuster, 1974.

Sanderlin, George. "Chaucer's *Legend of Dido:* A Feminist Exemplum." *Chaucer Review* 20 (1986): 331–40.

Schibanoff, Susan. "Taking the Gold Out of Egypt: The Art of Reading as a Woman." In *Gender and Readers: Essays on Readers, Texts and Contexts,* ed. E. Flynn and P. Schweickart, 83–106. Baltimore: Johns Hopkins University Press, 1986.

Schmidt, A. M. "Christine de Pisan." *Mercure de France* 305 (1966): 158–74.

Schulenberg, J. T. "Clio's European Daughters: Myopic Modes of Perception." In *The Prism of Sex: Essays in the Sociology of Knowledge,* ed. J. A. Sherman and E. T. Beck, 33–53. Madison: University of Wisconsin Press, 1979.

Seigel, Jerrold. *Rhetoric and Philosophy in Renaissance Humanism: The Union of*

Eloquence and Wisdom, Petrarch to Valla. Princeton: Princeton University Press, 1968.

Severs, Jonathan B. *The Literary Relationships of Chaucer's Clerkes Tale.* New Haven: Yale University Press, 1942.

Seznec, Jean. *The Survival of the Pagan Gods: The Mythological Tradition and Its Place in Renaissance Humanism and Art.* Trans. B. F. Session. New York: Pantheon, 1961.

Sherman, Claire R. "Representations of Charles V of France 1338–80 as a Wise Ruler." *Medievalia et Humanistica* 2 (1971): 83–96.

Simone, Franco. "La Présence de Boccacce dans la Culture Française du XVème Siècle." *Journal of Medieval and Renaissance Studies* 1 (1971): 17–31.

Skeats, W. W., ed. *The Complete Works of Geoffrey Chaucer.* Oxford: Clarendon, 1889.

Smith, Roland. "The Limited Vision of St. Bernard." *Modern Language Notes* 61 (1946): 38–44.

Smith, Sarah Stanbury. "Chaucer's Sight in the Prologue to the *Legend of Good Women.*" *Counterpoint* 4 (Fall 1981): 95–102.

Solente, Suzanne. "Deux chapitres de l'influence littéraire de Christine de Pisan." *Bibliothèque de l'Ecole des Chartres* 94 (1933): 27–45.

———. "Christine de Pisan." In vol. 40 of *L'Histoire littéraire de la France,* 335–442. Paris: Imprimerie Nationale, 1974.

Spisak, James. "Chaucer's Pyramus and Thisbe." *Chaucer Review* 18 (1984): 204–10.

Stadter, Philip. *Plutarch's Historical Method: An Analysis of the Mulierum Virtutes.* Cambridge, Mass.: Harvard University Press, 1965.

Stuard, Susan, and Brenda Bolton, ed. *Women in Medieval Society.* Philadelphia: University of Pennsylvania Press, 1976.

Sussman, Linda. "Workers and Drones: Labor, Idleness, and Gender Definitions in Hesiod's Beehive." In *Women in the Antique World: The Arethusa Paper,* ed. John Peradotto and J. P. Sullivan, 79–93. Albany: State University of New York Press, 1984.

Tatlock, John S. P. "Chaucer and the *Legenda Aurea.*" *Modern Language Notes* 45 (1930): 296–98.

Taylor, Beverly. "The Medieval Cleopatra: The Classical and Medieval Traditions of Chaucer's *Legend of Cleopatra.*" *Journal of Mediaeval and Renaissance Studies* 7 (1977): 249–69.

Taylor, Henry O. *The Classical Heritage of the Middle Ages.* New York: Frederick Ungar, 1957.

Taylor, Willene P. "Supposed Antifeminism in Chaucer's *Troilus and Crysede* and Its Refutation in the *Legend of Good Women.*" *Xavier Review* 9 (1988–89): 1–18.

Temple, M.E. "The Fifteenth Century Idea of the Responsible State." *Romanic Review* 6 (1915): 402–33.

Thompson, David. *The Three Crowns of Florence: Humanist Assessments of Dante, Petrarch, and Boccaccio.* New York: Harpers, 1972.

Thompson, R. Ann. "The Irony of Chaucer's *Legend of Good Women* Perceived in

1576." *Archiv für das Studium der neuren Sprachen und Literaturen* 213: 342–43.

Tupper, Fredrick. "Chaucer's Lady of the Daisies." *Journal of English and Germanic Philology* 21 (1922): 293–317.

Tuve, Rosemund. *Allegorical Imagery: Some Medieval Books and Their Posterity.* Princeton: Princeton University Press, 1966.

Utley, Francis. *The Crooked Rib: An Analytical Index to the Argument about Women in English and Scots Literature to the End of the Year 1568.* Columbus: Ohio State Press, 1944.

Verducci, Florence. *Ovid's Toyshop of the Heart*: Epistulae heroidum. Princeton: Princeton University Press, 1985.

Wasserman, Julian, and R. Blanch, eds. *Chaucer in the Eighties.* Syracuse: Syracuse University Press, 1986.

Weese, Walter E. "Alceste and Joan of Kent." *Modern Language Notes* 63 (1948): 474–77.

Weiher, Carol. "Chaucer and Gower's Story of Lucretia and Virginia." *English Language Notes* 14 (1976): 7–9.

Weissman, Hope Phyllis. "Antifeminism and Chaucer's Characterizations of Women." In *Geoffrey Chaucer: A Collection of Original Articles*, ed. George Economou, 93–110. New York: McGraw-Hill, 1975.

Wiesen, David. *St. Jerome as a Satirist: A Study in Christian Latin Thought and Letters.* Ithaca, N. Y.: Cornell University Press, 1964.

Wilkins, Ernest H. "Descriptions of Pagan Divinities from Petrarch to Chaucer." *Speculum* 32 (1957): 511–22.

———. "A Survey of the Correspondence between Petrarcha and Boccaccio." *Italia Medioevale e Umanistica.* 6 (1963): 179–84.

———. *Studies on Petrarcha and Boccaccio*, ed. Aldo Bernardo. Padua: Antenore, 1978.

Wilkinson, L. P. *Ovid Recalled.* Cambridge: Cambridge University Press, 1965.

Willard, Charity C. "The Manuscript Tradition of the *Livre des Trois Vertus* and Christine de Pizan's Audience." *Journal of the History of Ideas.* 27 (1966): 433–44.

———. "A New Look at Christine de Pizan's 'L'Epistre au Dieu d'Amours.'" In *Seconda Miscellanea di Studi e Ricerchi sul Quattrocento Francese*, 71–92. Turin: Centre d'études Franco-Italien, 1981.

———. "A Fifteenth Century View of Women's Role in Medieval Society: Christine de Pizan's *Livre des Trois Vertus*." In *The Role of Women in the Middle Ages*, ed. R. T. Morewedge, 90–120. Albany: State University of New York, 1975.

———. *Christine de Pizan: Her Life and Works.* New York: Persea, 1984.

Wilson, Katharina. "Wykked Wives and Blythe Bachelors." Ph.D. diss., University of Illinois, 1978.

———. "*Figmenta* vs. *Veritas*: Change in the Perceptions of the Literary View of Women in the Middle Ages." *Tulsa Studies in Women's Literature*, 4, no. 1 (Spring 1985): 17–33.

———. Introduction to *Women Writers of the Renaissance and Reformation*, ed. Wilson. Athens, Ga.: University of Georgia Press, 1987.

————, ed. *Medieval Women Writers*. Athens, Ga.: University of Georgia Press, 1983.

————. and Elizabeth Makowski. *Wykked Wives and the Woes of Marriage: Misogamous Literature from Juvenal to Chaucer*. Albany: State University of New York Press, 1991.

Wilson, M. S. "A Revaluation of Christine de Pisan as a Literary Figure." Ph.D. diss., Stanford University, 1952.

Windeatt, B. A. *Chaucer's Dream Poetry: Sources and Analogues*. London: D. S. Brewer, 1982.

Winny, James. *Chaucer's Dream Poems*. London: Chatto and Windus, 1973.

Winsor, Eleanor J. 'A Study of the Sources and Rhetoric of Chaucer's 'Legend of Good Women' and Ovid's 'Heroides.'" Ph.D. diss., Yale University, 1968.

Wisman, J. A. "L'Humanisme dans l'oeuvre de Christine de Pisan." Ph.D. diss., Catholic University of America, 1976.

————. "L'éveil du sentiment national au Moyen Age: la pensée politique de Christine de Pisan." *Revue Historique* 257 (1977): 289–97.

Woodbridge, Linda. *Women and the English Renaissance: Literature and the Nature of Womankind 1540–1620*. Urbana: University of Illinois Press, 1984.

Wright, H. G. *Boccaccio in England: From Chaucer to Tennyson*. London: Athlone, 1957.

Yenal, Edith. *Christine de Pizan: A Bibliography of Writings by Her and about Her*. Metuchen, N.J.: Scarecrow Press, 1989.

Yates, Francis. *The Art of Memory*. Chicago: University of Chicago Press, 1966.

Zappacosta, Guglielmo, and Vittorio Zaccaria. "Per il testo del 'De Claris Mulieribus.'" *Studi sul Boccaccio* 7 (1973): 239–270.

Index